THE SEVEN LIVES OF COLONEL PATTERSON

THE SEVEN LIVES OF
COLONEL
PATTERSON

*How an Irish Lion Hunter Led
the Jewish Legion to Victory*

DENIS BRIAN

With an Afterword by Alan Patterson

SYRACUSE UNIVERSITY PRESS

First Edition 2008

09   10   11   12   13   14   6   5   4   3   2

The paper used in this publication meets the minimum requirements of
American National Standard for Information Sciences—Permanence of
Paper for Printed Library Materials, ANSI Z39.48–1984.∞™

For a listing of books published and distributed by Syracuse University Press,
visit our Web site at SyracuseUniversityPress.syr.edu.

ISBN-13: 978-0-8156-0927-8   ISBN-10: 0-8156-0927-2

Library of Congress Cataloging-in-Publication Data
Brian, Denis.
The seven lives of Colonel Patterson : how an Irish lion hunter led the Jewish
Legion to victory / Denis Brian ; with an afterword by Alan Patterson. — 1st ed.
p. cm.
Includes bibliographical references and index.
ISBN 978-0-8156-0927-8 (hardcover : alk. paper) 1. Patterson, J. H. (John Henry), 1867–
1947. 2. Soldiers—Great Britain—Biography. 3. Great Britain. Army. Jewish Legion—His-
tory. 4. World War, 1914–1918—Regimental histories. 5. Israel—History, Military—20th
century. 6. Zionists—Biography. 7. Hunters—Africa, East—Biography. 8. Explor-
ers—Africa—Biography. 9. Roosevelt, Theodore, 1858–1919—Friends and associates. 10.
Authors, English—Biography. I. Title.
CT788.P375B75 2008
956.9405092—dc22
[B]
2008008870

Manufactured in the United States of America

To Martine, Danielle, Alex, and Emma, with love

DENIS BRIAN is the author of *Murderers and Other Friendly People: The Public and Private Worlds of Interviewers, Genius Talk: Conversations with Nobel Scientists and Other Luminaries,* and biographies of Ernest Hemingway, Albert Einstein, Joseph Pulitzer, and the Curies.

Contents

Illustrations

Preface

A MAN OF BREATHTAKING ACHIEVEMENTS, the charismatic and exceptionally courageous John Henry Patterson is a biographer's dream. He lived seven separate lives, any one of which would make a compelling biography. Yet his childhood and the identity of his parents remain a mystery even to his relatives. Three actors have portrayed him in movies about his life as a lion hunter. Another facet of his many lives inspired Hemingway's "The Short Happy Life of Francis Macomber" and provoked Winston Churchill into slandering him as an adulterer and murderer. President Theodore Roosevelt admired and befriended him, as did the greatest English actor of his day, Henry Irving. In the First World War, as a British officer, Patterson led a brigade of Jewish volunteers known as the Jewish Legion—the first such fighting force in two thousand years—in a successful battle against the Turks in Palestine. Then, to the end of his life in 1947, he kept fighting as an ardent and outspoken Zionist to help create a Jewish homeland in Palestine. Today he is recognized as a vital contributor to both Israeli history and British colonial history. Here are glimpses of his seven lives.

First life: Two lions on a rampage killed 128 men working on a railroad the British were building in 1896 in East Africa and "literally stopped the greatest colonial empire on earth from one of its grandest engineering feats absolutely cold."[1] Hundreds of terrified workers fled, and the rest went on strike. The British Colonial Office sent a thirty-one-year-old Irishman, John Henry Patterson, to get the fearful men back to work. To succeed, he killed the man-eating lions, foiled an attempt to murder him, and put down a mutiny. When he left, the workers who had tried to kill him presented him with a silver bowl inscribed, in part, "We add our prayers for your long life, happiness and prosperity."

Second life: Patterson's account of his triumphant ordeal, *The Man-Eaters of Tsavo*, made him an international celebrity. Both President Theodore Roosevelt and Ernest Hemingway were among his enthralled readers. Roosevelt called it the most thrilling book of true stories ever written, and began a correspondence with him that led to their friendship and Patterson's visit to the White House. The lions Patterson killed at Tsavo are on display in Chicago's Field Museum of Natural History.

Third life: Soon after Patterson returned to England, the Boer War broke out, and he was sent to South Africa to command a battalion of the Imperial Yeomanry, known as the Rough Riders. For his daring during the war—which included hijacking a locomotive, defeating a larger enemy force, and unmasking an enemy soldier disguised as a woman—he was awarded the Distinguished Service Order (DSO), which King Edward VII presented to him at Buckingham Palace, and promoted to lieutenant colonel.

Fourth life: In 1908 the British Colonial Office appointed Patterson the first game warden in East Africa, with orders to survey the unmapped territory. Leaving his pregnant wife in England, Patterson took the opportunity to combine his mapping trips with safaris to hunt big game. He once took a young married couple with him. The husband killed himself on the trip. An official investigation in the House of Lords hinted that because Patterson was probably having an affair with the wife, the sick, jealous, and despairing husband had committed suicide. Although Patterson was officially exonerated by the House of Lords, Winston Churchill charged him with adultery and murder. Hemingway was inspired by the incident to write "The Short Happy Life of Francis Macomber," though with a twist: he had the wife "accidentally" kill the husband.

Fifth life: Patterson became a man-about-London-town, idolized and befriended by members of high society and England's leading actor, Sir Henry Irving. With a passion for military history, he spent his leaves in Europe visiting the battlefields where Napoleon and Wellington had fought and inspecting foreign troops in Spain and Germany and colonial troops in Egypt, Kenya, Uganda, and West Africa.

Sixth life: When World War I broke out in 1914, Lieutenant Colonel Patterson led a unit, consisting mostly of Jewish volunteers and known as the Zion Mule Corps, which took part in the fighting at Gallipoli. Winston Churchill called him crazy for taking the job, saying that the Jews were too stubborn and fragmented. General Sir Ian Hamilton, the British commander at Gallipoli, wrote of them, "It is a purely Jewish unit (except for Patterson and a few other officers). As far as I know, this is the first time in the Christian era that such a thing has happened. They have shown great courage taking supplies up to the line under heavy fire."[2] Toward the war's end, as Lawrence of Arabia led an Arab force against the Turks, so Patterson of Palestine led a Jewish force, known as the Jewish Legion—among them Lieutenant Vladimir Jabotinsky—in a successful final battle against the Turks.

Seventh life: In 1920 Patterson left the British army as a colonel to become a political activist. From then on, he made common cause with Jabotinsky, head of the Revisionist Party, in the struggle to combat the anti-Jewish, pro-Arab bias of many British bureaucrats and politicians. Throughout World War II, Patterson continued to campaign with Jabotinsky and others in the United States, lobbying for a Jewish state and promoting the idea of a Jewish army to fight the Nazis. He also became a close friend of another member of this Zionist group, Benzion Netanyahu, and his wife, Cela, the parents of Binyamin Netanyahu (the Likud leader and former president of Israel). Because of their affection and respect for Patterson, in 1946 they named their son Jonathan after him. Patterson in turn became the boy's godfather. Jonathan (Yoni) was killed while leading the daring commando raid on Entebbe to free Jewish hostages in 1976.

Patterson retired with his wife in Bel Air, California, where he died at age seventy-nine in 1947, a year before the creation of his dream—the State of Israel. His only son, Bryan Patterson, became a noted Harvard paleontologist, literally following in his father's footsteps, to uncover and investigate the past in Kenya. His only grandson, Alan, a consultant on environmental problems, lives in Boston and wrote the afterword to this volume.

Three actors, Robert Stack, Gregory Peck, and Val Kilmer, have portrayed Patterson in films about his early life as a lion hunter. No film has been made about his later life, but he is remembered in Israel, where his military uniforms are on display in the Jewish Legion Museum in Avihavil and a Jerusalem street is named in his honor.

This book is his first full-length biography.

Acknowledgments

MANY THANKS for their help and encouragment to Cecil Bloom, Elaine Bloomberg, John Brady, Jennings Braun, Lawrence Cramer, Albert Edelson, Pesah Gany, Samuel Geshman, Sir Martin Gilbert, Grace Golden, Patrick Hemingway, A. Hershberg, George Higgins, Janet Hilman, Z. H. Hurwitz, Oscar Kraines, Jose Mirelman, Alan Patterson, Beatrice Patterson, M. Pearsall, Zeev Raphael, Harriet Schlosberg, Charles Schwartz, Jack Schwartz, Nathan Shapiro, Cyril Silvertown, Patrick Streeter, Martin Sugarman, Joan Travis, Roy Travis, Martin Watts, Robert Weintraub, Annette Wenda, Ilse White, Ernest Wodak, Glenn Wright, Eva Zimmerman, the British Record Office, Harvard University, the Central Zionist Archives, Jabotinsky Institute, *Jerusalem Post*, Chaim Weizmann Archives, Library of Congress, and especially my wife, Martine.

THE SEVEN LIVES OF COLONEL PATTERSON

1

The Man-Eaters of Tsavo, 1896–1901

BEING HUMAN, the British put a gloss on their questionable pursuits, so that their bloody conquest of foreign lands was to extend the blessings of their empire—appropriately red on maps of the world—by teaching East Indians to play cricket, Africans to wear pants, and everyone to worship Jesus Christ and to stop for tea and cucumber sandwiches at five. They were remarkably successful at converting some foreigners into imitation Englishmen. Their rivals in piety and plunder, especially the French and the Germans, saw the British through narrowed eyes and gun sights, as perfidious, pompous philistines with power and filthy lucre as their essential goal.

Some British Empire builders were unquestionably eager to bring the blessings of civilization to their backward brothers and sisters, even if they had to kill them to do it. No one has defended the British point of view with more verve and command of the mother tongue than Welsh author James Morris, who wrote with patriotic fervor:

> Whenever I hear some pip-squeak Asian or African mouthing the usual scurrilous platitudes about the universal frightfulness of colonial rule, my blood boils at the thought that it was through the presence of empire that his own hopeful little Power acquired all the roads, railroads, telegraphs, political parties, universities, newspapers and hospitals—had its slavery abolished as likely as not, discovered its tin or bauxite and was elevated from a condition of tribal savagery . . . into the semblance of an orderly modern State.[1]

Author Charles Miller largely agreed, writing in his *Lunatic Express:*

> The majority of British voters felt pride in witnessing the expansion across
> Africa of what they profoundly believed was the best way of life to which
> any human being might aspire. Britain's presence in the aboriginal regions
> of the planet was seen as an influence which could only bring justice,
> order and hope to peoples who had crept for untold centuries through
> the dark labyrinths of ignorance, superstition, disease and mindless hate.
> Certainly the Empire would bring material wealth to England as well, nor
> did many Britons find reason to apologize for this in an age when profits
> from the sweat of one's brow were almost universally considered the fruit
> of virtue. But even though the promises of riches may have been the drive
> shaft of imperial growth, this in no way detracted from the sincerity of the
> Englishman's belief in the rightness of his country's civilizing mission.[2]

Morris and Miller echoed the Anglophile enthusiasm of former U.S.
president Teddy Roosevelt who, after a big-game hunting trip to British East Africa and a visit to the Sudan in 1909, recalled in his *African Game Trails: An Account of the African Wanderings of an American Hunter-Naturalist* (in which he characterized Colonel John Henry Patterson as author of "the most thrilling book of true lion stories ever written"), "Most of the tribes were of pure savages. . . . Over this people—for its good fortune—Great Britain established a protectorate, and ultimately, in order to get easy access to the new outposts of civilization in the heart of the Dark Continent, the British Government built a railroad from the old Arab coast of Mombasa westward to Victoria Nyanza."[3]

Should his readers be inclined to think that the "pure savages" would have been better off without British "protection," Roosevelt elaborated: "[In the Sudan] I witnessed a native dance and was struck by the lack of men of middle-age; in all the tribes which were touched by the blight of Mahdist tyranny, with its accompaniments of unspeakable horror, suffered such slaughter of the then young men that the loss has left its mark to this day. The English, when they destroyed Mahdism, rendered a great service to humanity; and their rule in the Soudan [*sic*] has been astoundingly successful and beneficial from every stand-point." He described Sir William Garstin (1894–1935), an English engineer who played a vital part in building Egypt's Aswan Dam and the National Museum of Egyptian

Antiquities, as "one of the men who have made Egypt and the Soudan what they are today, and who have thereby rendered an incalculable service, not only to England, but to civilization."[4]

Empire building reached its zenith a few years before Roosevelt's appearance in Africa, at the end of the nineteenth century. Then, seventeen European nations and the United States ostensibly put rivalry aside and agreed on a joint humanitarian effort—to cooperate in ridding the world of the slave trade. The British already had a railroad in the works in their protectorate in East Africa, which they claimed would be their contribution to an attack on the slave traders. Slaves were forced to carry goods, especially ivory, over the primitive East African roads, and the railroad was expected to put the traders out of business by being a faster and more reliable means of transportation. It could also protect the country's rich resources and encourage European settlers by quickly moving troops to put down any native uprising by those individuals who resented foreigners.

They planned to build it from the east coast, near Mombasa on the Indian Ocean, to Lake Victoria, on the Uganda border, 572 miles away. It was part of this area, what would become known as the highlands of Kenya, that they would soon offer as a refuge for the world's persecuted Jews. Called the Uganda Plan, it received a thanks-but-no-thanks response. Skeptics were soon ridiculing the enterprise as the "Lunatic Line," because not only was the terra incognita, but so were the weather conditions; the availability and skill of the required workers; the reaction of the inevitably dispossessed Kikuyu, Kamba, Luo, and Masai tribes; the response of militant slave traders; the deadly animals and insects en route; and the cost.

The *Times* of London recalled the many difficulties—based on the reports of 389 men who had spent nine months surveying the 572-mile route. They concluded that the heavy steel rails would have to be manhandled to a plateau more than 3,000 feet above sea level, over ridges twice that height. Dense forests would have to be cleared, massive rocks shattered to make way for the rails, and bridges built over streams subject to sudden flooding from tropical rainfall.

Henry Labouchère, a charismatic, radical British member of Parliament (MP) and editor, published this satirical send-up of the enterprise in his muckraking newspaper *Truth:*

What It will cost no words can express;
What is its object no brain can suppose;
Where it will start from no one can guess;
Where it is going to no one knows;
What is the use of it none can conjecture:
What it will carry there's none can define:
And in spite of George Curzon's superior lecture:
It surely is nothing but a lunatic line.[5]

Queen Victoria was all for it, and damned Labouchère as a horrible man and a liar to boot. Britain's Parliament supported their queen, voting 218 to 52 to "protect" Uganda and 255 to 75 to build the railroad linking British East Africa with Uganda.

Ronald Preston, who had been raised in an Indian orphanage and had directed the building of railroads in India for eleven years, supervised the laying of the first rails in Mombasa on August 5, 1896. He had enormous resources at his command, including thousands of men, 800 donkeys, 629 bullocks, 350 mules, and 63 camels, as well as the financial support of the British government, and the company of his British wife, Florence.

Most native tribesmen in the area were unsuitable or unwilling to undertake the various tasks, and so Preston recruited 2,600 laborers known as coolies, and hundreds of stonemasons from India, Pakistan, and Afghanistan. Contemporary accounts emphasize the squalor of the crowded coolie camps and the trade in human flesh. The camps teemed with prostitutes, small boys, and other accessories of the vices that moralists claimed were practiced by Orientals.

Still, all went reasonably well until the track reached the Taru Desert, an area infested with tsetse flies, which killed more than 1,500 of the 1,852 animals and many of the workers. Then the sky became dark with vultures and the trail littered with the corpses of pack animals being devoured by ravenous hyenas. Many of the men who had escaped the deadly tsetse flies were dying in the primitive hospital—a group of leaking tents—from malaria, dysentery, tropical ulcers, or pneumonia.

Preston pressed on until he reached Tsavo, with its clear, swiftly flowing river fed from the snowcaps of Mount Kilimanjaro. There he learned that Tsavo, despite its pleasant appearance, had a grim history. *Tsavo* was the native (Kikamba) word for slaughter, as it had often been the site of bloody Masai battles. The natives warned him that the place was haunted by evil spirits that enticed men to their deaths, leaving nothing behind except a sandal or a cap.

He hadn't long to wait for an "enticement" to take place. A coolie disappeared overnight, and next morning someone found his dhoti (the loincloth worn by Hindus) on the riverbank. Told of the ominous discovery, Preston grabbed his Winchester rifle and led a search party. They eventually found parts of the missing man—his head and feet intact, but all the flesh torn from his body. And around his corpse were the paw prints of his killer—a lion.

Back at the camp Preston instructed the coolies to collect thorn bushes from the nearby scrubland to use as barricades around their tents as protection from marauding lions. While they were at it, he set off with a group of beaters to flush out the man-killer lion or lions, covering an area between the camp and the river. On the way they came across a few skulls and skeletons as evidence of previous killings, but none of the killers.

Days later, at two in the morning, Preston woke with a start to screams of "Sher!" (Tiger), the frantic beating of drums, and the banging of empty kerosene oilcans. Rushing outside with his rifle and a hurricane lamp, he got the dreaded news: another man had vanished. He searched for an hour before giving up, aware that the victim would almost certainly be dead, as a lion invariably kills its victim immediately with a blow to the head. In Preston's words, "The act of killing the victim, before devouring him is, to say the least, merciful."[6]

The corpse was found at dawn in much the same condition as the previous victim. Afterward, Preston reported, not surprisingly, the coolies were disinclined to work and many deserted. It looked as if the entire enterprise was doomed. Preston, who had behaved with courage and enterprise, was in desperate need of help.

In the glory days of the British Empire, his or her majesty's government often chose Irishmen or Scotsmen to bail them out of trouble. General Charles Gordon, a Scot, was sent to rescue a besieged British garrison in the Sudan from a Muslim agitator and his fanatical followers. Colonel T. E. Lawrence, an Anglo-Irishman, would be persuaded to lead an Arab revolt against the Turks, who were a threat to the British in World War I.

Faced with a massive work stoppage in East Africa because of lions devouring the workers, the British Colonial Office sent John Henry Patterson, a former army sergeant, to solve the problem. Purportedly the son of an Irish Protestant clergyman, nothing more is known about Patterson's father, Henry, and nothing at all about his mother. His entire childhood remains a mystery, except that his father, whoever he was, intrigued him with Old Testament tales. According to Patterson's daughter-in-law, Beatrice, his grandson, Alan, and several close friends, he never spoke of his childhood, of his parents, or of anyone who would have known them—as if hiding a secret. Patrick Streeter, author of *Mad for Zion: A Biography of Colonel J. H. Patterson,* suggests that Patterson was, in fact, illegitimate—born into a good Anglo-Irish family, or, as it was then euphemistically called, "on the wrong side of the blanket" (as was Lawrence of Arabia). Streeter believes that Patterson's mother may have been an Irish maidservant and his father an Anglo-Irish earl whose family employed her.

What is known from official documents is that Patterson was born on November 10, 1867, in the beautiful village of Forgney, Ballymahon, County Meath (now County Longford), also the birthplace of the writer Oliver Goldsmith. As Streeter discovered:

> The entire village is dominated by New Castle House, one of the seats of the King-Harman family—a cadet branch of the Earls of Kingston. (In 1883 they owned some 72,000 acres.) At the time of Patterson's birth, New Castle was occupied by Hon. Laurence Harman King-Harman, his wife and sons Edward, 29; Wentworth, 27; George, 22; Charles, 16; and two daughters. There is reasonable circumstantial evidence that Patterson may have been the natural son of one of the King-Harman family. His possible occupation as a groom indicates that he could have been part of the extended household at New Castle, living above the stables in the servants' accommodation.[7]

Also, the King-Harman family was among the 10 percent of County Meath's Protestants. So was Patterson.

Another clue to his childhood and youth was that when he married a Belfast woman, Frances Gray, in 1895, he listed his father, Henry Patterson, on the marriage certificate as a deceased gentleman. Of course, that description does not preclude him from being a clergyman, too.

Even less is known of Patterson's mother. When he joined the British army, he gave the name of an aunt as his next of kin, a Miss Coleston of the Kells, about thirty-seven miles from Forgney. Presumably, she was his mother's sister, and so his mother's maiden name was also Coleston. But despite Streeter's research into all the local sources, in Dublin and Belfast, he found no record of a Patterson-Coleston marriage.

This man of mystery, a contemporary of Winston Churchill and Rudyard Kipling, might have stepped out of a Kipling tale. The lean, almost six-foot thirty-one-year-old Irishman was steeped in military history and the Old Testament. He had the gift of the gab, a lively sense of humor, a friendly and optimistic nature, and an air of command, reinforced, perhaps, by the Bible he sometimes carried in one hand and, no doubt, by a gun he held in the other.

He had joined the British army at seventeen, on March 14, 1885, signing on for seven years, trained at Canterbury Barracks, and briefly served in South Africa. A year later, he sailed for India to join the Third Dragoon Guards at Chakrata in the Himalayan foothills. At twenty-four, on September 1892, he transferred to the Sixteenth Lancers, was promoted to sergeant, and moved with his regiment to Bombay. His commanding officer, William Robertson, was to have a spectacular and unrivaled career, rising from private to field marshal—unique in the British Army—and into the bargain he would be knighted by the queen. Robertson was obviously impressed by Patterson and encouraged him to make the army his career, and to study military history.

While in India, Patterson met his future wife, Frances Helena Gray, a teacher with a bachelor's degree in science and a doctorate in law. She had previously been engaged to a doctor who fell ill and died on the day they had planned to marry. The Pattersons were married in autumn 1895, when he was on home leave, then returned to India, where their first child, a girl, Ellen Moyra, died when she was only four months old.

In India, Patterson studied engineering, helped to build military forts, and picked up more than a smattering of Hindi, a language spoken throughout India. The British government picked Patterson for the job of building a railroad in East Africa because of his engineering know-how. And, with his elementary knowledge of Hindi, he would be able to talk directly to the many Indians eventually hired to do the hard work, without the foul-ups likely with an interpreter. Unlike Preston, when Patterson shipped out to Africa, his wife, Frances, who was eight months pregnant with their second child, returned to England to live in the London suburb of Beckenham.

After reaching Mombasa, Patterson caught a train at 5:20 A.M. on Tuesday, March 8, 1898, and arrived at Tsavo at seven that evening. As he recorded in his diary: "Have a hot and unpleasant journey [of 120 miles] through the Taru Desert. Dr. McCullock shot an ostrich from train—we pull up to take it with us. I have some of the feathers [which he later mailed to his wife]." Awaiting him were four Punjabi servants, hired to light his fires, clean his tent, draw and heat water from the river for his bath, and cook his meals. He also had a Sikh *jemadar* (overseer), Ungan Singh.

Patterson's main task was to build a three hundred–foot bridge on three massive stone piers needed to continue the track—fifteen feet above the highest flood level—across the Tsavo River and on its way to Lake Victoria in Uganda. He also had to construct all the railroad station buildings and thirty miles of cuttings, embankments, and permanent track on both sides of the river.

An equally difficult task was to overcome the influence of a rival German empire builder, Carl Peters, also at work in East Africa. Peters entertained the natives by demonstrating his spin on the relative size of Englishmen and Germans. The Englishman, he would say, are so high, as he held his hand about six inches from the ground, whereas the Germans are . . . and he would leap in the air, hand raised, to indicate a giant. After such behavior, Peters left his gullible audiences convulsed with laughter and invariably pro-German, although he conceded that the only thing that left a lasting impression on them "was a bullet from my double-barreled rifle and then only when in emphatic relation to their own bodies."[8] Not surprisingly, Peters became something of a hero to Adolf Hitler. Patterson took a more nuanced approach than his German rival to the south across the border in German East Africa and eventually got on good terms with several native chiefs.

To find out why hundreds of his workforce were on strike, he visited them in their tents, scattered for several miles on either side of the railroad tracks, and was immediately struck by the atmosphere of doom. Some men were literally paralyzed with fear. Only one was able to speak, and he told Patterson that it was useless to shoot the man-eating lions because they were the immortal and "angry spirits of two departed native chiefs [who] had taken this form in order to protest a railway being made through their county."[9] In the guise of lions, they were destroying the workforce to protect their country. Naturally, Patterson discounted the talk of bulletproof lions. Knowing that Parsee coolies traditionally left the bodies of the dead to be eaten by vultures, he thought it likely that lions sometimes got there first, and eventually developed a taste for human flesh. Also, because the two recent victims had been known to carry a lot of cash, Patterson suspected that they had been murdered for it and dumped in the forest, where the evidence would inevitably be devoured by wild animals.

A short-lived theory.

On Saint Patrick's Day, March 17, 1898, Patterson prepared to spend an all-night vigil near the site of the recent killings. It had been a very hot day, and he had a slight fever. One man followed him with a lamp and another with a goat, which Patterson tied as a decoy to a tree. Then he climbed to a high branch, where he sat, holding a loaded gun. The temperature dropped fast at night, and he was soon shivering and soaked to the skin by a steady drizzle. When it stopped raining, a cloud of mosquitoes attacked him. As he noted in his diary, he longed to be back in his beloved Ireland and missed his wife. About midnight he heard a heart-rending scream from a distant camp. Another victim, but too far from him to help.

The next morning an Indian watchman told him that while he guarded them, a gang of workers had gone to sleep in an open train wagon atop a pile of wood. About midnight, he saw a lion emerge from the jungle and, silent as a ghost, approach the wagon. When he raised the alarm by shouting and rattling empty tin cans together, the lion dived under the train and then crept toward the open guard's van, where a sick engineer, named Ogilvy, was asleep, waiting to be taken to Mombasa Hospital. As the lion was about to spring at Ogilvy, "dancing on his legs," the watchman called it, a noise made the animal dive back under the guard's van. It soon reappeared, moving fast, reached the open wagon that it had first approached, gave a huge spring, and landed among the men. As they screamed in terror, it grabbed one by the shoulder and leaped out and away with him into the jungle. The man's howls of fear and pain were soon replaced by the crunching of his bones and the lion's ominous purring.

A servant woke Patterson at dawn a few days later with news of another lion attack near the Tsavo station. Armed with a rifle, he and his visitor, Veterinary Captain Haslem, reached the tent of Ungan Singh, Patterson's Sikh overseer, which he shared with six other men. They were too traumatized, literally struck dumb, to answer his questions, except for one witness, who said, "Sahib, I was awake and lying next to Ungan Singh, who was fast asleep. I was looking out into the moonlight when suddenly I saw a big lion put his head in at the open door. My heart turned to water when I saw him so near me, and I could not move. His eyes glowed like coals of fire as he looked first at me and then at Ungan Singh. I almost died of fright lest he should choose me; then, by the kindness of Allah, he seized Singh by the throat, instead of your slave." He went on to say that the overseer had cried out, "Let go!" and had thrown his arms around the lion's neck. But it had lifted him off the bed and dragged him away, while the other men—now all wide awake—looked on, helpless and terrified as they listened to the gruesome death struggle outside their tent.[10]

Patterson and Haslem followed the lion's route—guided by pools of blood and the victim's heel tracks in the sand as he was dragged along. The spot where the killer had stopped to eat his human prey was littered with blood, bits of torn flesh and clothing, part of his skull with eyes wide open, a shin bone, and part of a foot. Deeply disturbed, the two men buried the remains under heavy stones. And there Patterson vowed that "I would avenge the foreman's horrible death and spare myself no pains until I had rid the neighbourhood of the brutes. I little knew the trouble that was in store for me, or how narrow were to be my own escapes from sharing poor Ungan Singh's tragic fate."[11]

That same night, Patterson and several coolies, who had implored him to let them join him, sat in a tree near the dead overseer's tent on the chance that the lion would return for fresh victims. Patterson was armed with a .303 rifle and a 12-bore shotgun. Soon after, he heard distant lion roars and then for the next hour or so an ominous silence—ominous because lions stalk their prey in complete silence—followed by a distant uproar and the now too familiar frenzied cries.

He had chosen the wrong spot. The killing was in another camp about a half mile away, where a lion had broken into a tent and dragged off one of the men. As the workers' camps were scattered for several miles on either side of the Tsavo River, Patterson concluded that however tempting he made the spot where he sat in wait with a decoy, the lions seemed to have an uncanny ability—as if they anticipated his plans—to choose their victims elsewhere.

Patterson lived in an unprotected tent in an open clearing, which he briefly shared with a visiting Dr. Rose. During the night they were awakened by a noise outside, as if someone was trying to get into their tent. They searched outside with a lantern but found nothing unusual. In the morning they saw what had caused the noise—a lion, whose paw marks repeatedly circled their tent, until, apparently, it got entangled in the tent ropes and decided to seek its dinner elsewhere.[12]

Patterson immediately moved to the other side of the river to share a hut of palm leaves and palm branches with Dr. Brock, the district's medical officer. It was surrounded by a high and thick thorn fence. Their servants lived within the enclosure, and the two men spent their evenings on the hut's veranda, reading by firelight, loaded rifles within reach, and anxiously awaiting the sight or sound of a man-eater.

During the day of March 25, Patterson met Bishop Alfred Tucker and another missionary going to Uganda—a British protectorate after a favorable vote in Britain's Parliament—and wished them well. That evening he again began an all-night vigil, this time on the far side of the river. While he watched and waited, a lion attacked a hospital tent on the near side of the river, but was scared off when the startled doctor's assistant, in a panic, dropped a cabinet of medical supplies. But the animal returned, badly mauling the arm of one patient who managed to struggle free, catching the leg of another who hit the animal so hard he let go, and seizing a third by the throat, carrying him off to the terrified shrieks of his tent mates, dragging him though the thorn barrier, and devouring him just outside. It seemed to Patterson that the thorn barriers were no obstacle to "the demons," as he now called them, and before dark he had moved most of the hospital tents and patients closer to the main camp, which he surrounded with a stronger thorn fence.[13]

That night he sat alone near the site of the recent killing, "in the hope of getting an opportunity of bagging" one of the raiders.[14] But the lion again outwitted him. Patterson knew it, by the shrieks coming from the hospital area.

At dawn Dr. Brock, who was in charge of the hospital, and Patterson went to the site of the attack—a tent where eight patients had been sleeping. Dr. Brock joined Patterson in following the lion's track and, some four hundred yards from the tent, discovered the victim's skull, jaws, a few large bones, part of a hand, his teeth, and a silver ring. Patterson sent the ring, and the teeth—the latter specially prized by the water carrier's caste—to the victim's widow in India.

On Sunday, March 27, Lord Hugh Cholmondeley Delamere (who would become a leading light among the early white settlers) passed through Tsavo on a hunting trip, followed by a detachment of the Uganda Rifles. Patterson went to bed that night for the first time in a week, only to be awoken by a leopard that broke into his goat shed and killed twenty-nine of the animals.

There were several more near misses. One night a lion attacked a man riding a donkey but then got tangled in a rope with oilcans attached that was wrapped around the donkey's neck, and the noise of rattling cans frightened him off. Another night a lion entered a tent and grabbed a mattress instead of a man before making a quick exit. On a third occasion, a lion broke into a tent of fourteen sleeping coolies, clawed the shoulder of one of them, and then took off with a sack of rice that—apparently not to its taste—it dropped on its way back to the jungle. Patterson again evacuated the hospital patients to other more secure tents.

On April 16 he received four letters from his wife, and reading them chronologically discovered in the last that his recently born son, Maurice Rupert, had lived only three days, dying of convulsions. A friend, Dr. White, stayed with him that night to console him.

A week later, he was back to lion hunting. Then he and Dr. Brock set up a trap for the killers. Late at night they waited in a wagon on a railroad siding, near the now deserted hospital tents. They opened the top half of the wagon door, intending to fire their rifles through the open space when the target appeared. They kept the door's lower half closed to protect them, but it was so dark they couldn't even see the few cattle tethered nearby as decoys. "The deadly silence was becoming very monotonous and oppressive, when suddenly a dry twig snapped, and we knew that an animal of some sort was about."[15] Patterson then proposed that he should leave the wagon and lie on the ground to get a better view of the animal—and, of course, act as bait. But Brock talked him out of it.

Listening anxiously, hardly daring to breathe, they heard a dull thud, as if a heavy animal had jumped over a fence, and the cattle began moving around restlessly, followed by dead silence. What neither knew at the time was that the lion was almost within springing distance of them. Patterson tried to pierce the darkness by staring in the direction from which the noise had come, and thought he saw an animal gliding to a bush nearby. But he wasn't sure.

They resumed their silent vigil. Patterson admitted afterward that the strain on his nerves was almost unbearable. Then, without warning, "a huge body sprang" at them. "The lion!" Patterson shouted, and both men fired simultaneously.

> Not a moment too soon, for in another second the brute would assuredly have landed inside the wagon. As it was, he was probably blinded by the flash and frightened by the noise. The double report which was increased a hundredfold by the hollow iron roof. Had we not been very much on the alert, he would undoubtedly have got one of us. The next morning we found Brock's bullet embedded in the sand. Close to a footprint, it could not have missed the lion by more than an inch or two. Mine was nowhere to be found. Thus ended my first direct encounter with one of the man-eaters. We realized that we had had a narrow escape."[16]

Patterson's diary entry read: "Had a most intensely exciting night and narrowly escaped being carried off."[17]

When he learned that a Swahili porter had just escaped from a lion attack but sustained terrible injuries, including several broken ribs, a fractured arm, and a shattered thigh bone, he thought there was no hope of the man surviving. The more optimistic Dr. Brock bound up the man's fractured bones and amputated his leg. Six weeks later Patterson was happily surprised to see the patient out of the hospital and even cheerful.

His was hardly the mood of most workers. Demoralized by the lion attacks, many threatened to quit. Patterson persuaded them to stay by organizing a defense strategy involving fire and noise. He also gave them time off to build higher thorn fences around the camp and hired a watchman to keep fires burning throughout the night and to regularly raise the alarm by pulling on a rope—while sitting in his tent—attached to several empty oilcans suspended from a tree. Despite these precautions, night after night, lions entered the camp and left with their human prey.

The killing by the lions alone did not explain why the railroad and bridge construction were far behind schedule. Patterson discovered another reason after visiting a ravine where workmen were quarrying rocks to provide piers for the bridge. Needing skilled specialists to shape the quarried rocks, he had hired masons, mostly Pathans from northern India, for forty-five rupees a month, three times the pay of unskilled coolies. But on inspecting their work, he discovered that he had been fooled. Many self-proclaimed masons were unskilled laborers who had lied to get the higher pay. Patterson solved that problem by instituting a piecework system. This setup made it easy for the skilled workers, but not the phonies, to earn the forty-five monthly rupees. The unskilled being in the majority, they attempted to intimidate the others into lowering the standards to match their own, hoping that it would force Patterson to drop the piecework system. He saw through their scheme, though, and stuck to his guns. Not that the genuine masons showed any gratitude: instead of shaping, or "dressing," the rocks, they wasted their time arguing ferociously about their respective religions—Hinduism and Islam—which at times escalated into violence.

Patterson separated the combatants and dressed their wounds, once ordering the worst troublemaker, Karim Bux, to attend a magistrate's court on a minor charge. He was told that Bux could not attend, as he had been severely injured during a religious argument and was confined to his bed. Not to be outwitted, Patterson arranged to have Bux brought to him on his bed, carried by four coolies. Several of the man's friends turned up, too, doubtless to watch one of their own hoodwink the sahib. When the bed was put on the ground near Patterson, he thoroughly examined Bux and determined that "it was pure budmashi [devilment]—I told him that I was going to give him some very effective dawa [medicine]." Patterson then grabbed an armful of wood shavings from a nearby carpenter's bench, put them under Bux's bed, and set them alight. "In a flash, Bux left the bed and ran off, and his amused comrades greeted me with shouts of 'Shabash, Sahib!' [Well done, sir!]." Bux eventually returned "with clasped hands imploring forgiveness, which I readily granted," instead of having him flogged.[18]

Despite Patterson's tough tactics, many workers still continued to goof off, as he would soon find out. Returning to the camp after another futile night vigil in a tree, he came across a group who should have been working but were either fast asleep or playing cards. As they had not yet spotted him, he decided to scare them by firing his rifle over their heads. The shot sent them, as if by magic, into instant action. Now, instead of snores or card talk, the air was filled with a cacophony of hammers and chisels. He shouted that, having caught them slacking, he would punish each man by reducing that week's pay and dismissed the foreman in charge.

As Patterson headed back to his hut, two workmen tottered after him, crying for heaven to witness that his gunfire had hit them both in the back, and they lifted their shirts to show him the multiple bleeding wounds. It didn't fool him. As he pointed out, the wounds must have been made by fellow workmen, because there were no corresponding bullet holes in their shirts. Furthermore, he said, he had fired a single bullet from a rifle, not a shotgun. As punishment for their attempted deception, he additionally reduced their pay.

That night, September 6, 1898, the angry workers held a protest meeting where it was proposed that the next day, when Patterson was to supervise their work at the quarry, they should kill him and leave his body in the jungle for the lions to eat. The plan was unanimously approved, and everyone took an oath of secrecy, leaving fingerprints on a strip of paper as a token of their binding agreement.

Patterson was forewarned. A worker—risking his own life—broke his oath of secrecy. But Patterson did not believe him, suspecting that he was a plant, sent by others to frighten him into going easy on them, and discounted the danger.

The next morning, as Patterson walked toward the quarry, about an hour away, Heera Singh, his trusted head stonemason, crept out of some bushes and advised him not to go to the quarry. He dared not explain exactly why, he said, but he and other stonemasons were keeping clear of the place because they anticipated trouble. Still unconvinced, Patterson assured Singh that there was nothing to fear. He began to change his mind, though, as he entered the quarry's narrow ravine and several workers glanced at him furtively. After a few more steps, a foreman stopped him to complain that some men were refusing to work and asked Patterson to go with him to confront them. He went with the foreman, who pointed out two men who were obviously slacking. Patterson asked for their names, wrote them in his notebook, and began to walk back.

It was a trap. From each end of the ravine, well over a hundred men rushed at him, yelling with rage and armed with crowbars and hammers, leaving him no room to escape. Fortunately, the first two to reach him were unarmed. The first grabbed Patterson's wrists and yelled incoherently but with obviously murderous intent. Patterson hurled him aside. The second used his neighbor as a weapon and pushed him at Patterson, who stepped aside, and the weapon collided violently with a rock.

Outnumbered about 160 to 1, Patterson sprang onto a rock. At least he now held the high ground, as he shouted in Hindi, "I know all about your plot to murder me!" Surprisingly, they stopped their battle cries and onward rush to listen. He put it down to their ingrained habit of obedience. Knowing that he had only a few seconds to subdue them, using remarkable grace under pressure and his Irish gift of the gab, he went on:

> But if you do [kill me] many of you will assuredly be hanged for it, as the government would disbelieve your story that I had been carried off by a lion. I know it is only one or two scoundrels among you who have induced you to behave so stupidly. Don't allow them to make fools of you. Even suppose you were to carry out your plan of killing me, would not another sahib at once be set over you and might he not be an even harder taskmaster? You all know I am just and fair to the real worker. It is only

the scoundrels and shirkers who have anything to fear from me. And are upright, self-respecting Pathans [men from southeastern Afghanistan and northwestern Pakistan] going to allow yourselves to be led away by men of that kind?[19]

The discontented, he said, would be allowed to return immediately to Mombasa. If the others resumed work and there was no more plotting against him, he promised to ignore their "foolish conduct."[20] When he called for a show of hands, everyone seemed to express his willingness to continue working.

He was under no illusion that one speech had saved his life. It had only given him time to plan his next lifesaving move. Aware of the still smoldering animosity, he pretended to be at ease by carefully measuring a slope in the quarry and approving work recently completed, before casually heading back to the comparative safety of Tsavo.

As soon as he left the quarry, the men held another mass meeting and agreed to murder Patterson that night. His timekeeper anxiously told him of the resumed plot and that the men had also threatened to kill him when he tried to do his job by calling the roll. Patterson decided to get help. He sent an SOS by telegram to the railroad police in Mombasa, and to George Whitehead, the district governor, who had a Swahili wife.

Whitehead immediately ordered a contingent of soldiers to march the twenty-five miles to protect Patterson and the timekeeper. They were still guarding them a few days later when the railroad police arrived and arrested the ringleaders of the murder plot. They had been exposed by a fellow conspirator, who turned queen's evidence, and identified by their fingerprints on the document meant to be Patterson's death warrant. Found guilty, British consul Clifford Crauford sentenced them to a prison chain gang.

There were no more threats or mass strikes—for a time. But Patterson was still losing workers to disease, desertion, and lions. One group of Swahili porters from Zanzibar, whom Patterson considered the laziest workers, took the lion attacks less seriously than most of the others.

They were camped together in a pleasant spot on the banks of the Tsavo River, shaded by palm tress, and with the flimsiest of protection around their tents—that is, until a lion seized one of them in the night

1. Many of these workmen at Tsavo, who tried to murder Patterson, later respected him as a demigod. From J. H. Patterson, *The Man-Eaters of Tsavo.*

and hurried off with him. Then they began to work overtime, feverishly cutting and collecting thorn bushes for protection and digging deep pits as traps around their camp, camouflaged with sticks and earth. However, because they failed to keep the home fires burning all through the night and neglected to post a guard to sound the alarm, a lion made its way safely and undetected past the pits, forced itself under a thorn bush, and grabbed Juma bin Aslimi by the shoulder. As the man screamed in pain and terror, and his panic-stricken tent mates cried out for Allah to help, the lion dragged him back under the thorn bush and away. But they didn't make it far. A loud crash announced that the lion and his prey had plunged into one of the pits. The fall must have scared the would-be man-eater, who leaped out and raced off into the jungle, leaving Juma bin Aslimi stunned, his shoulder injured, his flesh torn by the thorn bush through which the lion had dragged him. He was not rescued for several hours because no one had the nerve to reach him until daylight.

Patterson had heard the commotion while perched in a tree on guard some four hundred yards away. Later that morning he asked Juma bin Aslimi how he had felt when the lion attacked him, but the man was so shocked and dazed that he could not even recall falling into the pit. Dr. Brock, evidently a first-rate doctor, had him fit and back at work soon after.

For Patterson, sitting in a tree night after night, hearing the now too familiar sounds of the lions' attacks and screams of their victims, was exhausting and demoralizing. As he recalled years later:

> In the whole of my life, I have never experienced anything more nerve-shaking than to hear the deep roars of these dreadful monsters growing nearer and nearer, and to know that some one or other of us was doomed to be their victim before morning dawned. Once the lions reached the vicinity of the camps, the roars completely ceased and we knew that they were stalking for their prey. Shouts would then pass from camp to camp: "Beware, brothers, the devil is coming," but the warning cries would prove of no avail; and sooner or later agonizing shrieks would break the silence, and another man would be missing from roll call next morning.[21]

He was baffled. Every trick he tried had failed. He never discovered how the lions were able to get through the thick, seemingly impenetrable barricade of thorn bushes, nor why they seemed impervious to and totally unafraid of gunfire. He even began to wonder if these creatures were really immortal "devils" after all.

George Whitehouse, the tall, lean chief engineer in charge of building the railroad from Mombasa to Lake Victoria, had plastered posters throughout the city, offering a one hundred–dollar to anyone who killed a man-eating lion. The award attracted a motley crew of military men on leave, poachers, and sportsmen from Britain, who shot almost every animal in sight—but not one man-eater.

Meanwhile, Patterson had built a homemade trap made of wooden sleepers, tram rails, telegraph wire, heavy chains, and steel bars. It was a large box divided into two compartments by a grill of steel bars. Armed volunteers, serving as bait, were to enter their compartment through a sliding door and wait, guns at the ready and aimed between the steel bars. The lion, after entering its compartment, attracted, it was hoped, by the human bait in the adjoining compartment, would be instantly locked in by a spring mechanism. There it would be at the mercy of the human bait firing their guns through the steel grill at point-blank range. Patterson put a tent over this contraption and surrounded it with a thorn-bush hedge with a deliberate weak spot to let a lion get through without too much trouble. Though skeptics told Patterson that the lions were too cunning to walk into his trap, he spent several nights viewing the trap from a nearby tree, kept awake not only by the prospective lions but also by hordes of mosquitoes.

One pitch-black night a lion killed a man at the Tsavo railroad station and brought him to eat so close to Patterson's hut that he heard the dreadful crunching of bones and the lion's purring, a sound that would stay with him for days. It was too dark to see anything, and the man was obviously dead, so Patterson could do nothing to save him. But he did help the half-dozen workmen who lived nearby and pleaded with him to let them into his hut, which he willingly did. On inquiring about one of the group, whom he knew to have been ill, he was told that they had callously left him behind. Patterson took a lantern and several men with him to bring the ill man back to the hut. But they were too late. The man was dead, but not from a lion attack: he had apparently died from the shock of being abandoned by his workmates.

Until late November 1898 the lions had gone on their manhunts separately: while one killed, the other stayed in the bush. After that date they attacked as a pair—their first victims two Swahili porters. One was grabbed and carried off; the other was heard moaning for hours, caught in a thorn bush through which the lion had been unable to drag him. His companions were too scared to reach him until daylight, but he had been so badly mauled he died on the way to the hospital.

Patterson was not surprised when almost the entire camp went on strike a second time and confronted him, carrying their few possessions to indicate that they were on their way home—and not willing to be persuaded to stay. A spokesman explained that they had come from India to work for the British government, not to supply food for lions or "devils." At the sound of an approaching train, hundreds rushed for it; some even lay on the track to slow it and then, joined by the others, flung themselves and their possessions onto the train heading for lion-free Mombasa. Patterson ordered the engineer to stop, but he ignored him and kept the train moving along the track.

Patterson again sought help against the lions in a letter to Whitehead, the district officer, asking him to bring as many native soldiers with him as he could. Whitehead promised to do so. Expecting him to arrive for dinner on December 2, 1898, the day after most workers had deserted by train, Patterson sent his "boy" to meet him at the Tsavo railroad station at six that evening. Soon after six, the boy returned and, trembling with terror, told Patterson that Whitehead's train had not arrived and that the station was completely deserted except for an enormous lion on the station platform. Patterson did not believe him. He knew that the workers had been so demoralized by the lions that if they saw a hyena, baboon, or a wild dog or cat in the bush, they imagined it was a lion. As for Whitehead, he assumed that he had not arrived simply because he had postponed his trip.

During his solitary dinner he heard gunfire but, as guns were frequently going off, thought nothing of it. That night he resumed his now customary vigil at a camp where he expected the lions to seek their next meal. Instead of up a tree, he waited in his shelter made of wooden sleepers atop a girder. Almost immediately, he was surprised to hear the presence of lions—as they growled, purred, and crunched away on bones some two hundred feet away. He had not heard any screams from the camp, so he assumed that the lions had seized a native traveling through the area. As he stared in their direction he saw the lions' eyes glowing in the darkness and, aiming carefully, fired. Again they lived up to their immortal reputation and merely moved with whatever they were eating over a slight rise and out of sight.

At daybreak he walked toward where he had last seen the lions and en route, to his astonishment, met a pale and disheveled Whitehead. "Where on earth have you come from?" Patterson asked. "Why didn't you turn up for dinner last night?"

"A nice reception you give a fellow when you invite him to dinner," Whitehead replied.

"Why, what's up?"

"That infernal lion of yours nearly did me in last night."

"Nonsense, you must have dreamed it!" Patterson said.

Whitehead responded by turning around to show Patterson the evidence, saying, "That's not much of a dream, is it?" His clothing was ripped from the nape of his neck to his waist, and there were four red claw marks on his back.

After Patterson had taken him to his tent and washed and dressed his wounds, Whitehead spoke of his ordeal. The train had been very late when he arrived at the Tsavo station with thirty *askari* (native soldiers) and his sergeant, Abdulla. The soldiers went to eat at a nearby mess hut, while Whitehead, followed by Abdulla with a lighted lamp, made his way toward Patterson's campsite. Their route from the station led through a small cutting. About halfway through it, a lion leaped from the bank onto Whitehead, knocking him down and clawing his back. Luckily, White-head was holding his carbine, which he was able to fire. The noise and flash scared the lion into letting him go, only to pounce on Abdulla and carry him off. As he cried out, "Oh, Master, a lion!" Whitehead fired a sec-ond shot, but apparently missed, and the lion and Abdulla disappeared into the night.[22] Patterson now realized that the unfortunate Abdulla had been the prey he had heard the lions eating during the night, and that his "boy" had not imagined that he had seen a lion on the station platform.

Tracking the lions the following days, Patterson could move through the thick jungle undergrowth only by crawling on all fours. A dangerous disadvantage, as a dead twig invariably snapped at a critical moment and scared off what might have been a lion. Still, he persisted, spending all his spare time at it, often getting caught by the thorns of the intensely pain-ful "wait-a-bit" thorn bushes, when his gun bearer had to release him. Exhausted after one of these exasperating hunts, he returned to his tent and slept peacefully until the silence of the night was shattered by the now too familiar cries and shrieks.

The next day, the superintendent of police, Farquhar, arrived with a score of sepoys (Indian soldiers under British command), who took up positions in various trees. Whitehead joined Patterson in his perch on a girder, and two sepoys served as bait in Patterson's homemade lion trap consisting of two partitioned sections illuminated by an oil lamp. The sepoys inside one partition were armed with powerful Martini rifles and loads of ammunition and had strict orders to shoot at the lion as soon as it entered the adjoining partition. At about nine that night Patterson heard the lion-trap spring mechanism clatter down and waited anxiously for

2. Abdulla with his two wives. Patterson heard him being killed by one man-eater. From J. H. Patterson, *The Man-Eaters of Tsavo.*

the sound of gunfire. But there wasn't any. The two sepoys had been so unnerved when the lion appeared and repeatedly hurled itself against the steel bars between the two partitions that for several minutes they had been unable to fire. Then, as Farquhar shouted encouragement, they fired with a vengeance—anywhere, anyhow. Several almost hit Patterson and Farquhar, and succeeded only in blowing away one of the bars of the trap door, thus allowing the lion to escape. "How they failed to kill him several times over," Patterson wrote, "is a complete mystery to me, as they could have put the muzzle of their rifles absolutely touching his body."[23]

The entire group spent the next day crawling through the dense, thorny jungle, urged on by the distant sounds of growling lions but never sighting one, except for Farquhar, who glimpsed one as it bounded away from him. After two more unsuccessful days of crawling through the jungle, all the visitors left, and Patterson was again left to face the lions alone.

During the next three weeks Patterson and the few dozen workers courageous or crazy enough to stay built what they hoped would be lion-proof shelters. Despite his fears for himself and the workers, Patterson was amused to see the unexpected places some chose to build shelters—atop water tanks, roofs, and girders. A few lashed their beds to a tree's high branches. They soon wished they hadn't, as one night, when the lions appeared, a group of terrified men joined the tree squatters, overloading the tree, which came crashing to the ground. All survived on that occasion, as the lions had already seized their prey and were preoccupied with devouring him. Others, who dared to stay on the ground or had no head for heights, slept in gravelike pits they had dug and covered with heavy logs inside their tents.

On the night of December 9, 1898, Patterson used a dead donkey as a decoy. A lion had only partially eaten it before being scared off—and Patterson hoped it would return to finish the meal. As there was no nearby tree in which to perch, he had four wooden poles stuck in the ground and lashed at the top—with a plank as his seat. It was a fairly flimsy structure, and if the lion chose to test it, Patterson was likely to tumble to the ground at the lion's mercy. But he had reached the stage where he was willing to take desperate measures.

To prevent the lion from getting away with the donkey carcass, Patterson had secured it with wires to a nearby tree stump. There, throughout the night, he sat expectantly on his plank seat, until he "fell into a reverie." A snapping twig startled him awake, and he heard rustling, as if a large animal was forcing its way through the brush, followed by a deep sigh (a sign of hunger) and an angry growl (a sign that the lion sensed a human presence). To Patterson's horror, it began to stalk him, circling his flimsy perch twelve feet above the ground in diminishing circles. Suddenly feeling a slap on the back of his neck, he feared he was done for, and in his terror he almost jumped off his plank perch to escape. Just in time he realized that the slap was not from the lion but from a shortsighted owl that mistook him for a tree.

Now, despite his attempt to remain still and silent, he was trembling with a mixture of fear and excitement as the man-eater crept slowly and stealthily toward him. In almost total darkness, when he could just make it out—close at hand and headed toward him—he fired. The bullet hit home. The target gave tremendous roars and began thrashing around. Patterson continued to fire in the general direction, and the roars subsided to groans, then to sighs as the lion crept away, and, finally, to silence.

He assured the men yelling questions from a nearby camp that he was safe and the lion badly wounded if not dead, and they responded with cheers. It wasn't long before they came to see things for themselves, carrying lights, beating tom-tom drums, and blowing horns. When he climbed down from his perch to greet them, to his astonishment some prostrated themselves before him, crying out "Mabarak! Mabarak!"—which means "Blessed one," or "Savior."[24] Warning them not to look for the lion, as it might still be alive or its partner in crime might be in the vicinity, he walked with them back to the nearby camp, where Swahili and other African natives celebrated the victory with wild dances.

He had another shock the next morning when he returned to the site to find what he expected to be a corpse and saw instead a lion in his path, alive and about to spring. Fortunately, it was an illusion; the lion was dead. Again the men laughed, danced, and shouted for joy, and two carried Patterson on their shoulders as they marched around the dead lion. The male measured nine feet eight inches from its nose to the tip of its tail and was three feet nine inches tall. It took eight men to carry him back to the camp.

News of Patterson's success after eight months of hunting the elusive beast quickly spread throughout the country. Floods of congratulatory telegrams poured in, and scores from surrounding areas traveled to Tsavo to see the man-eater's skin.

But, of course, his job was not over. There was still another man-eater at large. On the dark night of December 27, 1898, in his bed for a change, Patterson was awoken by men who had left their tents to sleep in a tree, screaming that a lion was after them. The moon was hidden by dense clouds and Patterson could see nothing, but he fired off a few bullets and apparently scared it off. The next day he found the lion's trail: it had gone into every one of the men's empty tents, as well as around their tree.

The next brightly moonlit evening he climbed the same tree, almost grasping a poisonous snake curled around a branch. He hurriedly hit the ground and waited until one of his men killed the snake with a long pole before climbing back up together with Mahina, his Swahili gun bearer, who was to spell him during the night. At two Patterson roused the sleeping Mahina to take his place and slept for a while, leaning against the tree. Then he awoke, having suddenly sensed danger. He had neither seen nor heard anything but after staring intensely could make out a lion slowly approaching. The land in the area was open except for occasional small bushes dotted around. And the lion's skill in taking advantage of the bushes as cover showed Patterson that "he was an old hand at the terrible game of man-hunting."[25] The lion was some twenty yards away when Patterson fired his .303. Although Patterson heard the bullet hit home, the lion merely growled fiercely and bounded away. Patterson followed up with three more shots, and another growl told him that the last bullet had hit its target a second time.

At dawn he took a native tracker with him, while Mahina followed closely behind with a Martini carbine. Blood spatters led them for a few hundred yards into the jungle, where they were abruptly stopped by a fierce growl. Staring through a thicket, Patterson made eye contact with the man-eater, who glared at him as it bared its teeth in an angry snarl. As the lion charged, Patterson fired. It needed a second shot to knock it down, but the lion was up in a flash and, though crippled by the bullet, still headed for Patterson. A third shot had no apparent effect, so Patterson dropped his rifle and urgently held out his hand for the more powerful Martini rifle—and grasped empty air. Mahina and his gun were halfway up a nearby tree and climbing fast. Patterson joined them just before the lion arrived at the foot of the tree. When the wounded animal began to limp back to the thicket, Patterson took the carbine from Mahina and after one shot the man-eater fell and lay still. Too excited to be cautious, Patterson scrambled down the tree and approached the lion. To his dismay, it got up and charged at him. It was within five yards of him when one carbine bullet in the chest and one in the head dropped it dead almost at his feet. This lion, also a male, was the bigger of the two: nine feet six from the tip of his tail to his nose and three feet eleven inches high.

Prime Minister Lord Salisbury announced the welcome news in the British House of Lords, without naming Patterson, giving the credit to "an enthusiastic sportsman," and adding, "The whole of the works [at Tsavo] were put a stop to for three weeks because a party of man-eating lions . . . conceived a most unfortunate taste for our porters. At last the labourers, entirely declined to go on unless they were guarded by an iron retrenchment. Of course it is difficult to work a railway under such conditions, and until we found an enthusiastic sportsman to get rid of these lions, our enterprise was seriously hindered."[26]

An editorialist in the British magazine *Spectator* named Patterson as the hero and, in a piece titled "The Lions That Stopped the Railway," reported, "When the jungle twinkled with hundreds of lamps, as the shout went on from camp to camp that the first lion was dead, as the hurrying crowds fell prostrate in the midnight forest laying their hands on his feet, and the Africans danced savage and ceremonial dances of thanksgiving, Mr. Patterson must have realized . . . what it was to have been a hero and deliverer in the days when man was not yet undisputed lord of the creation, and that might pass at any moment under the savage dominion of the beasts."[27]

Patterson noted wryly that the same men who once wanted to murder him now treated him like a demigod and gave him a silver bowl. Translated from the Hindi, the inscription read, in part, "We, your Overseer, Timekeepers, Mistaris and Workmen, present you with this bowl as a token of our gratitude to you for your bravery in killing two man-eating lions at great risk to your own life, thereby saving us from the fate of being devoured by these terrible monsters who nightly broke into our tents and took our fellow workers from our side." It was dated January 30, 1899.[28]

A foreman of masons, Roshan, gave him a remarkable poem that Patterson had translated from the Hindi. A small part of it reads:

Patterson Sahib is indeed a brave and valiant man, like unto those
    Persian heroes of old.
So brave is he, that the greatest warriors stood aghast at his action;
Tall in stature, young, most brave and of great strength is he.
Lions do not fear lions, yet one glance from Patterson
Sahib cowed the bravest of them . . .

Previously, many Englishmen had come here to shoot but had been
disappointed.

Because the lion was very courageous and ferocious, and the Sahibs were
afraid.

But for the sake of our lives, Patterson Sahib took all this trouble, risking
his own life in the forest.

Patterson Sahib has left me, and I shall miss him as long as I live, and now
Roshan must roam about in Africa, sad and regretful.

Patterson cherished the silver bowl and the poem as his "most highly
prized and hard-won trophy."[29]

Before he shot the two lions it is believed that they had killed twenty-
eight Indian laborers and more than a hundred Africans. When he
finally completed the bridge on February 7, 1899, and proudly watched
it survive a fierce, flooded river, he estimated that, but for the lions, it
would have been finished seven months earlier. (The Germans blew it
up during World War I.) Rather than resting on his laurels, Patterson
pressed on with extending the railroad, and completed another bridge
over another river.

Killing the man-eaters did not leave him with a trouble-free existence.
Leopards, hyenas, wild dogs, and wild cats were constant unwelcome
visitors to the camps. A leopard especially enraged Patterson after it wan-
tonly slaughtered a flock of thirty sheep and goats he kept for food and
milk. He left their carcasses on the ground and waited for the leopard to
return to feast off his prey, and, when it did, shot it dead.

In March 1899 Patterson was supervising the building of another railroad station and killing the occasional lion when a caravan of some four
thousand porters arrived, carrying supplies for a Sikh regiment stationed
on the coast that had recently suppressed a mutiny by the Sudanese in
Uganda. The porters were astonished at the sight of a train and so terrified when, to entertain them, Patterson blew off steam and sounded
the whistle that they flung themselves on the ground, howling in terror.
Then, gradually, they got up and raced off in all directions. After Patterson shut off the steam and stopped the whistle, they slowly returned,
and he persuaded two of the chiefs to climb aboard for a short ride, which
both seemed to enjoy.

3. A train crosses the bridge at Tsavo shortly after its completion on February 7, 1899. From J. H. Patterson, *The Man-Eaters of Tsavo.*

Several days later the porters returned from the coast in a terrible state, many dying from dysentery. When thirteen left the column and collapsed near Patterson's tent, he boiled a bucket of water, added condensed milk and almost a bottle of brandy, and fed it to them. The few able to speak simply whispered, "Bwana, Bwana" (Master, Master). Six died that night, but he nursed seven back to health over the next two weeks, when they were fit enough to resume their walk to Uganda.[30]

During those two weeks Patterson left orders for the care of his patients and took a pony ride several miles away to plan for a bridge over the Athi River. En route he came across several swollen corpses before he saw a dying porter lying at the side of the road, wrapped in a scarlet blanket. Another porter walking by grabbed one end of the blanket and rolled the dying man out of it. Outraged, Patterson galloped his pony toward the callous thief and raised his rhinoceros-hide whip, as if to use it. The man began to draw his dagger, but stopped when Patterson dismounted and aimed his rifle at him. After Patterson made the thief replace the blanket, he marched him at gunpoint back to the camp and handed him over to the officer in charge—who had him whipped. Patterson then returned to his task.

On June 5, 1899, a train carried Patterson; Doctors McCulloch, Brock, and Waters; hundreds of coolies; Patterson's trophies; and his horse, Blazeaway, along the Uganda Railway as far as Nairobi, its most western reach, where Patterson set up camp. His job now was to build a bridge to continue the railroad across the Nairobi River.

It was there that Patterson heard of the dreadful death of Dr. Haslem, who had spent several months with him in Tsavo. Haslem had visited Kikuyu country to study the tropical disease rinderpest, from which scores of their cattle had died. To do so he dissected the animals' bodies. The superstitious Wa Kikuyu, believing that Dr. Haslam had bewitched the cattle, tortured and killed him. Patterson, of course, was deeply distressed. Despite this killing, and although the Wa Kikuyu were reputed to be cruel, cowardly, and treacherous, Patterson, who had hundreds of them working for him at Nairobi, found them to be bright, amusing, and eager to learn.

The workers who most intrigued him were the Swahili, the Wa Taita, and the Kavirondo. Swahili were generally well built, carefree, careless, and pleasure-loving descendants of Arab fathers and black mothers. He heard two versions of the derivation of their name. One had it derived from the Arabic for "coast"; the other called it a corruption of "sawi Biloi," which means equal-opportunity cheaters, or "those who cheat all alike." In Patterson's experience, the Wa Taita "like most other natives of Africa are exceedingly superstitious, and this failing is turned to good account by the 'witch-doctor' or 'medicine man.'" He judged the Kavirondo as the most interesting, calling them "simple, industrious, exceedingly hospitable, and a little addicted to thievery, perhaps, but that is hardly considered a sin in the heart of Africa."[31]

Patterson, in turn, must have intrigued the workers with his inflexible rituals. When not actively hunting lions—and he killed several more after the Tsavo man-eaters—he invariably awoke at dawn to breakfast on sugar-free hot tea, cold meats, and dry bread, after which he bathed in his portable India-rubber bath two-thirds full of hot water. He shaved while sitting in the bath, using a flat board across it to hold a mirror and his shaving kit.

4. Although Kikuyu tribesmen like these were reputed to be cruel, cowardly, and treacherous, Patterson found them to be eager, intelligent, and well behaved. From J. H. Patterson, *The Man-Eaters of Tsavo.*

Now clean-shaven, he stayed in the warm bathwater to read a few pages of the Bible—for the literature and history, rather than the message.

Warned that the Nairobi River that supplied all the town's water was dangerously contaminated, he went with Dr. Winston Waters to the crowded rat- and flea-infested bazaar nearby and came across a sleeping man with plague fleas on his skin. Dr. Waters put the man under quarantine, and when they returned to the camp, Patterson had the outside of his tent disinfected. But he knew that was not enough. Having seen how

5. At work on the Tsavo railroad in 1898. Courtesy of Alan Patterson.

the plague had devastated the Calcutta slums, he decided to take drastic action. Instructing his servants to load a cart with oil and cotton waste and follow him to the bazaar, he gave the Asian and Arab storekeepers there an hour to move their goods and evacuate the place. Then he burned it to the ground. "For this somewhat arbitrary proceeding," Patterson wrote, "I was mildly called over the coals," largely because the storekeepers had made outrageous claims to compensate for the loss of their property.[32] But Patterson felt entirely justified because it stamped out the plague. (In 1902 a Dr. Spurrier, the medical officer of health, emulated Patterson by having the rebuilt bazaar again set ablaze, spurred by the previous year's death toll of fifty from the plague.)

As Patterson was preparing to return to London, hundreds of workers begged him to take them with him as his children. He imagined the reception in England if he arrived with a bodyguard of almost naked "savages," and persuaded them to remain in their own country. However, a few of his best workers—his "ever-faithful Mahina," his "boy Roshan Khan," and his "honest chaukidar, Meeanh"—accompanied him to Mombasa to see him off on a ship to India en route to England.[33]

He was back in England on December 20, 1901, when the Uganda Railway was completed at what would be called Port Florence Station. The next day, watched by her husband, a few officials, and a pet dog, Ronald Preston's wife, Florence, took her pet parrot from her shoulder, exchanged her parasol for a keying hammer, and drove home the last key in the last rail. The *London Times* reported, "Within less than five and a half years of its inception this great and arduous undertaking has been brought to a successful conclusion. The railway is altogether 572 miles long, but its mere length conveys no idea of the difficulties which had to be overcome in carrying the steel tracks up from the shores of the Indian Ocean." The paper cited evidence that Uganda's untapped wealth would amply repay the huge investment of 5.5 million pounds, and did not forget to mention that "the Pax Britannica has secured order and security over a vast region of nearly 4,000,000 souls which until the advent of British rule was given over to a cruel and sterilizing tyranny."[34] But there was not a word about Patterson's vital contribution.

2

Boer War Bravado,

1900–1907

PATTERSON HAD HARDLY set foot on English soil before he was sailing for South Africa to fight in the Boer (or South African) War. It was a battle between the British and Dutch, known as Boers, over who should control South Africa's wealth—especially after gold had been discovered—and its native inhabitants. Patterson went as a second lieutenant, second in command of the Seventy-sixth (Cavalry) Company of the Imperial Yeomanry Company, known as the Rough Riders.

On arrival, he sent twenty men to guard a bridge. When one of them on sentry duty accidentally fired his rifle, Patterson had him tied to a cartwheel for two hours—Field Punishment no. 1. He showed considerably more kindness when he decided to commandeer a farmer's horses. The pleas of the man's teenage daughter weakened his resolve. But she would have to hand them over, he said, if his company ever really needed them. Apparently, they never did. Patterson went to another farm on a tip that a Boer spy was using it as a hideout, and encountered three women. Or so it seemed. On closer inspection, he saw that one needed a shave. Instead of having him shot as a spy, Patterson made him stay in the dress he was wearing for the trip under guard to Cape Town as a prisoner of war. At another farm Patterson made friends of the farmer by shooting baboons that were eating his crops.

His familiarity with trains came in useful in January 1901, when he, his men, and their horses had been traveling by train without water for twenty-four hours. When the train stopped near a stream, Patterson

34

ordered his men to take themselves and their parched horses to drink from the stream. The delay irked the guard, who warned Patterson, "When the train coming down the track passes us, I'll leave for Johannesburg whether your horses are back in the boxes or not"

"Will you?" Patterson challenged.

"Yes I will. I'm in charge of the train."

Patterson whispered to his sergeant major, and the next moment the guard was under arrest, an armed soldier on either side of him.

After the down train had passed by, and the thirsty horses and their riders continued to drink from the stream, the guard, though still under arrest, yelled to the train's driver, "Move off, even if you have to leave me behind."

Patterson asked the driver if he meant to follow the guard's instructions. When he said yes, Patterson put him under arrest, too.

When all the thirst-quenched horses and riders were back on the train, Patterson told the driver and guard that they were free to take over. But the driver refused. Patterson then mounted the foot plate, confidently moved the lever to start the train, and gleefully noted the driver's look of astonishment. Both driver and guard then resumed the journey.[1]

He proved his fighting spirit during the war, when he was on patrol with two men and encountered fifteen enemy soldiers. Instead of a stealthy retreat, he went on the attack. And it was the Boers who retreated, after Patterson and his partners had killed one, wounded one, and captured two of them. For that act of bravery, Patterson was promoted from second lieutenant to captain and awarded the Distinguished Service Order.

After home leave in the summer of 1901, he was expecting to return to the war front, but the new sovereign, King Edward VII, had other plans for him. (Edward's mother, Queen Victoria, had died in January of that year.) As honorary colonel of the Essex Imperial Yeomanry, the king cabled Lord Kitchener, commander of the British forces in South Africa, to inform him that he was keeping Patterson in Britain. As Patterson's wife, Frances, explained in a letter to her mother on July 8, 1901:

We came to Cromer on Saturday and Colonel Barclay met us at the Station and drove us out to his house . . . a most beautiful place and the grounds are lovely. Jack and I have a lovely "suite" of three rooms, so cosy and comfortable—and all lit with electric light of course. I am thankful to say that Jack is not going back to the war just at present—if at all—as the King requires his services at home for 4 or 5 months. He wants him to be adjutant of a new regiment of Imperial Yeomanry at which the King is Honorary Colonel.[2]

Instead of a gun, Patterson now toted a tennis or badminton racket, or a croquet mallet at frequent parties in the Home Counties around London. Describing one such affair to her mother in an August 22, 1901, letter, Frances Patterson wrote:

> Here I am back in Beckenham [a London suburb] after having such a nice time in Cromer for 3 weeks. Mrs. Locker-Lampson [a prominent politician's wife] had a tennis party in the afternoon and [the poet] Lord Tennyson's grandson, Charlie Tennyson, was there. . . . Jack was the hero of the evening as they all heard of his lion-hunting exploits. They were all tremendously interested. I paid my call on Saturday and met Lady Humphrey there and Miss Kate Greenaway the artist. . . . They all think very highly of Jack and are so pleased to have him as adjutant. The Rhinoceros [one of Patterson's African trophies] has arrived at last . . . a most dreadful looking monster."

Writing to her father on October 30, 1901, Mrs. Patterson said that the rhinoceros's head was so heavy it took three men to lift, adding,

> Yesterday Jack had to go to St. James Palace to be decorated by the king. The officers had to approach the throne alone, and kneel in front of the king and then kiss the king's hand and retire backwards from his presence. I met Jack immediately afterwards at the Carlton and we had lunch there. Jack wore his two decorations—the ordinary South African Medal, and the D.S.O.
>
> After lunch we drove to the Colonial Office, where Jack had an appointment with the Chamberlain's private secretary. He offered him an appointment in N.W. Africa with a salary of 1,500 pounds per annum, but he refused it as he would rather go to South Africa if he goes out of England again. Then Jack had to go back to Norfolk, to provide an escort for the King and Queen and the Duke and Duchess of Cornwall.

In January 1902, Patterson was promoted to lieutenant colonel of the Imperial Yeomanry's Thirty-third Battalion, with 460 men under his command, and after several months he was ordered to return to the Boer War in South Africa. But when he and his battalion arrived in May 1902, the peace had just been signed.

At year's end, Patterson's wife joined him in South Africa, where they partied with former enemy generals Cronje, De la Rey, and Botha. They also socialized with Robert Baden-Powell, a British general and national hero for his successful 217-day defense of the town of Mafikeng against a much larger Boer force. He later founded the Boy Scouts and the Girl Guides. During their conversation, Baden-Powell laughed so loudly that a senior general sent his adjutant to tell him to cool it.

In January 1903 they visited a gold mine and the schoolhouse where the Boers held British prisoners, and were driven to a park in a rickshaw. That same week General Louis Botha dined with when at their hotel. Frances Patterson told her father, "We had a long talk with Botha about the war. He is very sensible and pleasant and we all agreed that war ought to be abolished as it seems such a barbarous way of settling differences." Patterson befriended Botha's daughter, Anne, and her family, with whom he maintained a lifelong correspondence.

Back in England that summer, the Pattersons resumed their high-society whirl, wining and dining with such celebrities as Sir Henry Irving, the greatest British actor of his time. Patterson got up early to play tennis with a colonel friend, and then, after breakfast, the men joined their wives for golf in the afternoon, snacking on fresh peaches and strawberries.

In August 1905 Patterson attended a garden party given by the countess of Warwick (reputedly one of Kind Edward's numerous mistresses), where he met leading British generals, including Douglas Haig (who became chief of the British forces during World War I), Baden-Powell for a second time, as well as Lord Vane Tempest, Lord Errington, and Lord Innes. In the social pecking order, the chief guests were Prince Francis of Teck, brother of the princess of Wales, and the queen's maid of honor, who had recently married General Douglas Haig in Buckingham Palace.

Haig, inspector general of cavalry for India, was the son of the head of a whiskey distilling company. (He would became commander of the British army in France during World War I). Now, he was about to return to India and invited Patterson along as his guest. Instead, Patterson spent

6. Sir Henry Irving, England's greatest actor, admired and
befriended Patterson. Courtesy of the Library of Congress
Prints and Photographs Division, LC-USZ62-105316.

the early weeks of his long leave at home now in Holland Park, West London, working on his car. He hoped to improve the internal combustion
engine and patent the result.

With the Boer War over, he was also considering his career options. The
lure of East Africa won out. He was back there early in 1906 on a hunting
and sightseeing trip to as far as Lake Victoria, and equipped with a new
camera with a telescopic lens. The marquis and marchioness of Water-
ford went as far as Somaliland. Five others stayed with him for the entire
trip: Lord Warwick and his brother, Alwyn Greville; Winston Churchill's
cousin Moreton Frewen; a Canadian timber tycoon named Lingham;
and one woman, Mrs. Hinde. They traveled on the Uganda railroad from

Mombasa, and when they reached Tsavo at midnight, all but Patterson were asleep. He could not resist waking them to see "the strength and beauty of the Tsavo bridge" by moonlight.[3]

At Nairobi he was surprised to find a thriving modern town of some six thousand inhabitants. It even had a first-class racetrack. After Nairobi the group left the train to either ride or walk through a swamp, over hills, and through rivers and streamlets, looking for big game.

During the journey, Patterson noticed that their guide, a Masai named Uliagurma, was suffering from an earache. When they made camp that night, Patterson treated him so successfully that the guide spread the word. From then on, wherever they went, the natives greeted Patterson as a medicine man. As he recalled, "The consequence was that men, women and children in every state of disease and crippledom besieged our camps, begging for some of the magical dawa [medicine]. I used to do what I could, and only hope I did not injure many of them; but it was heartrending to see some of the quite hopeless cases I was expected to cure."[4] On another safari later in 1906 with the Honorable Cyril Ward and his wife, Irene, Patterson's hunting trophies included a new type of eland that he gave to the British Museum.

After his return home, his wife's letters give a lively picture of British army life: she attended military balls and garden parties, went with Patterson on a trip to Paris, and, back in England, watched him take part in army maneuvers at two in the morning. Patterson's wife described the event in a letter to her mother, from Grand Hotel, Clacton on Sea, on May 31, 1906: "On Monday morning there was a big [mock] battle until lunch time. We were driving and got right into the thick of it and the bullets were flying all round us. It was most exciting. Jack's squadron was defending the position against the three other squadrons & succeeded in holding out until time was up. One of the ladies in my carriage was hit by one of the bullets, but she was not hurt as they only use wads on these occasions."

From the Hotel Continental, Paris, on April 6, 1907, she wrote her mother again: "We went to the Madeleine on Easter Sunday & then on to Versailles. Afterwards we walked through the lovely gardens of the Trianon where poor Marie Antoinette used to spend so much of her time.

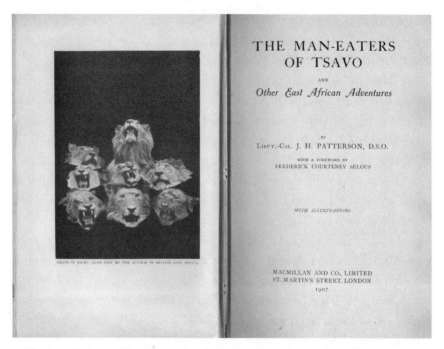

THE MAN-EATERS
OF TSAVO

AND

Other East African Adventures

BY

Lieut.-Col. J. H. PATTERSON, D.S.O.

WITH A FOREWORD BY
FREDERICK COURTENEY SELOUS

WITH ILLUSTRATIONS

MACMILLAN AND CO., LIMITED
ST. MARTIN'S STREET, LONDON
1907

HEADS OF EIGHT LIONS SHOT BY THE AUTHOR IN BRITISH EAST AFRICA.

7. The frontispiece of Patterson's book that impressed President Theodore Roosevelt and Ernest Hemingway.

On Monday we went down the Seine by boat to the races at Longchamps and enjoyed it all immensely. Yesterday Jack and I drove all about Paris, and went to the theatre in the evening."

Patterson had also been working on an account of his adventures in East Africa, with the telling title *The Man-Eaters of Tsavo*. Published in 1907, it got rave reviews, and was in print for more than eighty years. Ernest Hemingway kept two copies in his library. An enduring success, it has been the inspiration for three movies and still thrills contemporary readers, judging by the five-star accolades it gets.

The year of the book's publication, the British government needed a chief game warden to survey East Africa's northern and eastern borders to establish suitable areas for big-game hunting and other areas where the animals would be protected. Patterson, then forty, was the obvious man for the job, for which he was seconded from the army to the Colonial Office.

By that time some four thousand settlers, mostly British, had followed Lord Delamere's lead to make British East Africa, especially its fertile highlands, their homeland. The "lower orders" were discouraged from making the trip. In fact, so many settlers were aristocratic products of Eton or Harrow that their favorite meeting place, Nairobi's Hotel Norfolk, was called "The House of Lords."

3

Theodore Roosevelt's Friendship, 1907

AS PATTERSON WAS PREPARING to set sail for East Africa, he learned that American president Theodore Roosevelt had heard of his book and was eager to read it. Patterson wrote to him from his London club at 127 Piccadilly on October 1, 1907:

> At the special request of my friend Mr. Selous [a famous big-game hunter and explorer], who tells me you would be much interested in my book, I venture to send you a copy. . . . It was not until I had seen Mr. Selous's kindly introduction [to the book] that I was aware that you had ever heard of me, although my good friend Mr. E. N. Buxton is well known to you and has often told me of the enjoyable time he spent with you at Washington. It is entirely owing to Mr. Buxton's efforts that strenuous endeavours are now being made to protect the wild life in East Africa, which at one time stood in danger of being shot out. Perhaps one day you will find time to visit this beautiful country and see for yourself the glorious wild life which abounds there. I feel certain that you would find much more pleasure in tackling the King of Beasts than the King of Trusts! I am at present in charge of the Game Dept. in British East Africa and can assure you of a warm welcome there should you ever honour us with a visit.[1]

Roosevelt replied on October 25:

> I greatly appreciate the copy of your book. I quite agree with Selous that no lion story since the days of Heroditus [he doubtless meant the Greek

8. President Theodore Roosevelt sought Patterson's advice. Courtesy of the Library of Congress Prints and Photographs Division, LC-USZ62-134760.

historian Herodotus, called the father of history] equals yours; and even if this story were out the book would still be one of very great interest. I don't know when I have read a book of the kind that I have liked as much. What a trump Buxton is! I have watched with interest the successful effort being made to protect the wild life of East Africa. I wish there was any such good fortune in store for me as to be able to make a short hunting trip there. Is there any chance of your visiting Washington? It would be such a pleasure to see you.

Winston Churchill, Britain's assistant colonial secretary—like Patterson, an author and Boer War veteran—went on safari in East Africa when Patterson was there, hunting rhinos and lions and meeting the settlers,

9. Winston Churchill called Patterson an adulterer and murderer. Courtesy of the Library of Congress Prints and Photographs Division, LC-DIG-ggbain-04739.

which he described in his *My African Journey*. Halfway between Nairobi
and Fort Hall, on November 6, 1907, Churchill wrote to his mother:

> We left Mombasa after two days of functions & inspections & speeches
> & proceeded up country by the Uganda Railway [which Patterson had
> helped to build]. Everything moves on the smoothest of wheels for me—a
> special train with dining and sleeping cars at my disposal all the way,
> wherever I wished to stop—it stopped. When it went on, we sat on a seat
> in front of the engine with our rifles & as soon as we saw anything to
> shoot at—a wave of the hand brought the train to a standstill & sometimes
> we tried at antelope without even getting down."[2]

As Patterson was still on safari when he received Roosevelt's fan letter, he waited to mail this reply until he returned to Nairobi on January 15, 1908:

A thousand thanks for the very kind and flattering letter you wrote me. It was a most pleasurable one to receive in the wilds of Africa. I apologize for the delay in replying, but I have been out of touch with civilization for some time. I have just returned from a trip through the little-known districts of the country.

I was accompanied by an Englishman [Armand Sanderson] and his American-born wife [Anne] who bossed the show. She was delightful in every way and has pluck enough to tackle a "Trust King!" [Roosevelt had recently attacked the "malefactors of great wealth" by strengthening the Sherman Anti-Trust Act.]

This is our record for Xmas day. Started at 2.20 a.m. to search for lions we heard roaring some miles away. We failed to find them and went ahead. Mrs. S. shot a good Impala and Hartesbeest [hartebeest]. Mr. S. a Zebra and Duker [duiker]. Then we got into rhino country and the fun began. We were charged three times by these brutes, but as there were convenient trees about we easily got clear. Just on the fourth time, however, Mrs. S had a narrow escape. Soon after this Mr. S ran into two lions, three lionesses and five cubs, but he was so taken aback that he never fired a shot. Unfortunately, Mrs. S was away after eland or she would have accounted for some of the lions. We eventually reached camp after a very exciting and memorable Xmas day at 6.30 p.m. I hope sir you will be able, when the cares of state are over, to pay this country a visit, where I am sure you would enjoy hunting immensely. It is most kind of you to say I should be welcome at Washington. I heartily wish I saw any chance of going there. But alas, I fear I am condemned to a life in the wilds.

He left out a safari highlight, when Anne Sanderson defended herself from a charging rhinoceros with her umbrella. She later adopted two male lion cubs, which she fed on warm meat and hot milk. The cubs survived a sea journey to New York, where they found a new home in the zoo.

Patterson's main purpose on that first safari was to note the variety and distribution of the animals around the Athi Plain, which was comparatively uneventful. It was the next safari that would have a critical and indelible effect on his life.

4

Fatal Safari Leader, 1908

A WEEK AFTER he completed his hunting trip with the Sandersons, Patterson prepared to leave Nairobi on a second safari: to survey the northern and eastern territory for the British Colonial Office and to hunt en route. He had already hired porters to carry food and other supplies and a headman, Munyaka bin Diwana, to take charge of them. Whenever possible, he hoped to ride his Arab horse, Aladdin. He even decided to take along a recent gift from a friend, his dog, Lurcher.

He was about to leave, when Audley James Blyth, the son of Baron Blyth, an old acquaintance and a former officer in the Essex Yeomanry, asked Patterson if he and his slim, blue-eyed, blonde wife, Ethel Jane, could go with him. They had been hoping to go on safari, but the man who was to accompany them had backed out. As they were an attractive and amiable couple, Patterson got the official okay for them to join him. What happened on the trip would have an enormous effect on Patterson's future and be a catalyst for Ernest Hemingway's masterpiece "The Short Happy Life of Francis Macomber."

It got off to a bad start: even before they reached the foothills of the Kikuyu Mountains, six porters deserted. Patterson distributed their loads among the remaining porters, who were incensed at having to carry extra weight and vowed vengeance on the deserters if they ever caught up with them.

After a sleepless night, during which the gun bearers drove off several lions, the party headed north for Rumuruti. On the way, Blyth shot an oryx—a straight-horned African antelope. But his wife outdid him by killing a Grant's gazelle and a Thomson's gazelle.

A few days later, although mostly traveling on horseback, Blyth developed a painful abscess on his instep. Patterson urged him to return to Nairobi, but he was reluctant to go. As Blyth was also having trouble controlling his horse—so stubborn they called it "the mule"—Patterson swapped horses with him. They turned west for a while, crossed the plain of Eljogi, and made their way through undulating hills and beautiful grass valleys alive with rhinos, gazelles, giraffes, and zebras. By now, Blyth was so sick that Patterson had two porters carry him in a hammock. When a male rhino threatened to attack, he halted the safari to have Blyth carried to a safer spot in the shelter of a tree.

Patterson and Ethel Blyth then began to stalk the rhino, which had retreated into the nearby bush, and were surprised to find that he had joined a female rhino and her calf. After Patterson signaled for Ethel to take care of the menacing male, she knelt and fired her rifle, sending him wheeling around to disappear down a slope. Seeing the female was now about to charge, Patterson told Ethel to lie down and keep still. Then, to warn off the menacing female rhino, he put a bullet in her hide. It worked. She trotted off with her calf.

Later in the day when Ethel Blyth killed an oryx at 150 yards, the delighted porters and gun bearers gleefully shouted that the lady was a better shot than the men. They were especially gleeful because she had also provided that night's dinner. After the meal, Patterson sat in his camp chair, admiring the beautiful view from Turah, a cool spot fifty-four hundred feet above sea level, and was relieved to hear that Audley Blyth was in less pain and that his abscess had broken open.

The next day, though, as they approached the Kavai River, Blyth's fever returned. He was again carried by porters in the hammock, while Patterson and Ethel Blyth took turns walking alongside with an umbrella to shade him from the sun. Their journey was interrupted once by a lion blocking their path, but for some reason Patterson chose not to shoot it. Instead, he mounted his horse, Aladdin, and galloping at top speed toward the lion scared it out of their way into the thick bush. At midday, Blyth felt better, and all three of them rode ahead of the safari.

Near the Lungaya River, an enraged elephant came out of the shade of a tree as if about to attack. They quickly dismounted, and Patterson told Ethel Blyth to shoot it. Her first shot hit home. All three then opened up, and the elephant fell where it was, completely hidden by thick bush. Patterson ran to about thirty feet from where he thought the elephant had fallen but could not see it. After the Blyths had climbed a rock for a better view, they warned Patterson that the wounded animal was getting to its feet. Patterson joined them on the rock and watched it rampage through the bush toward the porters at the tail end of the safari. Telling Ethel Blyth to stay put, leaving his gun bearer, Abbudi, to guard her, Patterson and Audley Blyth set off on horseback to warn the endangered porters. When the bush became too thick, they left their horses with Indian attendants and continued on foot with a small Somali gun bearer, Abdi. They had almost reached the elephant when it turned and headed directly for Blyth. Patterson fired, but it only enraged the animal, which then changed direction and headed for Abdi. He made a dive for the nearest thicket, becoming trapped in its thorny branches. As Patterson frantically reloaded, the elephant brushed passed him, again heading for Abdi. As it swung its trunk and knocked off Abdi's turban, Patterson fired again. The second shot probably saved Abdi's life, as the elephant immediately lost interest in him and battered its way through the bush and out of sight.

After freeing Abdi from the thicket, the trio tracked the elephant for more than an hour, until they met some of the porters, who were astonished to find Patterson alive. They had been told that the elephant had crushed him to death, as well as killing Ethel Blyth and Patterson's horse, Aladdin. To their immense relief they found Ethel alive and unharmed. But Patterson was very upset to find that his horse, Aladdin, was dead. He rode "The Mule" through the bush until he found Aladdin's killer—now a corpse. As its only tusk was badly decayed, he assumed that the pain it must have endured explained its initial fierce, unprovoked attack. Before they moved on, Patterson photographed Ethel Blyth sitting atop what was considered to be her trophy. After all, she had fired the first shot.

Blyth's fever returned with a vengeance, and for most of the ongoing journey porters carried him in the hammock, while much of the night his

10. Ethel Blyth sits atop the elephant she helped to kill. From
J. H. Patterson, *In the Grip of the Nyika.*

wife stayed awake taking care of him. The next day, Patterson advised
them both to rest in their tent while he explored and mapped the area.

On his return he found Blyth sicker than ever and Ethel Blyth
exhausted. While he had been away, Blyth had ignored his advice, leaving his sickbed to bag a giraffe. Patterson suspected that he was suffering
from sunstroke and throughout the night sat up with him, keeping wet
bandages on his forehead and giving him cool drinks—a mix of lime juice
and water from canvas water bags cooled by the breeze. Meanwhile, Ethel
Blyth slept in Patterson's tent.

According to Patterson's subsequent account, because two *askari* guards
(native soldiers) had reported that lions giving low, sinister growls had
passed nearby on their way to a water hole, several times during the night
he had checked with the guards that there was no immediate danger. He
also kept the campfire ablaze, which frightened off another lion that was
approaching the tents. At about four in the morning, satisfied that Blyth

was sleeping peacefully, Patterson woke the cook, Paul, to make a cup of cocoa and sipped it as he sat in his camp chair outside his tent entrance, in which Ethel Blyth was sleeping. Occasionally, he dozed off, waking at about five thirty to hear Blyth moving about in his bed. They briefly spoke about the next morning's march, and then Patterson went to see the headman to discuss arrangements for that day, which included carrying Blyth in a hammock. During their conversation a young man named Edi joined them and complained about feeling ill. While Patterson was prescribing medicine for him, the three of them were startled by a gunshot from Blyth's tent. Patterson, the headman, and dozens of others, including Ethel Blyth, rushed to see what had happened. But only Patterson and his headman, Munyakai, entered the tent. Blyth lay on his bed, a bullet in his head and a revolver in his hand. "It was a terrible shock," Patterson recalled. "And one which I shall never forget. . . . He was quite unconscious when we entered and all was over in a few moments."[1]

As Patterson recalled, to spare Ethel Blyth's feelings he asked her to return to his tent, where he would explain everything to her. What he then told her was, of course, speculation, because no one had witnessed what had occurred. Patterson believed it was an accident. It seems that Blyth kept a loaded pistol under his pillow, and Patterson assumed that when he moved restlessly the gun had slipped under his shoulder. In trying to move it back he had accidentally shot himself. Had he known that Blyth kept a loaded gun under his pillow, Patterson said that he would have removed it, as "I have invariably found that a revolver is more dangerous to the owner than to anybody else." After he explained his theory to Ethel Blyth, he "hoped that she would, with her usual pluck, try to bear up under the terrible blow with what fortitude she could command."[2] But he was disappointed. She seemed dazed, apparently in shock, and not able to grasp the situation. So he decided it best to leave her alone, and told his "boy" to look after her while he buried her husband in a rocky hillside.

He then wondered whether to return immediately to Nairobi with the grieving widow or to complete his mission—surveying the boundary of the Reserve at Marsabit, which would take about four more days. He chose to press on. But back at the camp, before he could announce his decision, he faced a mutiny. During his absence, while he was burying Blyth, a few men had grabbed guns and ammunition and persuaded most of the others to join them. Although unarmed, Patterson walked through the crowd to the leaders of the mutiny, who were squatting on the ground. When he questioned them, they replied that if they continued the trek through the desert, they were afraid of dying of thirst. A spokesman insisted on turning back and said that Patterson could not stop them because they had all the weapons.

Patterson had previously talked his way out of a similar situation when helping to build the railroad. But this time the fate of Ethel Blyth was also at stake. Nevertheless, he refused to give in to their demands. He told them that he was an officer working for the government and meant to reach Marsabit, whatever the obstacles. If they refused his orders, he threatened to recruit a hundred spear-carrying natives to hunt them down and take them back to Nairobi as prisoners. There they would face severe punishment. The mutineers responded with jeers and counterthreats, though no one fired his gun at the defenseless Patterson. Still, he knew that his survival depended on what he said next.

During their trek through the jungle, Patterson continued, he had regarded them as his own children, concerned with their welfare and safety. And he had only punished those men who deserved it. He was reluctant to use stern measures, he said, but would not hesitate to do so if they did not give up the stolen guns and ammunition and return to duty. He gave them an hour to decide, then walked to his tent about fifty yards away and sat in the shade of a thorn tree.

Munyakai, the headman, and a few others immediately joined him. Munyakai explained to Patterson that the revolt was led by a few porters who were tired of the hard marches and strict discipline Patterson imposed. They had scared the others by claiming that Patterson would lead them to their deaths in the wilderness, to be slaughtered by savages or die of thirst. "They think you will not go on if they make trouble," Munyakai concluded, "as they know you are sad."[3] About an hour later a few mutineers turned up and before the deadline they had all gathered outside Patterson's tent. The revolt was over. As a concession, Patterson lightened their loads, junking nonessentials. Not wanting to disturb Ethel

Blyth, who had remained secluded in his tent, he made sure she knew nothing of the revolt.

Before moving on, he had part of her tent burned, perhaps because it was bloodstained with her husband's blood. He also packed up and stored away the rest of her tent, as, according to his account, "I did not wish painful memories to be recalled to Mrs. B's mind by the sight of it."[4]

Patterson maintained that even had he contemplated an immediate return to Nairobi, the mutiny made it impossible, because giving in to the mutineers would have put the lives of Ethel Blyth and himself at risk. He persuaded the dazed and grief-stricken widow who wanted to return at once to Nairobi that he must complete his work, which would take only a few more days. At Marsabit he could get fresh camels for their return to civilization—Nairobi was then a city of some 6,000 inhabitants, including 350 Europeans and 1,700 Indians.

As Patterson recalled, on March 21, 1908, the couple rode "in gloomy silence" across the Kaisoot Desert, "our minds full of the sad events of the morning," while from time to time the porters, agitated by the occasional distant roars, yelled, "Hurry! The lions are bad here!!"[5] Around midnight they stopped for a brief rest, and Patterson made a bed of rugs for Ethel Blyth. She slept fitfully for a couple of hours, waking sometimes with a cry of distress. He sat near her on a box, leaning against a tree stump, a rifle across his knees, trying to pacify and soothe her when she awoke.

At four in the morning, fortified with coffee, they continued their journey, stirring the red lava underfoot into dust clouds. By midmorning the fierce sun beat down on them, but there was some comfort in spotting their destination on the horizon—the cloud-covered mountains of Marsabit. Suddenly, a startled porter cried out, "Rhino! Rhino!" as one came trotting from the shade of a thorn tree. The porters panicked, dropping their loads and scattering. Patterson hurried Ethel Blyth to the shelter of a large tree whose branches, moments later, "were absolutely black with a swarm of porters."[6] When Patterson aimed his rifle at the rhino, it simply turned and trotted away.

For a second night Ethel Blyth slept on a bed of rugs while Patterson again sat nearby, guarding her. Once he dozed off and was awoken by the sound of stampeding frenzied ponies and mules, followed by rifle fire. A group of rhinos had scared the animals away, and the gunfire had driven off the rhinos. Patterson spent much of the remaining night rounding up the ponies and mules.

Soon after dawn they left the desert for what seemed paradise by contrast: mountains and forests full of wildlife—giraffes, rhinos, bushbuck, oryx, and female greater and lesser kudu. But it was still hard going, as they struggled through thickets, up and down steep ravines, across valleys, over hills, and along the edges of craters.

A few days later he left the headman in charge of the camp at Crater Lake, and with Papai as his guide and a half-dozen porters, he and Ethel Blyth set out for the eight-mile journey. At first they walked through a mist, and frequently stopped to rest, until they reached a hill. By then the mist had cleared, and from the hillside they clearly saw the Urray mountain range. Patterson marked it on his map as a natural border for the reserve's northern boundary. He had now completed his task, and, as he wrote, "it was with considerable satisfaction that I headed the safari southward and marched towards civilization."[7]

Patterson's next move was to be the subject of an official government investigation, the interrogation of native eyewitnesses, and questions in the House of Lords. As he saw it, if anything happened to him—such as being killed by mutineers or a wild animal—Ethel Blyth would be left alone in a savage land. He constantly worried about how to protect "the unfortunate lady, who had been so tragically left in my care."

> I was full of anxiety about her. I therefore decided to have my own tent divided into two compartments. I had a partition put along the centre of it, which made it into two tents, each with a separate doorway. Outside mine I always had a sentry posted; with instructions to call me at the slightest alarm, as I always lay down in my clothes with my rifle ready.
>
> I would have given Mrs. Blyth the whole tent for herself, only that on the day we got to Marsabit I fell seriously ill with dysentery. Rain also began to fall. It was therefore absolutely necessary that I should not only have shelter, but also the most careful nursing as, if neglected, dysentery can prove fatal [especially in the tropics].

Ethel Blyth became his nurse, which he believed "helped her to divert her thoughts and roused her a little out of her despondency."[8] He also believed that her nursing and preparing powdered milk, a new product, for him to drink helped to save his life. Afraid that the men would take advantage of his illness to mutiny again, he said that he forced himself, despite agonizing pain, to sit outside his tent to give daily routine orders.

Patterson never explained why he chose such a dangerous route back to Nairobi. Europeans were advised to avoid it, as it was the home of many hostile tribes. It also, of course, put Ethel Blyth at risk. Evidently, he thought he could protect her and handle the hostile natives. When he reached Meru country he had a chance to prove it. Then, although the safari was surrounded by some three hundred howling, spear-brandishing warriors, Patterson managed to break through and get an audience with their chief, Dominuki. He urged Patterson to join forces with him in a planned attack on a nearby enemy tribe led by a chief named Thularia. After an exchange of sheep, goats, camels, and various trophies, tribesmen celebrated the prospective military alliance with a spectacular war dance. But, after several more hours of talk, Patterson persuaded Dominuki to try to make peace with his enemy.

The next day, while Ethel Blyth stayed under guard, armed members of the safari and one hundred of Dominuki's men set out through a forest toward the enemy village. To avoid an ambush, Patterson sent scouts ahead. The scouts returned with news that Thularia and his prime minister were willing to talk with Patterson. After what seemed an endless conference, he talked Thularia into a peace treaty with Dominuki. Success encouraged him to stop at the next village to meet its chief and his advisers, who were also on the brink of war with their neighbors. Many hours later, Patterson had talked them, too, into calling off the war. At another village, Surah, he acted as honest broker at a gathering of the chiefs of three hostile tribes and persisted until they agreed to stop fighting each other—a diplomatic hat trick!

That visit was not the end of it. As the safari approached the village of Makinduni, Patterson heard the threatening noises of a tribal war dance and feared that his safari was again in danger. He sent a scout, who spoke the tribe's language, to discover if he should prepare for an attack. The scout returned with news that the tribe's young warriors had wanted to kill everyone on the Patterson safari and to steal their property. But a witch doctor had advised the tribe that the white man and woman

11. Some of the threatening warriors Patterson pacified. From J. H. Patterson, *In the Grip of the Nyika.*

had magic powers. Because the tribe's senior citizens believed him, they scared the younger men out of their planned massacre. Although Patterson seemed to have an extraordinary ability to pacify would-be warriors, nevertheless, he sat up all night, with a loaded rifle and, instead of using magic powers, fired off an occasional warning rocket, just in case. There was no attack.

The return journey was taking an unusually long time. It was now a month since Audley Blyth's death, but Patterson seemed in no hurry to reach Nairobi. When he saw a large herd of buffalo grazing in the distance, he could not resist stopping to take a photo. Sheltered by high grass and a slight ridge, he and Ethel Blyth moved stealthily toward the herd. Then Patterson came face-to-face with an enraged buffalo, which suddenly charged. With only a moment to decide, he told Ethel Blyth to shoot it, intending to hold his fire until it was close enough for a sure shot. But her bullet did the trick, and the buffalo took a dive to its death almost at their feet. The entire herd of some 150—led by a bull with huge horns—heads lowered for an attack, came thundering through the tall grass, straight for them. Patterson knew that the only way not to be trampled to death was to kill the leader, and possibly the herd would turn aside. As they both lay on the ground, Patterson shouted to Ethel Blyth, "We must drop the leading bull or we're done," and they both fired away.[9] The bull was within thirty feet of the couple when it fell and stayed down. The herd came to a halt, some just staring at the couple as they lay on the ground, partly hidden by the grass.

They were in even more danger when *askaris* from the safari began to fire wildly at the animals. To Patterson's immense relief, their bullets were wide of the mark. He knew that if any bullets had hit the animals, the entire infuriated herd would have charged again and trampled everyone to death. Fortunately, the gunfire and black powder from the *askaris'* Martini rifles panicked the animals into galloping away into a papyrus swamp.

Patterson admired Ethel Blyth's cool courage and asked her how she felt when the herd was charging at them. "Something like what I suppose an infantry soldier feels when he is resisting a charge of cavalry," she replied. "A case of beat them off or get trampled."[10] The next morning a gun bearer and *askari* found the body of the bull buffalo at the edge of a papyrus swamp and brought back his head, with horns more than four feet wide.

That afternoon, in crossing the flood-swollen Tana River, they almost lost the mule Patterson had ridden since the death of his horse, Aladdin. The mule had been pulled to safety by a rope on the far side, but had then plunged back into the river, apparently to rejoin another mule waiting to be pulled across. Patterson went into action and got both animals to safety by nine that evening. But that was far from the end of his problems.

5

Rumors of a "Sinister Character," 1908–1909

WHEN AT LONG LAST they reached Nairobi, the protectorate's principal medical officer thought that Patterson looked in terrible shape and sent him before a medical board for a second opinion. They ordered his immediate return to England. Before he left, Patterson wrote to the governor of British East Africa, Lieutenant Colonel Sir James Sadler, explaining, among other things, that Blyth accidentally shot himself while suffering from fever and sunstroke, leaving his devoted wife heartbroken. He added that Blyth and he were old friends and fellow officers, and that their wives were also close friends.

On May 7, 1908, Sadler sent his report to the British Colonial Office: "Patterson informs me that Blyth died on the morning of 21st March at Laisamis [224 miles north of Nairobi] . . . where he accidentally shot himself in the head with a revolver. Death immediate. He had been ill for two days. Patterson had been with him all night. Accident occurred early in the morning whilst temporarily alone. Patterson returned ill. . . . Mrs. Blyth comes today. Leaves for England on Hertzog."[1] In his second book, *In the Grip of the Nyika* (*nyika* means "wilderness"], Patterson does not mention on what terms he parted from Ethel Blyth, but notes that a few men went with him to Mombasa, where they wished him a quick recovery and return for another safari.

On March 20, 1908, the day before Blyth's death, President Theodore Roosevelt had written to Patterson, who did not get the letter until he had reached Nairobi:

Now Ready. 8vo. 7s. 6d. net.

IN THE GRIP OF
THE NYIKA

Further Adventures in British East Africa

BY

Lieut.-Col. J. H. PATTERSON, D.S.O.

AUTHOR OF

"THE MAN-EATERS OF TSAVO"

WITH ILLUSTRATIONS

MACMILLAN AND CO., LIMITED
ST. MARTIN'S STREET, LONDON
1909

12. Patterson's second book, in which he explained how a friend, the husband of Ethel Blyth, committed suicide while with him on safari. This incident inspired Hemingway's "The Short Happy Life of Francis Macomber," and roused the British House of Lords to launch an inquiry.

A year hence I will leave the Presidency and, while I can not now decide what I shall do, it is possible that I might be able to make a trip to Africa. Would you be willing to give me some advice about it? I shall be fifty years old and for ten years I have led a busy, sedentary life, and so it is necessary to say that I shall be in no trim for the hardest kind of explorer's work. But

I am fairly healthy, and willing to work in order to get into a game country where I would do some shooting. I suppose I should be absent about a year on the trip. Now, is it imposing too much on your good nature to tell me when and where I ought to get some really good shooting, such as you and your friends had last Christmas day, for instance. Would it be possible for me to go from Mozambique and come down the Nile? How much time should I allow in order to give ample opportunity for hunting? . . . It may be that I shall not be able to go at all but I should like mightily to see the great African fauna, and to kill one or two rhino or buffalo and some of the big antelopes, with a chance of a shot at a lion. . . . I am not a butcher, but I would like to kill a few lions.

Patterson replied on June 23, 1908, from 127 Piccadilly, London:

Please forgive me for not having replied earlier to your letter of the 20th March. I only received it when I got back to Nairobi, after my long expedition to the Jubaland Game Preserve. I was not at all well on my return and the doctors sent me home on sick leave, so I thought I would wait until I arrived here before writing to you. I certainly consider that it would be wise to spend the greater part of your time in B.E.A. [British East Africa]. It is a good healthy country and the shooting is—if I may use the word—"Bully." With ordinary luck you will be able to shoot good specimens of the following animals: Lion, Leopard, Elephant, Rhino, Hippo, Giraffe, Buffalo, Eland, Impala, Buchbuck, Reedbuck, Waterbuck (two kinds), Oryx (two kinds), Zebra (two kinds), Grants and Thomsons Gazelle, Roan Antelope, Gerenuk, Duiker, and possible Greater and lesser Kudu, Sable Antelopes etc., etc.

The place to land at is Mombasa which is reached from Marseilles by either French or German steamers. I prefer the former as there is more deck space for exercise although the ships are smaller. I enclose details of sailings etc.

You can shoot all the year round in E.A. so that it matters little what time you land provided you do not mind the rain or heat in the Red Sea. Personally I found little fault with either. You can obtain everything necessary for your expedition at Nairobi. The following are advisable: a good pith sun hat, a couple of khaki jackets Norfolk pattern with lots of strong pockets, a pair of riding breaches and pants, a couple of brown knee boots, or boots with putties or leggings. Personally, I like boots with soles like matting and with horses hide uppers. They are delightfully comfortable and silent for stalking.

As I shall probably be in England for some time, I could—if you cared to see me—run over to your side and tell you all about the expedition, the game, country and people. The trip is nothing nowadays. In fact I should dearly love to accompany you on your journey and take you through the best parts of the country from a sporting and health point of view. But for various reasons I fear that this is out of the question.

Patterson's letter gives no hint of the "various reasons." One was possibly the persistent gossip about him in East Africa. There, where wife swapping was as popular as big-game hunting, it was taken for granted that Patterson and Ethel Blyth had had an affair during the safari, which drove her sick and jealous husband to suicide. Had Roosevelt taken Patterson up on his offer, one can imagine a tabloid newspaper headline: "T. R. On Safari with Hunter Who Buried Previous Partner and Bagged His Widow!"

Apparently in the dark about the alleged scandal, Roosevelt replied from Oyster Bay on July 6, 1908, saying that Patterson's information was exactly what he wanted:

I already feel a real thrill of excitement. I never had dreamed that I would be able to go to Africa and see a real game country, where there was a good quantity of many kinds. . . . I leave the Presidency on March 4th, and as I am anxious to leave the country as soon as possible thereafter, it would suit my convenience to sail about April 1st. I will follow exactly the advice you give as to where to get my material. I have arranged to go for the National Museum at Washington, for I feel we ought to have at Washington a good series of big African animals, and I shall take one or two field taxidermists with me; but the shooting will be done by son Kermit and myself. Outside the one specimen—or, where the law permits it, two specimens—of such series for the National Museum, I shall simply shoot so far as it is permitted, to keep the caravan in meat; and then again, if it is permissible, I would like two or three trophies . . . for my own house. . . . I do not suppose I will see many lions, but if we get more than one I should like to keep the extra skin as a trophy for myself. . . . I am no game butcher, and will of course obey all the regulations. . . . Do you really mean that there is any chance of your coming to this side? I need hardly say how glad we should be to see you and Mrs. Patterson; but I rather hope if you do come it will be after the 25th of December, when we shall be in the White House, where I should particularly like to have you as guest. I have already had Selous and Buxton there. I am not fit for the hard work of the genuine African explorer type; and I freely confess that if I do meet lions I should hope to have far less thrilling experiences than you had; but when I go on a trip I hunt all the time and work as hard as I can up to the point where I think I may tend to lose time by breaking down, and if game is plentiful as seems the case, I shall hope to do fairly well. I have been asked by Sir Alfred Pease to stop at his ranch first to get some specimens of zebra, hartebeest, and gazelle while making the final arrangements for the caravan . . . then with a caravan take one or two trips from the railroad, and then go on any length of trip necessary to take me into a good country for the rhino, buffalo, eland, giraffe, hippo, and, if possible, elephant. . . . I do hope you can both get over here, although I am not sure you would find much to amuse you.

Patterson warned Roosevelt in a July 16, 1908, letter to be careful about the agents he engaged, as several game hunters had made bitter complaints to Patterson about the way they were "done" by Nairobi agents, who used to be all right but now were too much "on the make." If Roosevelt cared to see him to talk over the trip, Patterson wrote that he would be delighted to "run over. We could then map out the whole expedition and you can make certain of a lion or two."

Forewarned, Roosevelt replied to Patterson on July 27, 1908, inviting him and his wife to the United States.

Do you think you could make it after December 25th? For a man suffering from the effects of work in the Tropics, I think it would be better if he could get here not earlier than October 15th. Our American summers are pretty hot. Do come over after that date and spend two or three days at the White House.

Patterson, Wellington Club, Grosvenor Place, London, July 29, 1908, responded:

I have been more or less laid up so you must forgive me for not having replied earlier. . . . You should try to travel in comfort on the trip and be careful not to overdo yourself to begin with—take it easy at the start & generally harden up to the conditions. . . . I may be able to come in October and

13. Francie Patterson sits on the lion skins Patterson brought back from Africa. Courtesy of Alan Patterson.

if I come I shall bring some slides of the Wilds of East Africa to show you some evening if you would care for a "lecture." Perhaps if I can't go back to E.A. owing to my health I might stay awhile in Canada and America to recruit.

Frances Patterson, 33 De Vere Gardens, West London, August 24, 1908, to her mother in Belfast:

Jack's trip to Norfolk helped him to get over his sleeplessness. The Barclays were of course delighted to see him again and so was Frankie Ffolks. They were all delighted with his book [*The Man-Eaters of Tsavo*] and Frankie Ffolks told him he gave a copy of it to Prince Edward on his last birthday & he liked it ever so much. . . . I am enclosing President Roosevelt's last letter so you will see that we are both expected at the White House in October!

Patterson, 13 De Vere Gardens, wrote to Roosevelt again, on October 17, 1908:

I am extremely sorry to say that my doctor thinks that I should not travel just yet as I am still not very strong. Perhaps after Xmas I may be better & trust so at all events. When your elections are all over & you have a day or two for certain at Washington I should be glad to come. . . . I shall probably be returning to East Africa in April or May. By the way a very good man—eleven years in E.A.—also a good doctor—has written to me asking if you would take him with you on your expedition. He is a first-rate man and doctor. I have known him for the last 12 years off and on in the Wilds. He is a good cheery companion & would be most useful all round. Age about 45, very strong and fit. He asks 200 pounds for the trip and expenses. Of course I don't know if you want a man or not, but if you do you can get him.

Five days later, Patterson again wrote to Roosevelt:

I can arrange for a native guide who knows the country well. You must time it so as to arrive there for full moon and then you will have a fine sight of the beasts of the wilds. You must go there in the dry season so that the animals will not crowd to one water hole. A flashlight and a camera should be taken. I longed for one many a night. We can talk these things over when we meet.

When Patterson stayed with Roosevelt in the White House, he left his wife, Frances, now several months pregnant, at home. It was the start of his lifelong friendship with the president, and he made the most of his first visit to the United States. He saw the cavalry and artillery on maneuvers, East and West; watched the infantry in the Alaskan snows; and noted what excellent game preserves the cavalry troopers had made in Yellowstone Park, where a hungry bear gave him the run of his life. On horseback and on foot he followed Stonewall Jackson's footsteps up and down the Shenandoah Valley from Harper's Ferry to the Wilderness, and into Chancellorsville where friendly fire, a bullet fired from Jackson's own lines, killed him and ended all chance of victory for the South, in Patterson's opinion.

Several times during his trip, Patterson met Mary Lee, daughter of Robert E. Lee, whom he considered the army's best-loved general. Mary Lee told him that when the Civil war broke out,

her youngest brother at school disappeared and the family didn't hear from him for almost a year. One day while a furious battle was waging General Lee noticed some guns being moved from a hot position. He galloped up and ordered them back into the fight. He was surprised when a powder-blackened mud-grimed young soldier in a bloodstained shirt, said, "What, Dad, back into that Hell again?" And back into the hell his father ordered him. The son survived that battle and the war.[2]

On his return from America, aboard the Cunard HMS *Lusitania*, bound for England, Patterson wrote to Roosevelt on November 26, 1908:

> Just a line . . . to thank you most warmly and heartily for my pleasant and most enjoyable visit to you. I can't tell you how much I appreciate the honour of having been your guest at the White House. I must also thank you for having taken such an interest in my invention for carrying the rifle. I had a most satisfactory interview with General Crozier and my invention is to be tried properly in a practical way this time. Pray give my kindest salutations to Mrs. Roosevelt.

Back in England, Patterson got a letter from General William Crozier in the Office of the Chief of Ordnance, War Department, Washington, thanking him for *Man-Eaters of Tsavo,* which "I shall read with the greatest interest its wonderful stories, from what I already know of them, I think quite the most remarkable I have ever heard. We shall have the rifle slings [Patterson's invention] going before long. No difficulties have been met in supplying it to our equipment.[3]

On February 5, 1909, two months after Patterson returned to England from the United States, the district commissioner in British East Africa traced two members of the safari on which Blyth had fatally shot himself. The official questioned Patterson's account, doubting that at the time of Blyth's violent death Patterson was seriously ill, as he had stated. If the colonel was suffering from acute diarrhea brought on by dysentery, how then, the commissioner wondered, had he gone hunting buffalo? Furthermore, there was a report that Colonel Patterson told friends that he was going to take Ethel Blyth back to England—implying that theirs was more than a casual relationship. Under questioning, witness Saiewa Masai testified that Patterson and Blyth had a big quarrel but eventually made up and shook hands. At Sesamis, Blyth left his tent and shot a giraffe. He got back at seven o'clock and soon after was taken ill, behaving like a madman. The witness and others poured water on Blyth's head, and he gradually got better. This witness believed that Ethel Blyth must have been afraid of her husband, because, he said, she slept in Patterson's tent (evidence to bolster the commissioner's suspicion that Patterson and Ethel Blyth were having an affair). The next morning she came out and went to her husband's tent. Right after she lifted the tent flap, he shot himself. The witness concluded his testimony by saying that he helped to dig Blyth's grave, then buried him and burned his clothing.[4]

According to witness Karogi Mwertu, when he joined them Blyth had a bad foot and was being carried in a hammock, but later his foot was a little better and he rode a horse.

At the crossing of the Euaso Nyiro, Blyth said he was going to return (presumably to Nairobi), but Patterson persuaded him to stay with them. At Nachimunya, Patterson and Ethel Blyth went out alone every afternoon to shoot.

On reaching Linguya, they came across an elephant, and Ethel Blyth fired first and then her husband. It fell but got up again, and they followed it and came upon a great herd of elephants, one of which charged and killed Patterson's horse. They eventually picked up the tracks of the wounded elephant and found it dead.

In the evening the two men had a violent quarrel, and each went off to his own tent, leaving Ethel Blyth sitting outside. Eventually, she went to Patterson's tent and persuaded him to go to her husband's tent and shake hands.

The next afternoon Blyth shot three Grevy's zebra, his wife shot two, and Patterson one. Blyth returned to the camp at about six that evening, and the other two returned at about eight. Then the three of them had dinner together, during which Blyth fell back in his chair. After laying him on the ground, the witness and other porters carried him to his tent.

At midnight the witness and other porters were eating a meal of goat meat when they saw Ethel Blyth leave her sick husband's tent and go to Patterson's tent, where she stayed. At about seven in the morning Ethel Blyth left Patterson's and returned to her husband. Directly after she entered the tent the porters heard a shot, and Ethel Blyth came running out. They ran to the tent to find that Blyth had shot himself in the mouth. They now wanted to turn back, but, said the witness, Patterson threatened them and eventually persuaded them to continue the safari. They then buried Blyth and burned his clothes. Afterward, Patterson and Ethel Blyth occupied the same tent, and the other tent was never pitched.[5]

The testimony clearly implied that Patterson and Ethel Blyth had had an affair—despite his claim that the tent he shared with the widow was partitioned. Additionally, neither witness mentioned Patterson's dysentery, which surely would have precluded any romantic behavior. Patterson's plausible explanation is that none of the men would have known he was ill, because he deliberately hid his condition from them, for fear that they would take advantage of his weak state to mutiny again.

The Colonial Office's Sir Francis Hapwood gave his official view: "This is an ugly business and requires sifting to the bottom. I understand from Mr. Monson, the Secretary to the Administration, that the general impression in the Protectorate is that Mr. Blyth shot himself on account of too intimate relations between his wife and Colonel Patterson." Patterson responded to his critics: "My enemies out there are trying to work up some lies. . . . [T]here is not a vestige of proof in them. The whole thing has been worked up by scoundrels who wish to destroy me at all costs."[6]

It was a tough time for Patterson. Three months after his return to London from the United States, on March 10, 1909, his wife, Frances, gave birth to their son Bryan. About the same date the investigation of Blyth's death had been completed in East Africa and the report sent to England for further official investigation. Patterson obviously feared a verdict of at least unprofessional behavior and the resulting ruined reputation, which might explain why, to protect his newborn son from any future unpleasantness as the son of the infamous Patterson, he registered the boy's birth under a false name—Lionel Brown. Patterson's grandson, Alan, told this writer: "My father, Bryan Patterson, never knew about this until he was intending to come to the United States from Britain some thirty years later, and was also in the process of getting married to my mother. To get a passport, he had to produce his birth certificate, and lo and behold there was this totally different name—Lionel Brown. I don't know who it was the document said he was born to, because I've never seen it."[7]

A Patterson biographer, Patrick Streeter, did unearth the birth certificate, which states that Lionel Brown was born at 7 Gayton Crescent, Hampstead, London, to James Brown, a civil engineer, and Elinor Brown, née Miller (Ethel Blyth's maiden name was Brunner). Streeter suggests that if the child was Frances Patterson's, the birth certificate would have said so, but not if Patterson, intent on deception, had provided all the information to the official who issued it. Streeter continues:

> Bryan [Patterson] held the view shared by his son, Alan, that Effie [Ethel Blyth's nickname] may well have been his [Bryan's] mother. There are certain clues in the certificate. The surnames Brown and Miller are both common names. Were they chosen for this reason? The initials of the mother are E.B., Effie's initials. The occupation of the father is given as "Civil Engineer" the same as given for Patterson on little Maurice's birth certificate [the Patterson's son who died as a baby]. The name Lionel means "young lion." The address? 7 Gayton Crescent is not helpful in solving the mystery. The directories give it as the dwelling of Henry Carus-Wilson, 61, the son of a clergyman. Bryan's conception, the time of which cannot be calculated accurately, would have occurred around 10 June 1908, ten days after Effie and Patterson arrived back in England. The Blyth family does not consider the theory credible, on the grounds that if it were valid they would have heard of it. But then such secrets are better kept in the mother's family than the father's.[8]

Apparently, Patterson was never again in contact with Ethel Blyth, who during World War I was to run an auxiliary hospital in Chertsey, Surrey, for which she was awarded the MBE (member of the Order of the British Empire). She went to New Zealand in 1920 to live with a married man, Colin Anderson. Her death certificate in 1931 states the cause as cerebral thrombosis, but the undertaker disagreed, writing "a cut on her hand." Colin Anderson committed suicide ten years later. Ethel Blyth's son, Ian, three when his father died, studied at Cambridge University without getting a degree and was a playboy for many years, until 1928, when he married a nurse, Edna Lewis. He earned his doctor's degree at Queen's University, Belfast, in 1937, succeeded his uncle as Baron Blyth in 1953, and devoted the rest of his life to treating the poor in Northern Ireland.[9]

Testimony by the two native witnesses about Blyth's suspicious death was sent to Lord Crewe, Britain's colonial secretary, as part of the ongoing official investigation in Britain. Blyth's father, like Crewe, was a member of the House of Lords. To avoid embarrassing a fellow peer, Crewe chose not to question Ethel Blyth—who obviously would have been a critical witness—and to exonerate Patterson. Perhaps Crewe was also influenced by Colonel Sadler, governor of the East Africa Protectorate, who wrote to him suggesting that they avoid a public scandal by simply telling Patterson that his services were no longer required in East Africa.

The press inevitably got hold of the story when the affair was discussed in the House of Lords on April 1, 1909. According to the *Times,* Lord Zouche of Harynworth spelled out the case for

> Lieutenant-Colonel Patterson, D.S.O., late game warden in British East Africa, and inquired as to the circumstances under which he ceased to hold that position in the colony. He said that Colonel Patterson, having been appointed by the Earl of Elgin in 1907 to the post of game warden . . . took up duties which involved the delimitation of the northern game reserves and a survey of a certain part of the frontier.
>
> Those duties involved a long journey, which Colonel Patterson undertook with a native caravan. He was accompanied by some English friends, one of whom was taken ill and died when the party was within about thirty five miles of the end of the journey. It was, he believed, made a matter of comment that Colonel Patterson did not return at once after that tragedy, but within an hour after the death had taken place a serious mutiny arose among the natives. They refused to go on.
>
> The circumstances were extremely critical, and in a position so far from civilization it was literally a matter of life or death. Had Colonel Patterson given way the probabilities were that he and all the English members of his party would have been massacred. . . .
>
> After he had left East Africa certain rumours grew to such a pitch that Colonel Patterson felt obliged to take steps to vindicate himself. He went to the Colonial Office, where his representations were courteously received, and it was in order to follow up the matter that the case was now brought before their lordships.

Lord Crewe responded:

> The circumstances are so singular that it caused us at the Colonial Office some considerable degree of anxiety.
>
> Colonel Patterson has a distinguished record of service in South Africa and elsewhere. . . . He is also, I dare say, known to some of your

lordships through the account which he wrote of the extraordinary man-eating lions at the time of the making of the Uganda Railway, when the operations on this line were absolutely stopped by reason of the terror which those animals caused until they were finally disposed of by Colonel Patterson.

My predecessor, Lord Elgin, appointed him to the post of game warden—that is superintendent of game reserves in British East Africa. Last summer Colonel Patterson returned invalided from his post, and since that time rumours of a damaging and even of a sinister character have been prevalent regarding him, not merely in East Africa but, as I have been told, they have reached England.

The rumours . . . arose . . . out of the unfortunate death of Mr. Blyth, the son of a member of your lordship's House. . . . Colonel Patterson was going on duty with a safari of porters to the northern game reserve, and he was permitted by his superior officer to take [Mr. Blyth] with him.

. . . Mr. Blyth died in the course of the expedition, died by a revolver-shot wound, undoubtedly inflicted by himself, whether by accident or in a fit of delirium consequent upon a severe attack of fever from which he suffered throughout the journey. . . .

Rumours concerning Colonel Patterson arose, in some cases absolutely taking the form that he had the responsibility for Mr. Blyth's death. . . . I have examined all the documents relating to the case and I can assure your lordships that . . . there was no tinge of evidence—quite the contrary indeed—to connect Colonel Patterson in any way with the cause of Mr. Blyth's death. . . . Colonel Patterson throughout treated Mr. Blyth with nothing but kindness and humanity during the journey.

The best proof I can give to the House that we did not consider Colonel Patterson unworthy of continuing in His Majesty's service is that I sanctioned his return to East Africa. But his health is broken down . . . and this has prevented his return. I am glad to have been able to make this categorical and authoritative statement of the facts of the case, because it is one which, as the House will see from the facts, is of no small importance to the man concerned.[10]

Crewe said not a word about Ethel Blyth's role in the affair. In her testimony elsewhere, though, she had explained that it took them so long to reach Nairobi because of the extremely long peacemaking conversations Patterson had had with the native chiefs en route.

Despite Lord Crewe's report that Patterson was in no way responsible for Blyth's death, the rumors became the conventional wisdom such that the writer of a 1993 travel book on Kenya could confidently assert: "Before World War I an English aristocrat making a hunting trip in this area with Colonel J. H. Patterson, the martinet of The Man-Eaters of Tsavo melodrama, pitched camp near here. Returning from a foray in the Kaisut desert he found his wife locked in the Colonel's arms, in flagrante, and returned to the desert where he shot himself."[11] Even a mediocre defense attorney could have demolished that speculative account. But what really happened has never been reported. It calls for another Sherlock Holmes.

Ernest Hemingway (who also used a gun to kill himself) went on safari in Kenya in the 1930s and 1950s, and learning of Blyth's violent death put his own spin on the tragedy in his short story "The Short Happy Life of Francis Macomber." In it a wife, while on safari, kills her husband accidentally on purpose. Hemingway's son Patrick, an East African resident for some years, in a conversation with this writer, recalled:

> The story of Patterson was well known in East Africa, especially at the time my parents went there in the thirties. Patterson's book *The Man-Eaters of Tsavo* is a fascinating story, and you don't get any of the rather unpleasant aspects of Patterson's character. He obviously was involved in a very mysterious trip. In a sense, he was East Africa's first white hunter, in that he was employed by the British government to make a survey of the northern boundary of Kenya, which ran through some very rugged country, and required a person of considerable bush skills. And he agreed to take this couple with him. I suppose they were fairly wealthy or they wouldn't be doing that sort of thing. When they returned from the trip there was no husband, and, at first, no one was able to locate any of the safari help. They had all been discharged. It was too much of a public scandal. In those days in East Africa you didn't try white people. They were supposed to be setting examples. So all they could do was kick Patterson out.

"Although," I told Hemingway, "his relatives make him out to be a straight arrow, innocent of all charges." He laughed:

> I'm well aware of this sort of thing, you know. It seems that almost everyone who's ever achieved any reputation comes in for this treatment. The

relatives are all for him, and others, for various reasons, are against him. My impression of Patterson comes from conversations with old Philip Percival [a famous white hunter in Kenya who accompanied President Theodore Roosevelt and later Ernest Hemingway on their safaris]. He's a personal friend and a charming man with whom I spent a lot of time. His impression of Patterson was that he was a bit of a bounder. He was, after all, a contemporary [although they never met]. Percival's active involvement in Kenya was in 1914, and Patterson's last trip there was in 1909. That's only five years apart. Percival must have been reflecting the attitude of people there.

I pointed out that two native witnesses were located during the investigation into Blyth's death and that they had negative things to say about Patterson. Yet their somewhat damning testimony seems to have been discounted, even ignored. "One thing you have to watch there," Hemingway replied, "is the old tradition of the East, especially in India. And a lot of those traditions were imported very early into East Africa. Kipling is very amusing about this. You could have 250 witnesses, and it was the custom in the old legal trials in India for all of them to be perjured witnesses."[12]

Patterson's daughter-in-law, Beatrice Patterson, told me, "He was a bit of a rogue, it's true, but a nice rogue. I don't believe a word about an affair with Mrs. Blyth. He was a very handsome and charming man, but he was completely in love with his wife, who was in England at the time."[13]

Winston Churchill took a very different view, characterizing Patterson during a private conversation as an adulterer and murderer. Word got to Patterson, who threatened to sue him for slander, and Churchill appealed to his friend attorney F. E. Smith for advice. Smith responded on December 26, 1909:

The circumstances of which you write are extremely disagreeable. . . . The privacy of conversation in such an action is no justification, in such an action indeed it would be put against you that your official position should have made such a conversation impossible [as a member of the cabinet and soon to be home secretary, responsible for law and order in the country]. . . . If Patterson commences proceedings he will be shortly compelled to state in what persons' presence such statements were made, and when; you will probably then discover that P's informant (whom you will then be able to identify) merely repeated the story more or less accurately as gossip; greatly resents being charged with it; and is probably anxious to help you in every possible way. . . . If P can prove an actionable slander, only two courses would be open under the circumstances. 1. to withdraw & apologize, 2. to justify—say the story is true. No 2 is appallingly risky. . . . The C.O. [Colonial Office] dossiers may be positively damning, but . . . obviously weakened by Crewe's subsequent whitewashing. . . . I shall be in London on the afternoon of Jan. 4th if anything serious happens.[14]

The case did not go to court, and, strangely, none of Churchill's biographers has mentioned it.

6

Adventures in Africa and among the High and Mighty, 1909–1914

PRESIDENT THEODORE ROOSEVELT probably heard the rumors when he chatted at the campfire after a day of hunting in East Africa.

A hunter with a heart, although he relaxed from his presidential burdens by hunting panthers in Colorado, and bears in Mississippi, he could not bring himself to kill a small wounded bear that had been run down by dogs and tied up with ropes. Someone used a knife to put it out of its misery. Roosevelt's nickname was Teddy. And his reluctance to kill the captured animal inspired a cartoon of the incident, which led to the production of a now universally cherished toy, the teddy bear.

On Patterson's advice, less than three weeks after he quit the White House, on March 4, 1909, Roosevelt and his twenty-year-old son, Kermit, were on their way to what he called a great adventure. East Africa more than lived up to his expectations: he was euphoric about the beauty of the land and incredible variety of birds and animals. There, on an eleven-month safari, he even outdid Patterson—bagging nine lions. He brought fifteen native soldiers and two hundred porters on the safari to help him collect the more than 512 trophies—animals and birds—that were shipped to the United States, most of them for various museums, including the National Museum in Washington, D.C., and the American Museum in New York.

In his 1910 book about the safari, *African Game Trails*, Roosevelt acknowledged:

The most thrilling book of true lion stories ever written is Colonel Patterson's "The Man-Eaters of Tsavo." Colonel Patterson was one of the engineers engaged, some ten or twelve years back, in building the Uganda Railway; he was in charge of the work, at a place called Tsavo, where it was brought to a complete halt by the ravages of a couple of man-eating lions which, after many adventures, he finally killed.

At the dinner at the Mombasa Club I met one of the actors in a blood-curdling tragedy which Colonel Patterson relates. He was a German, and, in the company with an Italian friend, he went down in the special car of one of the English railroad officials to try to kill a man-eating lion which had carried away several people from a station on the line. They put a car on a siding; as it was hot the door was left open, and the Englishman sat by the open window to watch for the lion, while the Italian finally lay down on the floor and the German got into an upper bunk. Evidently the Englishman must have fallen asleep, and the lion, seeing him through the window, entered the carriage by the door to get at him. The Italian waked to find the lion standing on him with its hind feet, while its fore paws were on the seat as it killed the unfortunate Englishman. . . . The German, my informant, hearing the disturbance, leaped out of his bunk actually onto the back of the lion. The man-eater, however, was occupied only with his prey; holding the body in his mouth he forced his way through the window-sash and made his meal undisturbed, but at a couple of hundred yards from the railway carriage.[1]

Before returning to the United States, Roosevelt went to Norway to receive the Nobel Prize for Peace for helping to end the Russo-Japanese War, visited Germany to review German army maneuvers as the kaiser's guest, lectured at the Sorbonne in Paris and at both Oxford and Cambridge Universities, and also attended the funeral of King Edward VII.

Patterson's regimen in those days hardly matched Roosevelt's frenetic activity. He and his wife, Frances, with their one-year-old son, Bryan, had moved from London to Iver, in the Buckinghamshire countryside. When free of military duties, and meetings with Roosevelt, Patterson often played bridge in the evenings. One day in the spring of 1910 he and Frances rode on horseback to the Thames at Datchet. From there they rowed to Windsor for tea, and then rowed back to Datchet, picked up their horses, and rode home.

14. At home in Iver, England, in 1914 *(from left):* Patterson; his son Bryan; his sister-in-law; and his wife, Francie. Courtesy of Alan Patterson.

On May 6, 1910, from her home at Grove House in Iver, Frances Patterson wrote to her mother at Glenburn Park in Belfast:

> My most startling news is that Jack is off on Friday to America [for a second visit]!!! I forgot to tell you, he has been seeing a great deal of Roosevelt lately. He met him first at dinner at the Earl of Lonsdale's. There Mr. Buxton gave a lunch at Knighton to a few well-known sportsmen. Rhys Williams was there and Lord Warwick and Selous. Then tonight there is a big dinner given by the Fauna Society to Mr. Roosevelt, and Jack has just gone up to town for it. He will travel out to New York with Roosevelt as he is leaving also on Friday next.

Roosevelt doubtless told Patterson, as he had written in his book *African Game Trails:*

> The English rule in Africa has been of incalculable benefit to Africans themselves. . . . Mistakes have been made, of course, but they have proceeded at least as often from an unwise effort to accomplish too much in the way of beneficence, as from a desire to exploit the natives. Each of the

civilized nations that has taken possession of any part of Africa has had its own peculiar good qualities and its own peculiar defects. Some of them have done too much in supervising and ordering the lives of the natives, and in interfering with their practices and customs. The English error, like our own in similar conditions, has, if anything, been in the other direction. The effort has been to avoid wherever possible all interference with tribal customs, even when of an immoral and repulsive character, and to do no more than what is obviously necessary, such as insistence upon keeping the peace and preventing the spread of cattle disease. . . . Having said this much in the way of criticism, I wish to add my tribute of unstinted admiration for the disinterested and efficient work being done, alike in the interest of the white man and the black, whom I met in East Africa. They are men in whom their country has every reason to feel a just pride.[2]

The following letters give an idea of Patterson's active social life at this time. They are all from his wife, Frances, to "My own dearest Mother," in Belfast. July 6, 1910: "Roosevelt introduced him to everyone as the Colonel Patterson and announced in public that if all the books on sport in the world had to be destroyed and only one could be saved, then that should be Jack's book!! It is pretty warm at present over there he says, but then you know Jack likes the heat. He only stayed a day or two in New York and then went on to Washington where it was even hotter." And on one week later: "Even in America Jack continually meets people who say they are 'quite crazy' about his book."

Patterson had been back in England only a few months when he set off with three friends to Sierra Leone in West Africa on a business enterprise: to see if they could harness the power generated by a Sewa River waterfall to produce oil by crushing palm nuts. From the Sierra Leone coast, the four men traveled by a painfully slow train for the first 170 miles, then walked even more slowly in tropical heat for the next 25 miles, before reaching the first stop on their journey. As biographer Patrick Streeter reports, Patterson published an account of this adventure titled "The Devil of the Waterfall," in the magazine *Blackwood's* in June 1914.

Although Patterson's interpreter, Joe, was from the Mendi tribe, reputed to eliminate visiting missionaries by slicing them up with wire, the two got on well, and it was obvious that missionaries were no longer an endangered species. Patterson met one of them, a Moor, in a nearby village, who had survived intact, after walking 900 miles from his home in Timbuktu, trying to preach the gospel en route to hostile tribesmen. Now ill and half-starved, he seemed to be following Christ's lifestyle, and Patterson, who got to like and admire him, gave him food and other provisions.

Their next stop was in the land of the dreaded Leopard Society, a colorful and more gory version of America's Murder Incorporated. If a tribal chief wanted to get rid of someone, he hired a hit man, who dressed to kill in leopard skin and gloves with iron claws attached. The hit man clawed his victim to death and dragged him into the jungle, where he and his pals ate him. Patterson was pleased to learn that the government was trying to wipe out the death-on-command cannibals and was off to a good start: while Patterson was in Sierra Leone, a Leopard Society hit man was hanged in the capital, Freetown.

As Patterson and his partners approached their ultimate destination, a waterfall, the local tribal chief, surprisingly a woman, and her son, who was dressed in white robes and sitting in a hammock carried by four men, came to greet them. An accompanying band gave it a festive air, and attracted a small, curious crowd. Soon after, the local high priest, a tall, lean old man, made an appearance. Joe interpreted his warning that the devil guarded the waterfall and drowned anyone who dared to come near it. Consequently, none of the natives would dare to work for the visitors—that is, unless a white kid goat and a white chicken were sacrificed for the devil.

Patterson accepted the terms, and the next morning he and his partners, followed by a parade of hundreds led by the high priest, walked to the thundering waterfall, which dropped a hundred foot into the river. Staring at the water, the high priest told Patterson that the devil was satisfied and would move farther downriver while they worked at the waterfall. "Even now," he said, "I see him rising out of the water and floating with the current. So I must go and sacrifice before him at his new place."[3] When he left with his entourage, Patterson assumed that they were simply going to enjoy a picnic of the sacrifices.

Now free to hire native workers, without diabolical interference, Patterson had a road built to the top of the waterfall. That task done, he and his hydraulic-engineer partner, Hollenweger, chose the best spot for their powerhouse. After a lunch of cheese sandwiches, Hollenweger set out on a raft paddled by a local fisherman and Joe the interpreter to explore an island in the middle of the river.

Sitting on the riverbank above the waterfall, writing up his notes, Patterson heard shouts, looked up, and saw the raft being swept toward the waterfall. The only hope for the three men aboard was to reach a rock in the river. Hollenweger jumped and made it, but the other two were swept away into the rapids and over the waterfall. Horrified onlookers reported that two black men had been carried away to their deaths, but not the white man. Several hours later a rope made of vines was floated to Hollenweger. It needed the strength of twenty men to pull him from the rock to safety through the rough water. The bodies of Joe and the fisherman were never found.

The day after the drownings, Patterson told the high priest that something had obviously gone wrong with his pact with the devil. He replied that the white men paid for the sacrifices and a white man was saved; black men paid for no sacrifices, and the devil took them. Patterson thought that the wily old con man was wasted in the heart of Africa.

For various reasons, not least the refusal of the superstitious natives to resume work at the waterfall, the hydroelectric scheme to crush palm nuts and market the oil was abandoned. However, Patterson did not return empty-handed. He took three wild kittens with him, which probably ended up in a zoo.

After he had returned to England, his wife wrote to her mother on February 27, 1911: "Jack and I took a taxi to the Cavalry Club. . . . A few minutes afterwards Lord Zouche came in and . . . we all chatted until Mrs. Vanderbilt arrived. After dinner we paired off in taxicabs to the theatre."

The play was *The Princess Clementine*. Irving, Britain's leading actor, was the hero. Afterward, they went behind the scenes to meet Irving, who was still in his makeup. Patterson stayed to chat with Irving while he was changing, and Frances Patterson and three women friends went on the stage, as they wanted to see what it felt like to be "on the boards," behind the footlights. When they left by the stage entrance, a big crowd was waiting to see Irving. After several meetings with Patterson, Irving regarded him as a close and fascinating friend.

October 14, 1911:

Jack is still having a glorious time in Italy. He has been to both Rome and Florence. He certainly does not think much of rushing about the world, and started off the other day for Rome quite as casually as you would (even long ago) if you were going down to spend the day in Bangor. .

Patterson was fequently called upon to talk about his African adventures, and in a February 15, 1912, letter to her mother, Frances Patterson recalled one such lecture when

Jack's friends from West Africa came to tea. At dinner I sat between Sir Henry Seaton Karr, a very well known big game hunter, and Sir Herbert Sloley, the administrator of Basutoland [now Lesotho] home on leave. I had to hold a little reception after the lecture and, of course, so did Jack. Everyone said they had never heard him speak so well and fluently. He described everything most picturesquely and dramatically without a note of any kind and the audience were simply thrilled at some of the stories.

June 15, 1912:

We all met in the Piccadilly Restaurant lounge and I sat beside Irving and talked to him until we all moved into the big restaurant for lunch. There were fourteen of us. Marion Terry was there, and Sir Arthur Pinero [a fashionable playwright] and Dorothea Baird. There were ever so many courses—hors d'oeuvres, salmon mayonnaise, then eggs, then chicken and kidney beans, then iced fruit salad and coffee. A band played in the distance all the time.

June 26, 1912:

On Sunday we went to the Murrays for tea. It was a lovely afternoon and we sat out of doors on a terrace. A Miss Baker was there, the daughter of Sir Samuel Baker, the great African explorer who discovered the Albert Nyanza. She was talking to Jack for some time without discovering who he really was, and of course Jack never talks about his doings out there. At last she asked him if he had ever seen any lions while he was out there, and he admitted that he had come across one or two! Then she grew very interested and asked him if he had ever seen a place called Tsavo! Yes, Jack said, I lived there for some time! Just then Mrs. Murray happened to pass and overheard this, so she said, "Why he is the man that wrote The Man-Eaters of Tsavo." Miss Baker got tremendously interested and excited then and said, "You don't mean to say that you are the Colonel Patterson!! Why," she went on, "your name is honored all over the world, and your book has a worldwide reputation." Of course after that they had a great talk about Africa and lions and natives and exploring etc.—but isn't it curious how often we come across people like that who really know what they are talking about and all say exactly the same thing about Jack's book. Then, on Sunday afternoon, Bryan [the Pattersons' son] had his first lesson in cricket! On Friday Jack and I are going to the Lyceum Club to hear a lecture by the Renee of Sarawak. I had a letter from Lady Ffolkes who lives at Slough, asking us to go to tea there tomorrow. She is a relation of "Frankie" Ffolkes, who is the King's Chaplain and Jack's great friend.

July 4, 1912:

Jack had to stay in town for a private party, where he met a few kings, princes and grand dukes etc. at the Hyde Park Hotel. Jack had a long talk with Prince Christopher of Greece and the prince said he would love to go big game shooting in East Africa but he could not afford it!

December 10 1912:

At our lunch party at the Cavalry Club, our chief guests were a real live Prince and Princess!!! H.S.H. The Prince de Colleredo Mannseld sat at my right hand and H.S.H. The Princess sat at Jack's right hand. They are cousins of the German Emperor and rank higher than our Queen's family (the Techs). Jack saw a great deal of them in America and they think he is the very nicest man they ever met! They simply poured out praises of him all the time to me & said none of their parties were ever complete without him.

November 24, 1913:

I drove to the Ritz hotel to meet Jack. He had arranged that we were all to go to the Theatre after lunch to see H.B. Irving act in The Grand Seigneur at the Savoy Theatre. Irving himself was to be one of our guests at lunch.

The play was about the French Revolution & the guillotine & the terrible savage mob. It was most interesting especially to the Princess, as several of her ancestors were guillotined at that time, and she recognized lots of the people represented on the stage.

When it was over Jack and the Princess went behind the stage to talk to Irving and while we were waiting for them Captain Cartwright suggested we should all go to the Savoy for tea. There were no tables in the big Palm Court, and a waiter wanted to take us to a table off at the side somewhere. However, Captain Cartwright told him who we were, and the effect was magical! Instantly out came the manager & ordered a table to be brought at once & about a dozen waiters instantly rushed to get it and brought chairs & flew around to get everything we asked for! It really was very funny. The conductor of the band also came & asked what we would like the band to play. So we arranged the music for the rest of the afternoon.

Patterson's life was not just a perpetual round of theater and party-going with the high and mighty. Just before the outbreak of war in 1914 the German General Staff invited him to Germany to inspect their military might. On his arrival, an army captain escort looked surprised and said that he had expected a British lieutenant colonel to be a grizzled veteran. As they were walking together, Patterson, now in his early forties, explained that at thirty-three he had been "jumped" from lieutenant to colonel in charge of a yeomanry regiment during the Boer War. The German captain stopped in his tracks and gave Patterson a respectful salute and another promotion: "You," he said, "are a Napoleon!"[4]

If not yet a Napoleon, Patterson was on his way up. Since boyhood he had studied military history and the campaigns of great generals. He had followed the footsteps of Napoleon and Wellington in Spain and Flanders, and had been an official observer of Belgian, French, and Italian soldiers on maneuvers—as well as U.S. military exercises in Alaska.

In the summer of 1914 many in Britain feared that a war in Europe was imminent, triggered by a Serbian nationalist who had recently assassinated Austrian archduke Francis Ferdinand. That apprehension explains why France Patterson wrote to her mother on July 31, 1914, "Jack is waiting to see what will happen in Europe & whether the War is likely to be confined to Austria and Serbia or not. We are both invited to lunch at the

Murrays to meet the Marquis & Marchioness of Downshire! I suppose we will probably go unless Jack has anything more important to do that day." Because the archduke's assassination had activated a series of treaties, Germany declared war on Russia on August 2, 1914, and the next day on France. When Germany invaded neutral Belgium, the British were treaty-bound to join the fight against the Germans.

Patterson was lucky not be sent as cannon fodder to the western front, where World War I eventually bogged down in trench warfare. The massed armies of Britain and Germany faced each other in rat-infested trenches, leaving them to slaughter each other for a few feet of mud and the shelter of other rat-infested trenches. Though men were dying by the tens of thousands and reinforcements were desperately needed, Patterson remained kicking his heels in Britain, impatiently awaiting orders to join the fray on the western front, where he expected to be given an important command.

7

World War I, Patterson Leads the Zion Mule Corps, 1914–1916

AFTER A VISIT to the bloodbath on the western front in Belgium—which he told Theodore Roosevelt had horrified him—Patterson sought an appointment from the War Office, to be repeatedly told that his application was still being considered. He could not wait. At his own expense, he sailed for Egypt. His friend General John Maxwell was commander of the British forces there, and he intended to ask him if he could be useful on the Egyptian battlefront.

In October 1914, shortly after the war's outbreak, the Turks had joined the Germans and opened a second front—launching an attack across the Suez Canal against Egypt, then a British protectorate. The British beat them back. Needing reinforcements to beef up his defeated army, the Turkish sultan call for a jihad, or holy war, against the Allies. Learning of this mandate, a Russian Jewish journalist, Vladimir Jabotinsky, persuaded his editor at *Russkiya Vedomost,* a leading Moscow newspaper, to send him to Tunisia, Algeria, Morocco, and Egypt to assess the Muslims' response to the sultan's battle cry. His most informed contacts in the first three countries were not Muslims but Jewish storekeepers, attorneys, and journalists. They assured him that, over the past century, despite the Turks' many appeals for military help to protect their Ottoman Empire, not one fellow Muslim country had come to their rescue.

Meanwhile, Djemal Pasha, commander of the Turkish Fourth Army, had gone into action in Palestine—an outpost of the Ottoman Empire. Accusing Palestinian Jews of being British sympathizers—which no doubt many were—he deported thousands, ordered the torture and hanging of Jews suspected of spying, and announced that after the war, no Jews would be allowed to settle in Palestine. Almost daily, shiploads of Jewish refugees expelled from Palestine arrived in Egypt. The good-natured captain of an American battleship, the USS *Tennessee,* which carried some of these refugees, tried to boost their morale by having the ship's band play cheerful music.

Patterson and Jabotinsky were both heading for Egypt from different directions. Jabotinsky was on the last leg of his investigation in North Africa of Muslims' response to the call for a holy war. As a teenager in Odessa, where the Russians treated Jews like hunted animals, he had helped to organize a group to hit back. This deterred pogroms in his town, made him a neighborhood hero, and strengthened his view that, in order to survive, Jews must be ready to fight.

When his ship docked in the Egyptian port of Alexandria, Jabotinsky overheard a British customs officer say that a shipload of almost a thousand Zionist Jews the Turks had kicked out of Palestine had just arrived from Jaffa. The news switched Jabotinsky from reporter to recruiting officer. Told that the British were already feeding and sheltering some twelve hundred Jewish men, women, and children in three barracks at Gabbari, he headed there to rally volunteers to form a Jewish fighting force.

Among the first of the refugees he met was Joseph Trumpeldor, a tall, slim one-armed Russian Jew whose looks and easygoing manner made people mistake him for a Swede or an Englishman. Possibly the only Jewish officer in Czar Nicholas's army, he had lost his left arm during the Russo-Japanese War of 1904–1905. Released from the hospital, he had insisted on returning to the fight. Having only one arm, he seemed an unlikely prospect for Jabotinsky's military force. On the contrary, he was among the best: he had trained himself to be self-reliant and could shave, dress, polish his shoes and tie the laces, ride a horse, and shoot with precision—using his remaining arm. After the Russo-Japanese War, despite having a law degree, he had settled in Palestine as an agricultural laborer—until the Turks made life unendurable. Jabotinsky believed that Jews could never lead a peaceful life in Palestine until the Turks were driven out. Trumpeldor agreed and joined him in his recruiting drive.

They first approached Patterson's friend General Sir John Maxwell, commander of the British forces in Egypt, and offered to help the British free Palestine from Turkish control. Conversing in French, which all three understood, Maxwell said that there was no immediate plan to invade Palestine, and, in any case, foreigners could not join the British army. But he suggested a way to skirt the rules. They could form a separate, independent unit, a Corps de Muletiers (Mule Transport Corps), to deliver supplies to Allied soldiers fighting on various fronts. A Mule Transport Corps? Jabotinsky flinched at the idea as a humiliating insult, and would not even consider it. But Trumpeldor said that they would think it over and get back to the general.

They were arguing as they left the room and were still at it when they and six others met in Mordechai Margolin's Alexandria home to discuss Maxwell's proposal. Jabotinsky shot it down immediately. First, he said, it was an unflattering, even shocking suggestion to associate mules with Zion, with the rebirth of a nation, with the first prospective Jewish troops in history since the exile (except for the Jewish regiment that Berek Yoselovich formed in Poland in 1794 to fight the Russians). Second, Maxwell had made it clear that they would not be sent to liberate Palestine, but would go to some other front.

Trumpeldor calmly disagreed, saying that transporting ammunition and food to troops in the trenches anywhere was vital and dangerous war work. He considered Jabotinsky's reaction to the word *mule* childish. A Jabotinsky supporter remarked that a mule was almost a donkey, and to call someone a donkey, especially in Yiddish, was an insult.

"In Yiddish, 'horse' is also not a compliment," Trumpeldor replied. "Yet if it were to be a cavalry detachment you would all feel terribly proud. In French, to call a person chameau [camel] is grossly offensive, but they have a Camel Corps in the French army and in the English army, too, and to serve in them is considered a particular honor. It's all nonsense." He also explained why it was stupid to refuse to serve anywhere except Palestine: "To get the Turks out of Palestine, we've got to smash the Turks.

Which side you begin smashing, north or south, is just technique. Any front leads to Zion."

They argued through the night until dawn. But Jabotinsky held his ground. And when they left the meeting together he told Trumpeldor, "You may be right, but I would not join a unit of that sort."[1] Jabotinsky then left Egypt for England to agitate for a Jewish fighting unit to attack the Turks in Palestine alongside the British, while Trumpeldor continued the recruiting drive in Egypt.

He was still at it in the spring of 1915 when Winston Churchill, first lord of the Admiralty, masterminded a plan to launch a massive Anglo-French naval attack in the Turkish Dardanelles, then to steam north, force a way through the straits of the Sea of Marmara, and on to the capital, Istanbul. Eventually, Churchill hoped for the invaders to link up with their Russian allies, and to supply them with Allied munitions for a surprise attack on Germany's vulnerable, poorly defended rear.

Soon after Jabotinsky left Egypt, Patterson arrived. And just at the right time. General Maxwell was looking for someone to command a unit of Jewish volunteers awaiting him in Alexandria. Was Patterson interested? If so, his second in command would be a one-armed Russian, Joseph Trumpeldor.

The prospect of commanding a Jewish regiment amazed and delighted Patterson. As a boy in Dublin, he had been spellbound by his father's Old Testament accounts of Jewish history, laws, and customs, but especially, he recalled, "the battles, murders and sudden deaths."

> It was strange, therefore that I, so imbued with the Jewish traditions should
> have arrived in Egypt at the psychological moment when General Sir John
> Maxwell, the C-in-C in Egypt, was looking for a suitable officer to recruit
> a Jewish unit. A Jewish unit had been unknown for 2,000 years, since the
> day of the Maccabees, those heroic sons of Israel who fought so valiantly,
> and for a time so successfully, to wrest Jerusalem from the Roman Legions
> [except, as already mentioned, in Poland in 1794, when a Jewish regiment
> fought the Russians].
>
> It is curious that General Maxwell should have chosen me [to com-
> mand a Jewish unit], because he knew nothing of my knowledge of Jew-
> ish history and my sympathy for the Jewish race. When as a boy I eagerly
> devoured the records of the glorious deeds of the Jewish military captains,

such as Joshua, Joab, Gideon, Judas Maccabee, I never dreamed that I in a small way would become a captain of a host of the Children of Israel.[2]

On March 19, 1915, Trumpeldor stood on a platform in a dimly lit, converted stable in Mafruza, and told several hundred exiled Jews, "History is giving us an opportunity which has not been given to us in almost all the centuries of our exile. We will be the first to fight with our blood for the liberation of our land. We will be followed by thousands of other Jews."

Next, Patterson spoke of Maxwell's proposed Zion Mule Corps and, according to Elias Gilner, the author of *War and Hope: The History of the Jewish Legion*, "captivated the audience with his amiable, humorous and persuasive manner." He was followed by Major General Sir Alexander Godley, who said, "The English people is now speaking through me to the Jewish people, seeking friendship which will undoubtedly continue in Jewish Palestine. Do you have it in your hearts to shake the extended hand or to reject it?" When almost 200 men stood to volunteer, the general responded: "Today the English people have entered into a covenant with the Jewish people." As Gilner points out, "The irony of the situation was obvious: what centuries of ethical, self-disciplined living, and the most gruesome persecution could not accomplish, a few mules did. A door to international recognition had been opened."[3]

Trumpeldor's ongoing recruiting drive raised 470 more volunteers, and on March 23 all 650 of them paraded before Colonel Patterson. He had divided the men into four troops, each commanded by a British and a Jewish officer, and divided each troop into four sections with sergeants in charge, and each section into subsections led by corporals. There were 20 horses for officers and senior noncommissioned officers (NCOs) and 750 pack mules. Patterson appointed a Dr. Levotin as the medical unit's surgeon and was pleased to find many other highly educated men among the volunteers: lawyers, medical men, divinity students, Professor Goro-dissky of the Lycée in Alexandria, and a rabbi.

At the swearing in, the corps' honorary chaplain, Chief Rabbi della Pergolla, compared them to their forefathers whom Moses had led out of Egypt. Now, he said, Patterson was their leader. It was a hard act to follow. But the Irish Protestant hoped to outdo Moses, asking the men to pray with him that he should not only behold Canaan from afar, as Moses had done, but be divinely permitted to lead them into the Promised Land. The British *Jewish Chronicle* reported the event with chauvinistic fervor: "The formation of the Zion Mule Corps—a Jewish Legion composed almost entirely of Palestine refugees—marks an event in the history of the Jews as well as in that of England. Never has England been known to depart from its policy of admitting none but British subjects or colonials into its army, and the step which has now been taken, namely the formation of a Jewish battalion under the Union Jack, adds one more rung to the long ladder of kindly acts that have gained England her superiority over all nations."[4]

Patterson must have thought he had reached the proverbial Tower of Babel: besides Hebrew, the men spoke twelve other languages, and few were fluent in English. He partly solved the problem by having them drilled and trained in a colorful and occasionally comical mixture of English, Yiddish, and Hebrew.

Language caused another problem. Because the pharmacist Patterson had hired to serve the entire Jewish community did not speak to the students from Jaffa in Hebrew, they refused to collect the quinine necessary for their health from him. Patterson fixed that dilemma by persuading him to speak enough Hebrew to meet their demands. He also organized a school for the refugee children.

The recruits wore the Magen David emblem on their British battle uniforms—a reproduction of David's shield that he had carried while fighting Goliath. They were armed with rifles and ammunition recently captured from the Turks in their unsuccessful attempt to invade Egypt from Palestine across the Suez Canal. Owing to a warning of the imminent attack by Aaron Aaronsohn, an internationally famous Jewish agronomist working for British intelligence, most of the invading Turks had been wiped out before even reaching the canal.

From dawn to dusk Patterson and his officers taught the incipient Zion Mule Corps how to fire captured Turkish rifles, to use the attached bayonets in hand-to-hand combat, saddle and unsaddle their mules, load and unload the packs, exercise the mules and horses, and to feed and water them three times a day. And how to march. Before he left for England,

Jabotinsky had watched them on parade and scoffed that they walked like geese. Patterson soon corrected that issue and, overjoyed with the overall rapid improvements, recalled the Old Testament tales he had read as a boy in Dublin:

> Never since the days of Judas Maccabaeus had such sights and sounds been seen and heard in a military camp. Had the redoubtable General paid us a surprise visit, he might have imagined himself with his own legions, because here was a great camp with the tents of the Children of Israel, where he would have heard the Hebrew tongue spoken on all sides, and seen a host of Sons of Judah drilling to the same words of command he used to those gallant soldiers who fought the Romans: he would have heard the plaintive soul-stirring music of the Maccabaean hymn chanted by the men as they marched through the camps. Although it was only a mule corps, yet it was (potentially) a fighting unit and of this the men were all very proud.[5]

Each morning Patterson was pleased to see the arrival of an Australian soldier stationed nearby. He drove an army wagon pulled by two huge Australian horses and welcomed refugee children aboard for a ride. Patterson also enjoyed the presence of a beautiful Frenchwoman, the Gentile wife of the Jewish Baron Felix de Menasseh, who was helping the chief rabbi to collect clothes, food, and money for needy refugees. "Whenever she brought a wagon-load of fresh bread to Gabbari," Patterson recalled, "I wondered at the clever manner in which she was dressed. Very simply and yet with chic. It seemed as if the French modists had a special model—styles for visiting the poor."[6] It was at the Gabbari refugee camp, Patterson believed, where the Zion Mule Corps was in training, that the eventual Jewish Legion—a real fighting force—would be born.

Before Passover, Patterson talked reluctant War Office officials into providing kosher food and unleavened bread for the Passover celebrations, which he attended. Afterward, the corps marched to the Great Synagogue in Alexandria—cheered on their way by the sympathizers in the local population—where they were blessed by the grand rabbi.

On April 12, 1915, Patterson wrote from Alexandria's Palace Hotel to his presidential pen pal, Theodore Roosevelt:

My Dear Colonel, I must write you a line to tell you how in the midst of "alarums and excursions" I found time to read and thoroughly enjoy your book on your travels in Brazil. I quite envied you and Kermit [Roosevelt's son] at times! When I read of where he was wrecked in the rapids, I was reminded of my own sad experiences in West Africa. It was a closer shave for Kermit & I heaved a sigh of relief when I found that his adventure had no worse ending than the loss of the canoe-man. I hope you won't go on any more of these dangerous trips. . . . I have been in Egypt for some little time organizing a corps of Russians from various parts of the Russian empire, mostly Jews. They are a very useful body of men & we are off to the front in a day or two & hope we shall do some useful service. We are doing our best to keep our end up and not one of us has the slightest doubt about our being able to lick Germany. We will do it handsomely in time.

Roosevelt replied:

I am glad that you are able to realize what I know is your heart's desire, by doing your part in the great war. Confidentially, I and my four sons are exceedingly sorry that we are not in the fight also. The sinking of the Lusitania [on May 7, 1915, a German U-boat sank the British liner, drowning half the two thousand civilians aboard, including four hundred Americans] made me feel that the time had come to speak out, and if you see any American papers you know that I did so. [Roosevelt wanted to declare war on Germany; Woodrow Wilson was satisfied with an apology.] I would not be much use, however, excepting that I believe I could raise a division of mounted riflemen, composed of nine regiments like the one I commanded in Cuba in the Spanish War, and these men would fight well. I am glad you like my book on my travels in Brazil [*Through the Brazilian Wilderness*, in which he recorded his dangerous and agonizing journey in 1914 through the Amazon rain forest to map fifteen hundred miles of the unexplored River of Doubt, now called the Rio Roosevelt]. It is the last kind of thing I shall ever attempt to do, for I am too old [fifty-seven, but the Brazilian ordeal had aged him]. . . . I was immensely interested in your organizing a corps of Russian refugees and in the fact that these are mostly Jews. A cousin of Mrs. Roosevelt's is a captain in the Artillery and he informs me that his three best gun-crews are exclusively Jews, either born in or sons of men born in Russia.

A British army captain, Eric Wheler Bush, had watched the Zion Mule Corps about to embark and made a condescending comment in his memoir, *Gallipoli:*

> On my way down to the harbour I overhauled the Assyrian Jewish Refugee Mule Corps at the Wardian Camp. Their Commander, author of that thrilling shocker, "The Man-killers [sic] of Tsavo," finds Assyrians and mules rather a mouthful and is going to tabloid [organize in small, compact units] bipeds and quadrupeds [men and mules] into the "Zion Mule Corps." The mules look very fit, so do the Assyrians and, although I did not notice that their cohorts were gleaming with purple or gold, they may help us to those habiliments; they may in fact serve as ground bait to entice the big Jew journalists and bankers towards our cause, the former will lend us the colour, the latter the coin. Anyway, so far as I can, I mean to give the chosen people a chance.[7]

Singing "Hatikvah," Patterson and his men boarded two transports, HMT *Hymettus* and HMT *Anglo-Egyptian,* at Alexandria on April 16, 1915, and sailed with their mules and the Twenty-ninth British Division, fresh from England, toward enemy territory.

With massive naval bombardment failing to dislodge the Turkish and German defenders at Gallipoli, the Zion Mule Corps was part of an attempt by ninety-three thousand British, French, New Zealand, and especially Australian troops to succeed where the navy had failed. Spearheading the landing at Cape Helles, the Twenty-ninth Regiment suffered heavy casualties. A British pilot, Air Commodore Samson, flying in a reconnaissance plane, saw, to his horror, that the sea was red with blood for a distance of fifty yards from the shore. Survivors were scrambling up the sunlit slopes and digging in a few miles inland, where they faced more savage fighting, as the Turks, under uncompromising orders to fight to the death, tried to drive them back into the blood-drenched sea.

A few days later the Mule Corps landed on the beach under cover of a fierce and freezing hailstorm that lashed the soldiers like a whip. Apart from the ammunition, the animals also carried huge sides of frozen meat, bully beef, biscuits, plum and apple jam, and cans of water brought from Egypt, seven hundred miles away.

15. Lieutenant Colonel John Henry Patterson in London in 1915, during World War I, about to leave for Gallipoli as leader of the Zion Mule Corps, a group of Jewish volunteers. Courtesy of Joan Travis.

Because a Zion Mule Corps soldier left in charge of the luggage had a Turkish rifle and seemed to be speaking Turkish, the French arrested him as a spy. In fact, he spoke a mix of Russian and Hebrew, which apparently, to French ears, sounded Turkish. After a quick court-martial he was sentenced to death. He was standing against a wall, about to be shot, when a Zion Mule Corps sergeant came on the scene. Fortunately, he spoke French and rescued the man just in time. The suspected spy was so traumatized it took him months to recover.

By now the Zion Mule Corps had set up their camp in a valley, a few hundred yards from the beach and protected by a light rise in the ground. To reach soldiers at the battlefront, the men and their mules slogged through the mud, following the few goat tracks that had not been washed away by the hailstorm, through gorse and prickly oak, across rock-strewn slopes, up and down hills, and across flooded wadis, anxiously skirting the precipitous ravines, so steep that nothing grew there.

Moving at night, confused by the dark, the rain, and the constant shell fire, the men sometimes accidentally led their mules into no-man's-land, where they were shot at by friend and foe. Luckily, only a few of these men and mules were wounded, and at first there were no fatalities.

They worked nonstop for thirty-six hours until they were ready to drop. Then the equally exhausted Patterson ordered them to take a short rest. One man was so exhausted that although he was shot in the foot during the night, it did not wake him; he only discovered that he was wounded and couldn't walk upon waking the next morning.

On May 1 some of the men had just delivered their loads to the front when Turkish heavy guns opened up and a tremendous hail of shrapnel poured down, stampeding the terrified animals. At the same time masses of Turks under cover of darkness crept forward to launch an attack. As Patterson recalled,

> The Turkish General Staff had not calculated on the Zion mules. Scared and wounded by the shrapnel, they careened over our trenches and clattered down with clanking chains on the stealthy foe. The Turks undoubtedly took them for charging cavalry, for they poured a volley into them and thus gave away their position. Our men instantly lined the trenches and opened such an intense fire that the Turks were routed, and those left alive fled back to their trenches. . . . These mules helped to save the British army in much the same way as cackling geese once saved Rome.[8]

During the fighting, Private M. Groushkowsky was shot through both arms. Despite his wounds, when the Turkish shrapnel stampeded many of the mules he held on to his mule and delivered ammunition to men desperately in need of it. Patterson promoted him to corporal, and recommended him for the Distinguished Service Medal, which General Frederick Stopford pinned on his chest in the field. A horse-drawn ambulance took another casualty, Sergeant James Matin, to a field hospital, where enterprising surgeons saved his shattered shinbone with a graft from a dead mule's leg.

Although the Zion Mule Corps was officially forbidden to join in the fighting, the men were armed with rifles, bayonets, and ammunition, and soon broke the rule. It happened, Patterson explained, when "our Inniskilling Fusiliers had suffered terrible losses in the early battles and had very few men left to man their trenches. . . . The Turks made a determined onslaught upon them when a party of the Zion Mules Corps was close by, unloading a convoy. The Zionists left their mules and led by Corporal Hildersheim, leapt into the trenches and assisted in repelling the Turks." None impressed him more than Nissei Rosenberg, "who, throughout shot and hell, led his mules with their loads of ammunition into the firing line, while all others, Jewish and British," were being killed or retreating.[9] Patterson promoted him to sergeant and recommended him for the Distinguished Service Medal. Two weeks later Rosenberg was severely wounded by shellfire, from which he made a good recovery.

Patterson never doubted the courage of Trumpeldor, his one-armed second in command, and was amazed by his indifference to pain and death. What surprised him most was how sharply he differed in temperament from his compatriots. When one of them was wounded, his friends would weep and sometimes embrace him tenderly, but Trumpeldor showed no emotion. He once calmly remarked to Patterson over the body of a badly wounded Zionist, "Ken, ken! A la guerre comme à la guerre!" (Hebrew and French for, "Yes, yes! That's what happens in war"). He reveled in the fighting, and the hotter it got, the more he relished it, quipping to Patterson, "Ah, it is now plus gai! [more fun]."[10]

What Trumpeldor had in common with the others was his determination never to abandon their dead on the battlefield. They always retrieved the body—however dangerous the situation—and the entire corps attended the funeral, during which a little shield of David was placed on the victim's grave located among colorful outcrops of spring flowers: scarlet poppies, blue cornflowers, wild thyme, and tulips.

Patterson rated the Australians and New Zealanders superb fighters. He was also impressed by the Turkish enemy's daring and originality, especially two snipers who had the audacity to hide between British heavy guns, their faces, hands, clothes, and rifles painted green and with green twigs tied to their wrists. In that camouflage they killed and wounded several British officers and men before being hunted down and shot. Mostly illiterate conscripts from the country, poorly fed and treated harshly by their officers, often outgunned and outnumbered, the Turks were ferocious fighters and never panicked. It helped, of course, that they were defending their homeland, spurred on by their mullahs urging them to die—if that was their fate—for Allah and Muhammad.

Patterson also got a kick out of their sense of humor, such as the time during a lull in the fighting when they threw gifts of grapes and candy to the entrenched British troops, who responded with cans of meat, only to have a note thrown back: "Bully beef—non, Envoyer milk." And it wasn't just one funny Turk. For example, when a British sharpshooter missed his target, there was sometimes laughter from Turkish trenches and yells in English, "Better luck next time Tommy!" On another occasion, after a devastating shelling of Turkish trenches by enough field guns, siege guns, and howitzers to destroy an army, the Turks raised a huge placard on which was printed in large letters NO CASUALTIES.[11]

Patterson respected the Turks as a gallant enemy and believed that they treated prisoners humanely; "I never heard anything but praise for the Turk and the way he played the game. I only knew of one prisoner, a Sikh being mutilated and that may have been the work of a German. The Turks are clean fighters, and more than once have pointed out that they'd be glad if we'd move a hospital ship further from the transports, for they feared that, firing at the transports they might hit the hospital. This is more than would have been done by the Germans."[12]

On May 10 a Jewish officer in the British East Lancashire regiment, Captain Arthur Behrend, sent to get supplies from the Zion Mule Corps, recorded the event in his diary:

I found the Mule Corps in an open meadow. With much saluting I was taken to the C.O., Colonel Patterson . . . and he handed over a corporal, six men and fourteen mules. "Take care of my men and don't expose them," he said, as he wished me goodbye, "The mules don't matter so much as they can be replaced more easily." I returned to our lines followed by the stolid Zionists and the equally stolid mules, and handed all over to our astonished Transport sergeant. . . . Half an hour later I strolled along to see how they were getting on and found them all sitting around a big fire with our own transport section, a Dixie of tea boiling merrily in the middle. East Lancashire Arabic quickly became the lingua franca because our men had picked up a number of Arabic words in Egypt, equally quickly too the Zionists won respect and affection, because despite their over fondness for saluting, they showed a curious disregard for shell fire.

Behrend also noted that on May 11 the Mule Corps moved two miles inland. Nine days later Turkish guns killed a dozen horses and mules and wounded several men.

On Sunday May 22, as the Christian chaplain began a service, a Turkish shell landed among the worshipers, who all ran for cover. Private Katznelsohn of the Mule Corps, who had been standing nearby, calmly grooming his mule, continued to do so. A second shell killed him, but his mule survived.[13]

At the height of a battle in June, Patterson called for a volunteer to brave the intense fire and take two mules with urgently needed ammunition and food to the front. British troops as well as members of the Mule Corps were reluctant to go. The Zionist who did volunteer, Private Ben Wertheimer, was the frail, timid, and deeply religious son of an elderly Orthodox Jew. When Trumpeldor had signed him up, he had declared that although he was "ready to fight for the Land of Israel in the name of the Lord," he feared that he would not live up to expectations. Trumpeldor reassured him that he would make a good soldier.

The slight and stooped young man left the safety of the trenches with laden mules, crossing open terrain under heavy fire. He and the mules had almost reached the front line when he was hit by shrapnel. But he was so close, the soldiers waiting for the vital supplies were able to drag him and the mules into their trench. During a break in the battle he was rescued, and before he was evacuated to a hospital, in Alexandria, he told Trumpeldor, "Now, sir, I shall never know the meaning of fear." He later died of his wounds.[14] From May to July, Patterson frequently received letters from the transport officers saying how well the Zion Mule Corps had worked under enemy fire, especially Corporal Nehemiah Yahuda, a cheerful young man who inspired his men to great effort.

The Gallipoli campaign stalled in the intensifying summer heat that brought a plague of insects. No one could take a bite of food without catching a mouthful of flies. Some blew constantly and vigorously to keep the flies at bay until their lips quickly closed over the food. Mosquitoes drove some men half crazy. Patterson also had to contend with growing friction between Ashkenazi and Sephardic Jews, as well as a disgruntled group convinced that they would never succeed in liberating Palestine and demanded immediate shipment back to Egypt. Though Patterson assured them that an eventual invasion of Palestine was inevitable, they did not buy it.

The Turks continued to hold the high ground where they had a constant supply of drinking water, but the water the Zion Corps needed for themselves, their mules, and the men in the trenches came by sea from Egypt, seven hundred miles away, and was pumped ashore. Things became desperate when two ships bringing water ran aground far out in the bay. As writer Alan Moorehead reported, "Many of the soldiers, frantic with thirst, came crowding down to the shore, their tongues blackened, their faces smeared with dust and sweat, and they simply could not wait: they had to drink. Some waded into the sea and drank the salt water. One destroyer captain cut out his water tank and sent it ashore along with his canvas bath and kept both full with pumps, and later in the day all the other vessels in the bay were ordered to follow suit. But it was still not enough."[15] Then Sergeant Schoub of the Zion Mule Corps found a deep well hidden in the corner of a demolished building. Suspecting it was poisoned, Patterson got hold of a Turkish prisoner and with a little pressure persuaded him to taste the water. He sipped it cautiously, then drank freely. Still, Patterson waited for a while to see if he survived, and when he did gave the well water to the mules, and later allowed his men to drink it.

Trumpeldor deplored the few shirkers and grumblers among the Mule Corps but opposed the ferocious flogging sometimes meted out with Patterson's approval. Things came to a head in June after the mounting casualties, exhaustion, unfair and humiliating treatment by some British officers, and lack of promised leave. Seventy-five of them went on a hunger strike and on June 15, 1915, petitioned Patterson to send them home. Instead, the next day he ordered the entire corps to assemble. He then appeared with officers from other units carrying whips. When three leading troublemakers said that they would continue refusing to obey his orders, he had them tied to posts and flogged, then tied to wagon wheels for three hours, after which they were put on a diet of bread and water for three days. It worked. The men returned to duty. Even Trumpeldor reluctantly conceded that such punishment was justified if the corps was to become the nucleus of a Jewish army intent on freeing Palestine from the Turks. Although Patterson made light of the difficulties, he admitted that "the unit posed severe disciplinary problems, and punishments such as public flogging had to be meted out. In addition, the differences between the idealists and those who joined only in order to escape from the misery of the refugee camps resulted in clashes between Trumpeldor 'the Russian,' and the Sephardi Jews. It was Patterson's goodwill and patience, coupled with Trumpeldor's devotion, that held the unit together throughout the Gallipoli campaign."[16] Patterson gave an Irish spin to it, with a little help from the Old Testament:

> It must not be supposed that all the Zionists were saints, or that I did not have my times of trouble and difficulty with them. Because some would hanker after the "flesh-pots of Egypt." Moses in his dealings with his troublesome children had a tremendous pull over me, because when my men grumbled about lack of water, I could not strike a rock and make it gush forth for them, neither when food was scarce could I call down manna or quails from Heaven. Nor were there any black clouds to hide us from the devastating fire of our enemy. With the great example of Moses before me I felt it was up to me not to fail in shepherding through our trials the little host confided to my charge, so like Father O'Flynn with his flock, I kept my children in order by, "Checkin' the crazy ones, Coaxin' unaisy ones, Liftin' the lazy ones on with the stick."
>
> I found that the racial characteristic of the Israelite made it necessary to hold him with a thread of light silk and yet strong as steel cable, and it required a tremendous amount of tact and personal influence to weather the storms which sometimes threatened to wreck our family life.[17]

One soldier remembered that Patterson used something more effective than a thread of light silk to keep him in line—and was "scared to death of him," finally deserting and making his way back to Alexandria with a shipload of wounded Turkish prisoners.[18]

Even the Patterson-Trumpeldor mutual-admiration partnership was not always an easy one. Patterson accused him of "running unacceptable personal risks and failing to supervise his men, especially the shirkers."

> Once when he found two misplaced sacks, he accused Trumpeldor of idling. Trumpeldor lost his temper and sent in his resignation. The Colonel angrily replied that Trumpeldor could prepare immediately for the journey to Alexandria and offered the popular Lt. Gorodissky the post—which he refused. Trumpeldor began to pack his things [but] as news of his journey spread through the camp dozens of men surrounding his tent, crying, "Let's all go. We don't want to stay here without our Captain!" After many apologies and much persuasion from the Colonel, Trumpeldor agreed to stay.[19]

By the end of July the intense heat and disease-bearing flies had caused almost as many casualties as the Turkish guns. The corps was down to less than half its original strength, so the workload and danger for each man were more than doubled. To get replacement recruits, General Ian Hamilton ordered Patterson back to Egypt. He took Trumpeldor and two soldiers, Rolo and Groushkowsky, with him, and they explained their purpose to Cairo's leading Jews gathered in General Maxwell's office. Jack Mosseri, a Zionist and Hebrew scholar, also held meetings in Cairo synagogues to raise recruits. In a few weeks 150 men volunteered to join the fight. More came from Alexandria.

In that city Patterson deplored the inefficiency of the police and the tactics of car drivers, who scorned traffic directions and drove off at top speed. The police would race after them, stop them for a few minutes of heated conversation, then let them go. The same scene was repeated ad nauseum. He was also appalled by the callous way the natives treated animals.

But he had no complaints about two women he got to know in the Egyptian sultan's court. One, from Baghdad, was "as fair as a lily, had gloriously red hair, and was entertaining as Scheherazade." The other, with whom he was equally infatuated, he "took to be Cleopatra herself returned to life."[20]

While in Alexandria, staying at Claude Rolo's comfortable home, he became bedridden with a fever, and Rolo's wife and two nieces took care of him. When he had recovered, he told a correspondent for London's *Jewish Chronicle* about the Mule Corps:

> These brave lads who had never seen shellfire before, most competently unloaded the boats and handled the mules whilst shells were bursting in close proximity to them. . . . Nor were they in any way discouraged when they had to plod their way to Seddul Bahr, walking over dead bodies while the bullets flew around them. For two days and nights we marched. Thanks to the Zion Mule Corps the [British] 29th Division did not meet with a sad fate, for the ZMC were the only Army Service Corps in that part of Gallipoli at that time.[21]

In Cairo Patterson visited both Allied and Turkish soldiers in various hospitals, and befriended a Turkish officer who had survived fourteen sword wounds in a battle with Indian Lancers near the Suez Canal. The Turk and Patterson resolved, despite the war, to remain friends.

Returning to Gallipoli on a calm and beautiful moonlit night, Patterson and his men were greeted with joyous shouts of "Shalom!" He missed Lieutenant Gorodissky in the crowd and was told that he had died of an illness in August and been buried at sea. Formerly a railroad engineer and math teacher at the Lycée in Alexandria, and the only son of a widowed mother, he had rejected the offer of a top engineering job to serve in Gallipoli. Trumpeldor noted in his diary that Patterson sat for a long time ignoring all around him, grieving for his friend. Corporal Zalman Cogan, writing to the *Jewish Chronicle* from an English hospital, called Gorodissky "an officer and at the same time best friend of all the soldiers. Owing to his knowledge of English he was an intermediary between us and the Colonel. . . . I never heard from him one complaint . . . an honest and just man. . . . [W]e have lost one of the best men in the Corps." Patterson himself wrote, "He was one of the best. He was passionately fond of music and he had written out for me the words of Hatikvah. He told me that the

Germans claimed to be the world's most musical nation, but that all the best musicians were either Jews or had Jewish blood."[22]

For the next six weeks Patterson wondered why the Turks were so stingy with their ammunition. Previously, they had wasted dozens of rounds on a solitary horseman, and Patterson often had to gallop at breakneck speed to avoid being peppered with shrapnel. Now he assumed that they were simply short of ammunition. Testing his theory, he held drills and parades in full view of the Turkish positions and once rode his horse close to Turkish trenches without being shelled or shot at.

He also joined Canadian troops in a sport called tent pegging, where the soldiers on horseback tried to scoop up tent pegs with a spear. In the evenings he organized campfire sing-alongs, where his men sang "It's a Long, Long Way to Tipperary," in English, and other songs in French, Russian, Hebrew, and Arabic—the two latter, Patterson recalled, "made rather melancholy by the plaintive wail of the East. Some were first-rate Russian dancers and expert wrestlers, so we had many excellent little side-shows."[23] The shows always ended with the British national anthem and "Hatikvah."

Patterson was wrong about the enemy. They had plenty of shells and bullets and were saving them for a mass attack bolstered by Bulgarians, who had joined their side. Launched on October 22, 1915, in cold, driving rain that drenched the troops and flooded their trenches, it lasted for hours. But the British and Australians held fast, helped by the Mule Corps that kept them supplied.

Malaria, dysentery, and blinding blizzards that affected both sides almost brought the fighting to a standstill. To avoid spending the winter in freezing tents and waterlogged trenches, Patterson decided to build a solid stone house to shelter his men, with a perpetual fire burning. He obtained building material from a nearby ruin. During an excavation of the basement, his men dug up a slab of marble with a filigree carving around its edge. To everyone's surprise, in the center of the stone was a carving of the shield of David. They brought it back to the camp in triumph and kept it in the new building as a good-luck charm. Patterson assumed it was very old, and surmised that it had been looted from Solomon's Temple in Jerusalem. But its origin and where it is today remain mysteries. It proved to be a very good good-luck charm—shells exploded all around it, but the building itself was never hit and no one in its vicinity was ever injured.

By October the men had finished digging deeper and wider trenches, so that, after walking to deliver supplies to the front, on their return they could ride their mules, through the trenches. They became known as the "Allied Cavalry." That same month Patterson gave leave to fifty of his men, who sailed for Alexandria.

In November, he developed jaundice, and Captain Blandy of the Royal Army Medical Corps evacuated him to the hospital ship, *Assaye,* aboard which he had sailed to Africa during the Boer War, when he was in charge of twelve hundred troops. His faithful orderly, Corporal Yorish, who had been a dental student in Palestine, went with him. Patterson admired Yorish as a man who could turn his hand to anything, and was never happy unless he was working.[24] He left Trumpeldor in charge of the Zion Mule Corps—now down to 5 British and 2 Jewish officers and 120 men. Lieutenant Gye remained, too, as Trumpeldor's translator.

On Patterson's arrival at Gallipoli the entire peninsula had been a blaze of color, with green pastures, cultivated fields, groves of olive and almond trees, and beautiful wildflowers everywhere, especially the blood-red poppies. When he left, "the smiling land had become a desolate, God-forsaken place, nothing but row upon row of unsightly trenches and not a single blade of grass to be seen."[25] A padre on the hospital ship enjoyed Patterson's company, and noted in his diary:

> We have one particularly interesting personage among the officers—Lieut. Colonel J. H. Patterson, D.S.O., the writer of the thrilling story The Man-Eaters of Tsavo, the great African traveler and the discoverer of a new kind of antelope, to which he has given his name. I had read his book some years ago, so I viewed the author with a good deal of curiosity.
>
> During the last year he has commanded a transport battalion at Gallipoli. All the men enlisted were Russian Jews [most, not all], who had fled from Palestine to Egypt. I have been sitting with him this morning and have heard stories of his travel in Central Africa and the war galore. I have learned a lot about the secret societies among the natives in Western Africa. Colonel Patterson has had a good deal to do with attempts to

crush the Leopard Society a few years back, and he gave gruesome, sickening accounts of some of the horrors perpetrated by the natives. One is thankful to think that British rule does not make such things possible.[26]

Patterson had recovered enough to walk off the ship when it docked at Southampton the day after Christmas, 1915. During his stay at a London hospital at 40 Upper Grosvenor Street supervised by Lady Violet Brassy, his actor friend Sir Henry Irving came to see him with a ticket for a box at the Savoy Theatre, where soon after Patterson, his wife, Frances, and a dozen friends enjoyed the play *The Case of Lady Camber.*

Convalescing in the hospital, Patterson started to write his third book, *With the Zionists in Gallipoli.* It included his account of how, late in December 1915, though Trumpeldor was shot through the shoulder, he refused to go to the field hospital and kept fighting.

Soon after, the Allies withdrew from Gallipoli as a lost cause. Before they left, the survivors of the Zion Mule Corps paid tribute to their eight dead comrades, who were later buried in the War Cemetery on Mount Scopus in Jerusalem, the Star of David on their tombs testifying to their role as precursors of the Israeli Army. A last gruesome task had to be completed, to save their mules from lingering and painful deaths—the men in charge slashed the animals' throats.

Things looked grim for the Allies. The German army had overrun Poland. Recuperating in the hospital, Patterson remained optimistic, concluding that "our terrible losses and disastrous failure in the Dardanelles were not entirely futile. We held up and almost destroyed a magnificent Turkish Army, and by doing this gave invaluable aid to our Russian ally."[27]

Back in Egypt the corps was ordered to Ireland to help suppress a revolt by the Irish fighting for their freedom from British rule. They refused, one saying that they had enlisted to fight the Turks, not Irish patriots. Soon after, on March 26, 1916, the Zion Mule Corps was disbanded, and most of its members scattered.

However, some 120 agreed to stay together and join Vladimir Jabotinsky in England, where he had been campaigning to create a separate Jewish fighting force within the British army. The War Office had stalled, or ignored his proposal, especially as the secretary of state for war, Lord Kitchener, was against it. So, with rare exceptions such as Chaim Weizmann, were most Zionist leaders in Britain, who feared that their support of the Allies would endanger Jews living or trapped in enemy territory. Patterson knew of Jabotinsky's fervent efforts to raise a Jewish regiment within the British army.

A Russian Jew rebuffed by Britain's established and influential Jews, Jabotinsky had turned to those Jews living in London's working-class East End, many of them refugees from czarist Russia. Fiercely opposed to fighting as allies of their enemy, the czar, and exempted as aliens from military service in Britain, they ridiculed his impassioned oratory, shouted him off various platforms, and pelted him with tomatoes. At times he even needed police protection. Undeterred, he prepared a document that read: "Should the [British] Government create a Jewish Regiment to be utilized exclusively for Home Defense or for operation on the Palestine front, I undertake to join such a regiment."[28] Hoping for thousands of signatures, he got three hundred.

One morning he was pleasantly surprised to receive a note with a London postmark signed by J. H. Patterson, saying that he was on convalescent leave from Gallipoli and suggesting a meeting. Though Jabotinsky had left Egypt for England just before Patterson arrived there, they had briefly corresponded while Patterson was still in Gallipoli. Jabotinsky had outlined his efforts to raise a Jewish Legion in Britain, and seemed somewhat misinformed about the Zion Mule Corps. Patterson replied on November 15, 1915, pointing out that the Zion Mule Corps did not simply deliver food, water, and ammunition to soldiers in the trenches, but was a fighting force, armed with rifles, bayonets, and ammunition, just like a British infantry unit. Moreover, its men had fought in defense of the British trenches and had suffered substantial casualties. The commanding officer of the Australian and New Zealand Expeditionary Force, General Birdwood, thought a Jewish Legion was a great idea, Patterson wrote, and had even suggested to Patterson that he should return to Britain to help form one. "Nothing would give me greater gratification," Patterson concluded, "than to raise, train and command a Jewish fighting unit."[29]

Several members of the Zion Mule Corps had kept Jabotinsky informed throughout the Dardanelles campaign about the Irish-born Protestant's tough time in controlling some of the men, including the obstinate holy man, as Jabotinsky called Trumpeldor. He also knew that Patterson was famous for building a railroad bridge in Africa, and admired by big-game hunters in Europe and the United States as the prince of lion hunters. Maybe here was the vital partner he needed for his plans.

8

Patterson's Fight to Create
a Jewish Legion,
1916–1918

JABOTINSKY'S FIRST IMPRESSION of Patterson at the Dover Street convalescent home was of a tall, thin man of youthful middle age, with intelligent and cheerful eyes, the personification of what the English called Irish
charm, but with no hint of those so-called Irish qualities of gloom and
hair-splitting. He was soon to learn that Patterson was a great student of
the Bible for whom Gideon and Samson and David were living figures.

Patterson spoke enthusiastically about the Zion Mule Corps, said
he had been surprised how quickly they became excellent soldiers, and
praised Trumpeldor, now in command of them, as the bravest man he
ever met. When he asked Jabotinsky how well his plan to raise the Jewish
Legion was going, Jabotinsky replied that Kitchener, the influential British secretary for war, opposed it. "Realities are stronger than Lord Kitchener," Patterson assured him. (So was fate: shortly after their conversation,
on June 5, 1916, Kitchener, en route to confer with the czar of Russia, was
drowned at sea when his ship sank after hitting a German mine.)

Finally, Jabotinsky asked, "Will you help me?"

"Of course," Patterson replied, and beckoned him to follow.

Leaving the convalescent home, they took a cab ride to the houses of
Parliament where, in a hall between the Lords and the Commons, Patterson handed a note to an attendant. Five minutes later a small man in army
uniform emerged from the House of Commons. Patterson introduced him

as "Captain Leopold Amery, who knows our project," and asked Jabotinsky to give Amery the latest details.[1]

A Harrow schoolmate and friend of Churchill's, and now a Conservative MP, Amery had been in the same war zones as Patterson, as the *London Times'* chief war correspondent during the Boer War, and more recently in Gallipoli as an intelligence officer. He appeared extremely well informed about the British government's plans. More important, he wholeheartedly supported a Jewish Legion. (He was also capable of keeping secrets. Not until 1999—forty-four years after his death—was it revealed that he was Jewish.)

There was still strong resistance to the legion, especially from wealthy, established Jews, who regarded themselves first and foremost as British. Resistance, too, came from poor Russian Jews in London's East End, who were more than reluctant to fight on the side of the czar—their deadly anti-Semitic enemy. The turning point came in the fall of 1916. Then the ship evacuating the Zion Mule Corps from Alexandria, survived being hit by a mine near Crete, and delivered the men safely to London, where they were promised that, although the Mule Corps had been disbanded, they would be kept together as a unit, for future military service.

The very next day, Trumpeldor appeared at Jabotinsky's Chelsea home with a message from Nissei Rosenberg, a former Zion Mule Corps sergeant: "We arrived yesterday. There are 120 of us. Come to see us at the London barracks."[2] Patterson and Amery made sure the promise was kept, and the Zion Mule Corps veterans were assigned to the same Twentieth London Battalion. Jabotinsky joined them, signing up as a private, still pushing for a Jewish Legion in his off-duty hours from a training camp near Winchester.

Although he had once ridiculed the Mule Corps as "the donkey battalion," he realized that it was his trump card and that stressing its achievements would be a way to persuade the British government to create a Jewish Legion. Captain Amery agreed, telling him and Patterson, "Everything depends upon this group. Your whole plan must stand or fall by this small company of Zionist soldiers."[3] Patterson also hoped that the book he was writing, *With the Zionists in Gallipoli*, would arouse public support for a Jewish fighting force in the British army.

After recovering from his illness, he was sent to Kildare, in east-central Ireland, to command the Royal Dublin Fusiliers. Ireland itself was now a battleground, after an Easter uprising by a small group of men fighting for independence from Britain. They were quickly suppressed and their leaders executed, but, although he sympathized with the Irish nationalists, Patterson was not involved. Shortly after, he was assigned to the Curragh, also in Kildare—a British military training ground since 1646—to command the Sixth Battalion of the Royal Dublin Fusiliers, and to ready its recruits for the slaughter on the western front. From there, on February 25, 1917, he wrote this prophetic letter to Theodore Roosevelt:

I feel sure that it can't be many days now until the Professor's hand is forced [President Woodrow Wilson had been a professor and president of Princeton University] and you are in with us [in World War I as a British ally]. It has taken a long time—but better late than never for the sake of America no less than for ourselves. I see that you are raising an army, or taking steps that way. [Roosevelt also hoped to raise a volunteer army to fight on the side of the Allies.] I expect you will want instructors in all the latest "dodges" in trench warfare. If you do I hope you will ask our W.O. [War Office] for my services. You know that thanks to you I saw quite a good bit of your army and know its ways and liked it (please see my "Zionists in Gallipoli") and nothing would please me more than to go into the firing line with such a fine lot of men—under you—if the W.O. gave permission—and I am sure they would gladly do so—I could bring out a select small staff of expert officers and N.C.O's for such subjects as "Trench fighting," "Bombing," "Trench bayonet fighting," "Lewis and machine gun fighting," "anti-gas measures," and all the little odds and ends of the trench warfare that we have picked up at such cost during the past $2^1/_2$ years. I would start a school of instruction wherever you were located with your army and in a very few weeks you would be able to take your men into action with perfect confidence in their ability to hold their own.

Roosevelt replied on March 15, 1917: "Indeed, if I am given a division, there is nothing that I would like more than to have you with us, in just such a capacity; but I am utterly sick to heart about things here. I haven't an idea whether any action will be taken, or whether I shall be allowed to do anything; but I shall make a tremendous effort to get to the front."

On April 6, 1917, less than a month after Roosevelt wrote to Patterson, the United States declared war on Germany, spurred by the kaiser's decision to resume submarine warfare against ships of neutral nations. Less than two weeks later, on April 19, British prime minister David Lloyd George advised his ambassador in Paris that after the war the French would have to accept a British protectorate over Palestine, to protect Britain's security in the Suez Canal and adjoining Arab areas. At the same time Lloyd George decided to encourage Zionists and their aspiration for a homeland in Palestine—under British protection and auspices. Two members of his war cabinet, Jan Christiaan Smuts and Lord Milner, were all for it. So were several political allies: Leo Amery, William Ormsby-Gore, Philip Kerr, and Mark Sykes.

Sykes had been converted to Zionism after meeting Aaron Aaronsohn, leader of a group of Jews in Palestine spying for the British. He had warned them that the Turks intended to attack their troops across the Suez Canal. Admiration for Aaronsohn's courage and gratitude for the help he gave the British explained why General Sir George Macdonogh, director of military intelligence, and Colonel Richard Meinertzhagen, chief field intelligence officer to the Egyptian Expeditionary Force, supported the Zionists.

On July 17, 1917, Zionist leader and scientist Chaim Weizmann, a British Jew, advised British foreign secretary Arthur Balfour of the vital importance of an official declaration of British support for a Jewish homeland in Palestine. Already sympathetic to the Zionist cause, Balfour asked Weizmann and fellow Zionists to draft a pro-Zionist statement to be presented to the British War Cabinet and promised that he would support it. The draft read: "His Majesty's Government accepts the principle that Palestine should be reconstituted as the National Home of the Jewish People. His Majesty's Government will use its best endeavors to secure achievement of this object and will discuss the necessary methods and means with the Zionist Organization." Leo Amery advised Jabotinsky and Trumpeldor that now was a good time to send Prime Minister Lloyd George a formal petition calling for a Jewish Legion to fight on the side of the Allies in the war. Lloyd George and his War Cabinet approved the plan in principle, and instructed War Minister Lord Derby to work out the details.

Private Jabotinsky was staying in Chaim Weizmann's London home on Passover leave when he got a letter from Lord Derby requesting his presence at the War Office that afternoon. As a lowly private in the British army he felt anxious about discussing a matter of international importance with the secretary of state for war, and asked Trumpeldor, who was at least an officer, to go in his place. He declined, saying that his English wasn't up to it, but agreed to accompany him for moral support.

Derby, an affable type, though obviously surprised to see a private in the War Office on such an important mission, put his visitors at ease, told them that he approved of the legion, and asked them to name the man to lead it. Jabotinsky had a letter from Patterson in his pocket that read: "It is my honest opinion that you should find a Jewish colonel. I would be happy to lead Jewish soldiers again, but justice and your national interests demand that this honor should be given a Jew." But Jabotinsky was convinced that this historical privilege had been earned by a man who had stood by them when they were scorned and ridiculed, who had not been ashamed to lead the Mule Corps, which he had converted into a respected fighting force, and who, even while in a hospital and convalescent home, had celebrated their achievements in writing *With the Zionists in Gallipoli*. "There is only one nominee," Jabotinsky said. "Even though he is not a Jew, he must be our colonel, and I hope that one day he will be our general: Patterson."[4] Trumpeldor agreed, the War Office approved, and on July 27, 1917, Patterson accepted the job.

After his return from Ireland he asked Jabotinsky to join him. "From then on," Patterson recalled, he and Jabotinsky "worked together, fought together, and stood four square together, facing all kinds of troubles during those long trying years. Never could one have a better comrade or a truer friend than Vladimir Jabotinsky."[5] Trumpeldor was not with them, because the British army did not accept one-armed recruits. Instead, he returned to Russia to discuss with the new liberal Kerensky government his plan to raise an army of one hundred thousand Russian Jews to drive the Turks from Palestine.

Jabotinsky continued his recruiting campaign, circulating posters in London's East End and addressing public meetings at which he was sometimes pelted again with tomatoes and even physically attacked.

The confrontations stopped when he had the protection of former Zion Mule Corps members. But there was still much bitter opposition to his recruitment efforts. He told Amery that the strongest inducement for Jews to join the legion would be an official announcement in favor of Palestine as a Jewish homeland. Amery thought so, too.

To Patterson's astonishment some influential British Jews were hostile both to the idea of a Jewish homeland and to the creation of a Jewish Legion. Determined to change their minds, he invited them, as well as those individuals in favor of the legion, to a meeting at the War Office on August 8, 1917. The distinguished and powerful gathering included Lord Rothschild; Major Lionel de Rothschild; Major Neil Primrose; Captain Ormsby-Gore, MP; Edmund Sebag Montefiore; Dr. Chaim Weizmann; Joseph Cowan; Dr. Eder; M. J. Landa; I. J. Greenberg, editor of the *Jewish Chronicle*; the Reverend S. Lipson, senior Jewish chaplain; Jabotinsky (recently promoted to sergeant); Mark Sykes, MP; Leo Amery, MP; and Major Radcliffe Salaman, Royal Army Medical Corps (a cousin of Sir Herbert Samuel, who became the first high commissioner for Palestine).

Leading opponents, Major Lionel de Rothschild and Sebag Montefiore claimed to speak on behalf of the Jewish community. They had already stated that the Jews of London's East End were so thoroughly cowed that they believed the War Office intended to send the proposed Jewish battalion not to Palestine but to the most dangerous front in France—to have them exterminated. Patterson, then, according to Chaim Weizmann, gave Rothschild and Montefiore "a slashing reply—which cut the ground from under their feet," and Jabotinsky "lifted the debate to a level immeasurably above their point of view."[6] Finally, Patterson said that the matter was official British policy, and anyone not prepared to support the plan should leave the room. No one moved and the conversation continued.

Former opponents Lord Rothschild—though not Lionel de Rothschild—and Major Salaman now agreed to support the legion. Salaman, a member of an old Anglo-Jewish family, explained his decision, saying that the Zionists "have confronted us with an accomplished fact and thus stopped all discussion. There is only one thing left for us—to try to make the regiment a success and a credit to the Jewish people."[7] Salaman later joined the legion.

During the meeting, Neil Primrose, Lord Rosebery's son, handed Patterson a note asking if he could dine with him that evening, as he would like to join the regiment. "Patterson had another appointment that evening and the meeting never too place. Primrose went out to Palestine with another regiment and was killed leading his men in a charge. Patterson always felt that if he had been able to make the appointment and Primrose had joined him, he would not have been killed."[8]

Five days after the War Office meeting, Patterson held another at Jews' College, presided over by Lord Rothschild. Patterson reported the results to Lord Chichester, a War Office official, saying that almost everyone had approved of calling the regiment "Jewish" except for a few elderly English Jews who suggested "Russian Jewish Regiment." They had been howled down by some prominent English Jews who claimed:

> There was no such thing as a Russian Jew or an English Jew, that a Jew was a Jew and that the men composing the regiment were to be Jews. Therefore, the War Office had done the right thing in calling it a Jewish Regiment. . . . There are, I know, a few so-called English Jews headed by the Montagus and some of the Montefiores, who wish apparently to forget that they are Jews, because they have been settled in England for two or three generations and . . . are afraid that this regiment might possibly not do them credit. And, therefore, they are afraid to risk their reputations as Jews. But it was strongly pointed out to them at the meeting that the trumpery [paltry] two or three generations reputation in England was but a very small thing compared with the 6,000 odd years which the Jewish nation have behind them. . . . The Jewish Regiment is so popular that I am inundated with applications for transfers from British Jews now serving in the army.[9]

Yet Lord Derby still wavered, telling Philip Kerr (Lloyd George's private secretary, and later Lord Lothian) that "Rothschild himself has written suggesting it should be called the Maccabean Regiment and I am to see a deputation when I get back next week on the subject. Personally I am ready to call [them] the Joppa Rifles or Jerusalem Highlanders, or anything else as long as I get the men. Of course we shall employ them in Palestine, but I don't think they ought to be specially told that that is what they are going to be employed for."[10] Jabotinsky biographer Shmuel Katz notes that Lord Derby's "own view of Jews was, as he made clear, that they were indeed a nationality and not a religion."

> He had surely imbibed that truth as a family tradition, coming down from his great-grandfather and his grandfather, who had both been colleagues of [former prime minister Benjamin] Disraeli, and who had frequently heard Disraeli's creed that "all is race" and that a Jew was a Jew (and could be proud of it) even when he changed his religion. He may well have compared in distaste the assimilationists' denial of their nationality with the courageous and dignified stance of the Christian Disraeli, who did not hesitate to endanger his whole political career by insisting not only on his identification with Jewish nationality but on the superiority of the ancient Jewish tradition.[11]

Still, the opposition persisted. Lionel de Rothschild and Lord Swaythling led a group on August 30 to persuade Lord Derby to cancel his approval of the Jewish Legion. And he largely gave in, assuring them that the battalion would not be called Jewish, they would not get kosher food, and he would not pledge that they would be sent to Palestine, although they might be.

Enraged by the news, as he had already recruited several hundred men by promising that they would fight in Palestine in a Jewish Legion with a Jewish badge, Patterson risked a court-martial by rattling off a furious letter of protest to General Geddes, calling Derby's decision a betrayal and a disgrace, and as a result he was immediately resigning his command.

Chaim Weizmann and Leo Amery also protested Derby's decision, complaining to a member of the War Cabinet, Lord Milner. Shocked and surprised, Milner confronted Derby, who agreed to see a counterdeputation. Meanwhile, having told Derby that "the world's ruling caste are the Journalists," Milner left for the offices of the *London Times* to confer with its pro-Zionist editor, Wickham Steed. Apprised of the situation and of Colonel Patterson's threat to resign, Steed promised Milner, "Tomorrow the Times will tell the War Office not to play the fool."

"But," Milner said, "Patterson doesn't want to stay and I can't do without him."

"The Times," replied Steed, "will tell him to stay."

Steed's editorial the next day ridiculed the War Office for listening to a small group of plutocrats and ignoring the idealism of millions of Jews. He emphasized that the Jewish character of the regiment must be strictly safeguarded and the men sent only to Palestine. He concluded: "We hope that Colonel Patterson, with whose indignation we can sympathize, will change his decision."[12]

Embarrassed by the *Times* editorial on September 5, Derby declared that the all-Jewish legion would be sent to Palestine, and have the title "Jewish" and a Jewish insignia after earning them as good soldiers. Until then, it would be known as the Thirty-eighth Battalion of the Royal Fusiliers. Nevertheless, it was popularly known in writing and speeches as the Jewish Legion or the Jewish Regiment, even in some official documents.

Most of the War Cabinet approved of a Jewish homeland in Palestine, yet the fiercest exception was the only Jew in the cabinet, Sir Edwin Montagu, secretary of state for India. He spoke so vehemently of his fears that the statement would alarm Muslims in India and raise the sensitive issue of the dual loyalty of British Jews that Lloyd George postponed a final decision until October 4.

Bitterly disappointed, Chaim Weizmann wrote, "The 'dark forces' in English Jewry have gone into action again, and this time they have mobilized their famous fighter who even though he has now become a great Hindu nationalist, feels obliged to fight against Jewish nationalism. I cannot understand, I admit, how British statesmen still attach importance to the attitude of a few wealthy Jews and allow their opinion to be weighed against the almost unanimous voice of all sections of Jewish people."[13]

When Foreign Secretary Arthur Balfour presented the Zionist case to the War Cabinet on October 3, Montagu again opposed it so intensely that, according to Weizmann, he almost wept. Eventually, despite Montagu's continued objections, a compromise statement, known as the Balfour Declaration, was accepted on November 2, 1917. It appeared as a letter from Balfour to the president of the British Zionist Federation:

Dear Lord Rothschild, I have much pleasure in conveying to you on behalf of His Majesty's Government, the following dedication of sympathy with Jewish Zionist aspirations which has been submitted to, and approved by the Cabinet. His Majesty's Government view with favour the establishment in Palestine of a national home for the Jewish people, and will use their best endeavours to facilitate the achievement of this object, it being clearly understood that nothing shall be done which may prejudice the civil and religious rights of existing non-Jewish communities in Palestine, or the rights and political status enjoyed by Jews in any other country. I should be grateful to you if you would bring this declaration to the knowledge of the Zionist Federation.[14]

Later, Lloyd George said that the Zionist leaders had promised him that, if the Allies committed themselves to a national home for the Jews in Palestine, they would do their best to rally to the Allied cause Jewish sentiment and support throughout the world. They kept their word.

Overjoyed, Jabotinsky thanked Ronald Graham of the Foreign Office, a Scot he regarded as a good friend of the Zionist cause. Graham had helped Weizmann get the Balfour Declaration, and helped Jabotinsky in his campaign for the legion. Graham replied on November 7, 1917, "I congratulate you most heartily on this important step towards the realization of Jewish aspirations. The Jewish cause is now inseparably bound up with that of the Allies, and they must triumph or fall with them."[15]

On hearing the news, Jewish communities throughout the world danced in the streets, cheered British and Americans officials, and flooded Whitehall and Washington with telegrams of thanks. Some 150,000 people celebrated in the streets of Jabotinsky's Russian hometown, Odessa, and marched to the British Embassy singing "Hatikvah" and "God Save the King."

That night, Patterson and other Zionists held a celebratory supper in Chaim Weizmann's Kensington home. And the grandfather of the future Israeli statesmen, Abba Eban, attended a meeting in London's Kingsway Hall to hear Weizmann speak. A fervent but pessimistic Zionist, the old man had frequently said that hair would grow on the palms of his hands before the Zionist dream was fulfilled. Now, as he sat in the back of the hall and saw Weizmann raise his arms and announce the victory, he broke into silent and uncontrollable tears.[16] Jabotinsky and Weizmann agreed that the prospect of a Jewish Legion to help Britain win the war played a vital role in obtaining the Balfour Declaration, and the declaration in turn encouraged several hundred more men to join the legion.

However, Trumpeldor's plan to form a Jewish Legion in Russia had failed. The Bolsheviks, in power since October 1917, after toppling Kerensky's brief liberal government, were not interested in continuing the war and had sued for peace. With the Russians out of the war, refugee Russian Jews in Britain had no reason to oppose Jabotinsky's appeal to them to fight on the side of the Allies, especially if it meant freeing Palestine from the Turks.

Patterson, of course, was disappointed not to have the bravest man he ever knew with him in the legion, and was eager to have all who had served with him in Gallipoli join him in his new training headquarters at Plymouth. Most agreed. They would not only form the nucleus of the legion, as men who had proved themselves under fire, but also help in training the batches of raw recruits frequently arriving at the Crown Hill Barracks, Plymouth, Devon, a southern seaport town from which, in 1588, Sir Francis Drake set out to defeat the Spanish armada. Patterson screened each volunteer carefully, questioning him about his family, motives, and experience, before signing him up. Jacob Epstein, thirty-seven, a natural-ized British subject born in the United States, and later a famous sculptor, passed the test, though he eventually had a nervous breakdown and did not go overseas. Patterson had generally chosen his men well, proudly not-ing that they were doubtless unique among military units, because not one of them was arrested for a civil or criminal offense in all the time they were at Plymouth.

Muslim troops under British command received special food, but the army declined to provide Patterson's men with kosher meals or to let them rest on Saturdays, the Hebrew Sabbath. So Patterson threatened to resign unless the army catered to their religious beliefs and customs. And the army caved in.

The wet canteen to supply the Jewish battalion with beer was closed because it did not have a single customer. But there was plenty of enter-tainment. Music hall artists and musicians in the unit formed a concert party and an orchestra, which entertained the men in the evenings and performed by popular demand throughout the town.

Training was a challenge for Patterson. Many new recruits were devoted Orthodox Jews, and their beliefs and military life were hardly compatible. The Russian Jews, especially, after vicious treatment in their homeland, were wary of anyone in authority. Almost all of them had led a sedentary life and were unprepared for hard physical work outdoors in the cold winter. Still, Patterson was surprised to find that "a little tailor, snatched from the purlieus of Petticoat Lane [London's East End], who had never in all his life wielded anything more dangerous than a needle, soon became adept in the use of a rifle and bayonet, and could transfix a dummy figure of the Kaiser in the approved style."[17] Every commander who inspected the group on parade mentioned their rocklike steadiness, including General Macready, who said that he would advise General Allenby to make use of the men as soon as they arrived in Egypt. In January 1918, the legion was ordered to Palestine and its members given ten days' leave.

Macready had never refused a reasonable request from Patterson. He did refuse, however, when Patterson asked for Jabotinsky to be promoted to lieutenant. Impossible, Macready replied, because no foreigner could hold a commission in the British Army.

Prepared for Macready's response, Patterson asked, "Isn't the Czar of Russia a colonel in the British army?"

"He holds only honorary rank," countered Macready.

Patterson responded, "That will do for Jabotinsky, as well."[18] It was no contest. As usual, Patterson prevailed. And not for the first time, Macready bent the rules. Jabotinsky was made a lieutenant in the Thirty-eighth Battalion of the Royal Fusiliers, subtitled "the Judean," soon to become known as the Jewish Legion.

Biographer Terence Prittie points out that language was still a problem. For example, one night, when a Yemenite Jew was on guard duty and a British officer approached, he remembered to challenge him with "Halt! Who goes there?" When he got the correct response, "Friend!" he amazed the visitor saying, "Advance friend, and be circumcised."[19]

A controversy as to whether the legionnaires should display a Jewish or a British flag was settled by a War Office compromise: they carried both a Royal Fusiliers standard and a blue flag with a Star of David on it.

On February 4, 1918, the day Jabotinsky became an officer, General Macready got special permission from the mayor for some five hundred members of the Jewish Legion to march through the city of London with fixed bayonets. They spent the previous night quartered in the Tower

16. Patterson on horseback leads the Jewish Legion through London streets in February 1918, greeted by tens of thousands of cheering Jews. First published in the *Jewish Chronicle*, 1918.

of London and in the morning were led by the band of the Coldstream Guards playing stirring music, followed by Patterson on horseback and Jabotinsky walking behind him proudly carrying a Jewish flag. Their inaugural march took them from their temporary barracks in the Tower to Aldgate and through Fenchurch and Lombard Streets in the city of London to Whitechapel in the East End. En route, they passed the Mansion House, where the lord mayor, Major Lionel de Rothschild, and several generals from the War Office took the salute. "Rothschild," Jabotinsky noted, looked "important and proud, taking a delight in something he had narrowly failed to destroy."[20]

At Whitechapel, where Jabotinsky had once been subjected to derision and denigration, as he recalled, "there were tens of thousands of Jews in the streets, at the windows, and on the roofs. Blue-white flags were over every shop door, women crying with joy, old Jews with fluttering beards, murmuring 'Shehecheyanu' [prayers]; Patterson on his horse, laughing and bowing, and wearing a rose a girl had thrown him from a balcony; and the boys, those 'tailors,'" as he called them, "shoulder to shoulder, their bayonets dead level, each step like a single clap of thunder, clean, proud, and drunk with the sense of a holy mission."[21]

9

Patterson's Jewish Legion
Fights for Palestine,
1918–1919

ON THEIR JOURNEY to the war zone through France and Italy, the Jewish Legion's talented musicians and actors—several of them professionals—stopped at army camps to entertain Allied troops. On Patterson's orders, they always ended with what became Israel's national anthem, "Hatikvah."

Jabotinsky recalled how, throughout the journey, "The padre, Reverend Falk, held out bravely against the general attack of the whole regiment of skeptical lieutenants, who pleaded that being a Zionist had nothing to do with eating kosher food. He stood like a rock by his principle. 'It isn't a question of eating,' he said. 'It is a principle that the Jew must always fight against all temptation, control and discipline himself at every step, and build a Zion of purity in his heart, before building a Zion for his people.'"[1]

There were lively discussions between the Zionists and the anti-Zionists who had volunteered to join the legion only to avoid being drafted into ordinary British regiments where there would be no kosher food and no respect for their religious views. No one, especially Jabotinsky, disputed that the best Zionist among them—with Jabotinsky himself and the chaplain surely vying for second place—was the Irish Protestant Patterson, who bolstered his fervent Zionist views by quoting Old Testament accounts of Gideon, Deborah, David, and Migdal. The padre

17. Lieutenant Vladimir Jabotinsky of the Jewish Legion. Courtesy of Dr. Oscar Kraines.

attempted to prove that Patterson's actions indicated he was a Mizrahist rather than a Zionist (Mizrahi was the religious aspect of Zionism). It was not an unreasonable assumption, because Patterson not only quoted the Old Testament to support his Zionist views but, every Saturday morning, found a place for a synagogue parade, where Jewish and Christian officers and men stood together beneath the Zionist flag flying from the nearest flagpole, at the end of which the choir sang "Hatikvah" and "God Save The King."

In Taranto, Italy, while waiting for three Japanese destroyers to escort them to Egypt, the camp commandant warned Patterson not to let Jabotinsky go into the town, because he was Russian and Russian soldiers recently passing through had angered the residents by preaching Bolshevism. Patterson laughingly reassured the commandant that when he and Jabotinsky went to town together, he addressed him as Lieutenant Jackson. And Jabotinsky explained in a letter to his wife, Yohana (in England with their son, Eri, after leaving Russia, via Norway), "In the town I am a living puzzle. I babble in Italian as much as possible and surprise the populace. Quite often I am told, 'You, an Italian, how come you are not an Italian officer?'"[2]

While still in Taranto, the padre had a carpenter make an ark to house the Scroll of Law, and Patterson assured the men that as long as they had the ark, nothing would prevent their safe arrival in Egypt. He proved prophetic. But on its next voyage the ship, *Lascoe Castle*, was torpedoed and sunk.

In Alexandria, the same people who had welcomed the Zion Mule Corps three years earlier again greeted them with wild enthusiasm. Rabbis in ceremonial robes, British generals, neutral consuls, and Arab notables attended a special service to celebrate their arrival. Buoyed by the reception, the legion headed for more military training at Helmieh, a village near Cairo. There, immediately, Patterson felt hostility from the brigade commander to everything Jewish. Hoping to convert him, one night, chatting with him after dinner, he steered the conversation to the enormous contribution Jews had made toward civilizing and humanizing the rest of the world, and how, despite centuries of oppression, they had never lost their dream of returning to Palestine. Unimpressed, the brigadier scornfully warned Patterson that he was wasting his time as commander of a Jewish unit.

During the legion's training from dawn to dusk, when they practiced bayonet charges, grenade throwing, and signaling, Patterson got a telegram from the United States. It was from David Ben-Gurion, a Jewish refugee from Palestine and founder of the Hehalutz (Pioneer) Organization. He reported that legion recruiting offices had been opened in New York City, Greece, and Argentina. Patterson forwarded the news to General Allenby, now in possession of Jerusalem, since driving the Turks out of the city. He asked the general for a meeting to discuss the legion's role in the planned offensive to drive the Turks out of the rest of Palestine. Allenby's chief of staff, General Louis Bols, replied, inviting Patterson to army headquarters but advising him that Allenby did not want to deploy the legion.

Patterson was astonished by the reply. He knew that Allenby had recently lost many of his troops to the western front. There, the German general Ludendorff had launched a dangerous attack on Paris and the channel ports, and Allenby had to send several of his divisions to France to shore up the Allied defense, leaving him with a very diminished army. In those circumstances, Patterson could not believe that the general would refuse to employ trained reinforcements.

Hoping to talk Allenby into changing his mind, Patterson and Jabotinsky took a train ride to the general's Beer-Jacob headquarters. But he stood firm. He explained that a Jewish Legion would upset the Arabs, who, led by a British colonel, T. E. Lawrence, were fighting the Turks in Arabia. Still, he conceded that the British government wanted to be fair to Jewish interests. So he compromised. He would not let them join the fight, but they could continue recruiting for the legion. Baffled and disappointed, they returned to Helmieh to celebrate Passover, for which Patterson had prodded a reluctant military into supplying unleavened bread.

Chaim Weizmann visited the camp with a man named Aaronsohn, who told the legionnaires that the Turks had tortured his father, Aaron (who had helped the British army in Egypt), and his aunt, his father's sister, Sarah, for spying in Palestine for the British. To escape further torture, his aunt had committed suicide.

Patterson was now convinced that the anti-Jewish General Bols was intent on destroying the legion, especially after receiving a letter from military headquarters inviting his men to transfer to labor units away from the front lines. Incensed, Patterson called his battalion on parade and exhorted them to decline the offer, and to remain loyal to the legion. Twelve out of a thousand opted to transfer, until Patterson made a passionate appeal to each of them. Then only two decided to leave.

In April 1918 the Thirty-ninth Jewish Battalion, many of them Americans and Canadians, arrived in Egypt. Among them were two future Israeli prime ministers and one future president: David Ben-Gurion, Levi

Eshkol, and Yitzak Ben-Zvi. They were led by an Australian Jew, Colonel Elizier Margolin.

The positive news for Patterson was that the British government was sustaining its pro-Jewish policy and had created a Zionist Commission in London to cater to Jewish interests. The bad news: the British military in Palestine was still resisting the policy. Nevertheless, Patterson won out: early in June the legion was ordered to join the fighting front in Palestine, where Allenby planned a fall offensive.

With a dangerously reduced force, Allenby decided to dupe the Turks into believing that he had a massive army at his command. It would take several months to prepare. Meanwhile, unknown to Patterson, the role of the Jewish Legion would be to keep the Turks at bay in almost unendurable conditions. Not realizing what they faced, all through the night, too excited to sleep, they traveled by train across the Sinai Desert in open trucks, heading for the Turkish front lines. At sunrise on June 6, 1918, they passed the town of Gaza, a vital bridgehead to and from Egypt and the site of Samson's exploits. The Bible was coming alive for Patterson, who recalled how the strongman was said to have carried the gates of Gaza on his shoulders to the top of a hill now just in sight. In biblical times the Jews had failed to capture Gaza from their enemies. In the present war, the British had twice failed to take it from the Turks, but had succeeded in a recent third attack. Still, the battle for Palestine was far from over.

By midday the troop train steamed through a grove of olive trees and reached Lod, the ancient town of Lydda. From there, Patterson marched his men with full packs under a scorching summer sun to Surafend—an agonizing feat of endurance. They all made it and were revived by the incredibly joyful reception they received from hundreds of Jews. They had come not only from Surafend but from as far as Jaffa, traveling on foot, horseback, and even by chariot to greet the legion. Patterson was amazed by the horsemanship of the young men and women—the equal of American cowboys he had seen at rodeos. Even children of eight or nine managed horses with ease. Eliyahu Golomb, a founder of the original Palestine Jewish self-defense force, said, "The anticipation of Jabotinsky's arrival was almost hysterical. We had been waiting for the man whose name was connected with our greatest dream—the Jewish Army."[3] Thousands of men and many women volunteered for the fight, but only several hundred men were accepted.

The legion stayed three days at Surafend, refreshed by a gift of casks of Richon wine and encouraged by a visit from General Allenby, who inspected the battalion and judged them first-rate and ready for battle. Patterson, however, had to return to Egypt to preside over the trial of three Royal Air Force pilots charged with performing unauthorized stunts. The results are unknown, but chances are that Patterson let them off with a warning. He rejoined his men, who had moved on to Suffah, in the Samaria hills, a few miles from the Turkish lines.

The legion's baptism of fire came on Saturday, June 15, 1918, when the men were at Shabbat prayers and the Turks shelled their camp. Though no one was hurt, Patterson was quick to respond. From then on he sent out patrols every night, down a hill and up the other side, often reaching the Turkish barbed-wire defenses two miles away. In daylight he had two men with telescopes report to him by phone any movement of Turkish troops. He also had an intelligence officer, Lieutenant Simon Abrahams, to pair up with a scout, Private Angel. Together, they made a daring exploration of no-man's-land, and gave Patterson detailed maps of the territory that they had sketched out right under the noses of the Turks. Recalling that time in *With the Judeans in the Palestine Campaign,* Patterson wrote, "After a night's vigil, after a hasty breakfast, the men had to fix up barbed wire entanglements, build stone redoubts and gun emplacements, make roadways down the hills and bury dead animals which had died or been killed in others' camps."[4]

British intelligence officer Richard Meinertzhagen records in his *Middle East Diary* the occasion when a peppery little brigadier of the Indian army, named Edwards, while inspecting the legion called one with unpolished buttons "a dirty Jew!"[5] Patterson immediately ordered his men to fix bayonets and to form a square to surround the brigadier, and didn't let him out until he had apologized. Edwards reported Patterson to headquarters. Meinertzhagen was then ordered to investigate the incident and give Allenby the facts. As a result, Patterson was reprimanded and the brigadier was transferred for duty in India.

Patterson's version of another similar event describes an unidentified visiting general who rode into camp on July 16, 1918, when Patterson was elsewhere, and abused and insulted the men, threatening some, and striking one with his whip. When Patterson heard eyewitness accounts of the incident, he imagined that the general had gone insane. After interviewing those individuals involved, he sent their complaints to the general, together with the sick report of the man who had been whipped. The general asked for a chance to speak to the men, and Patterson agreed. To prevent a hostile demonstration, he confined the rest of the legion, who were not involved, to their tents and posted NCOs at every tent door to ensure they stayed put.

On his arrival, the general apologized, but the men insisted that he do so before the entire legion on parade. He agreed, and they accepted his apology. According to Patterson, "The General never again came near us and every indignity, slight, and petty tyranny that could be invented was put upon the Battalion. The whole subsequent attitude of GHQ [general headquarters] showed us that his apology was eyewash and had been extracted from him by fear of the consequence of his outrageous behavior. In the end I had to bring this conduct to the notice of the Commander-in-Chief [Allenby] and the General was removed from his command and no longer troubled Israel."[6]

Patterson was occasionally cheered by recalling how well the British military staff in Gallipoli had treated the Jewish Mule Corps. "Sir Ian Hamilton saw a tremendous force would be won over in the cause of England by dealing justly with Israel. I felt that the Adjutant-General [Macready] had confided a great trust to me when I was selected for the command of the Jewish Unit . . . a complete change from the command of an Irish Battalion, but the Irishman and the Jew have much in common— temperament, generosity, love of children, devotion to parents, readiness to help those down on their luck, and great personal bravery."[7]

In July 1918, shortly after the general's wild—and probably alcohol-fueled—performance, Chaim Weizmann invited Patterson and a few of his officers to Mount Scopus. General Allenby and leaders of the Jewish, Christian, and Muslim communities were also there to witness the laying of the foundation stones for the Hebrew University. At lunch afterward with Lord William Percy, Patterson was pleased to learn that Percy was passionately concerned with preserving Palestine's animal life. So was Patterson, who had strictly limited the shooting of wildlife in territory under his control.

Grim news awaited him on his return to his unit. A young soldier had been sentenced to be shot at dawn for sleeping at his post. Patterson sympathized with the condemned man, knowing that he had worked hard for forty-nine hours straight before he was found asleep. He telegrammed General Allenby, requesting a reprieve and citing the extenuating circumstances. But the anti-Semitic brigade commander, Bols, prevented Allenby from getting the telegram. Someone at the Signals Office warned Patterson, who dashed off a letter to Allenby some thirty miles away and handed it to a motorcycle dispatch rider saying, "Ride for all you're worth. A man's life depends on your speed."[8] Allenby not only reprieved the condemned man but gave him a suspended sentence, on condition he proved a credit to the legion. He was naturally overjoyed at his release, and lived up to Patterson's hopes.

The frustrated brigade commander, apparently disappointed that the young man was still alive, complained about Patterson to Sir John Shea, the divisional general. Shea called for Patterson and warned him that sending telegrams to Allenby would get him into trouble. Shea also said that he was so shocked by Patterson's behavior that he needed a cocktail to revive him—then laughed and invited Patterson to join him. Shea obviously admired Patterson's chutzpah, telling him that his children were Patterson fans who had once insisted that he read them a lion story from *The Man-Eaters of Tsavo.*

But Bols did not give up. He phoned Patterson to report that the Thirty-eighth and the Thirty-ninth Jewish Battalions were to be merged with two West Indian battalions. To stop this second attempt to destroy the Jewish Legion's identity, Patterson wrote to Allenby, stressing that the merger would renege on General Macready's promise and be regarded as a slight by Jewry worldwide. He asked for the order to be canceled or, if not, to be relieved of his command. Allenby replied, "I see the undesirability of brigading Jews with West Indian Battalions, and I have decided not to do so. I shall form a provisional Brigade of the two

18. British general Edmund Allenby, leader of the successful Palestine campaign against the Turks. Allenby broke his
promise to Patterson. Author's collection.

Jewish Battalions until a complete Jewish Brigade can be formed, and
they will be under you."[9]

In August 1918 headquarters retaliated by ordering Patterson's battalion to leave the cool hills of Samaria and march to the hot, dusty, and
malaria-ridden inferno of the Jordan Valley, about fifteen miles from the
Dead Sea. Here, in a ravine through which a saltwater stream flowed, Patterson made his headquarters, and his men built a reed hut as their mess
hall in the shade of the only tree in sight.

The Turks occupied the north swampy end of the ravine, where they
were plagued by mosquitoes. When the wind blew from that direction,

Patterson and his men became the mosquitoes' victims, too. Each night he led a group through their barbed-wire fence for about a half-mile toward the enemy lines on Operation Mosquito-Removal, digging in the sand to divert the stream that attracted the pests.

The legion was stationed on the right flank of the British army in Palestine, with the Turks almost on three sides of them. Patterson considered it "the post of honor and danger . . . the most exposed piece of front to guard which it is possible to conceive, and we were so badly supported with guns that had the Turks attacked the force, we would probably have been annihilated." He assumed that they had been sent to this hazardous hellhole because "the authorities must have had great faith in our fighting abilities."[10]

Armed with six thirteen-pound guns and a couple of howitzers, Patterson's men had to defend seven miles of land on the banks of the Mellahah river, as well as small hills in the ravine, against the Turks' seventy thousand men and more than seventy heavy guns. The enemy also had the advantage of possessing a strategically vital ford on the Jordan River.

On moonlit nights Patterson would stroll to an observation post on cliffs overlooking the Jordan, lie on the warm sand, and look for enemy movements while jackals and hyenas howled nearby. The only animal he actually saw was a reddish colored hare as it darted from a tangle of trees and shrubs on the riverbank to disappear among some reeds.

He welcomed the appointment of Major General Sir Edward Chaytor of the Anzac (New Zealand) Mounted Division, as overall commander of troops in the area. He found Chaytor "to be a man of wide sympathy and understanding, a demon for work and efficiency, but always ready to give honor where honor was due—even to Jews."[11]

To Patterson, the endurance of his men in that "desolate, nerve-wracking region" was astonishing and magnificent. "All day long the sun beat down mercilessly on them, their only shelter being a flimsy bit of canvas, and the nights were stifling. Even when at rest, perspiration streamed from every pore. Flies and mosquitoes deprived everyone of sleep, for our mosquito nets soon became torn and worthless and could not be replaced. Every drop of water had to be carried from the Auja river some five miles away. Every mouthful of food was full of sand and grit."[12] The Jordan Valley was considered uninhabitable during August and September, and even the Bedouins who fed their goats there fled the area during those dreadful months. Yet, Patterson wrote, although "no British soldier had been called upon to endure the horrors of the Mellahah even for a week, the Jewish Battalion was kept there for over seven weeks at the most deadly period of the year. Some of my men assured me that they saw the Devil himself there."[13]

Perhaps the only compensation was the legion's fair and considerate treatment by General Chaytor and his New Zealand troops. "That the Battalion found favor in the sight of these famous fighters is the proudest feather in its cap. Their minds were as broad as the wide spaces whence they had come and there was—without exception—no room for petty spite or discrimination."[14]

Patterson even enjoyed the frequent need to ride eight miles south in scorching heat for conferences with General Chaytor—who always welcomed him with a cool drink from the icebox. Chaytor agreed that in their isolated, vulnerable position the legion's best defense was to fool the Turks into thinking they faced a large enemy force by constantly going on the attack. This tactic, of course, was part of Allenby's not yet realized overall secret strategy still in the planning stage.

The legion's new tactics worked. The Turks went on the defense, frantically built more barbed-wire fences along their entire front, and shelled the legion's positions day and night. Fortunately, they were poor shots, and caused few casualties.

When Turks began to desert, at first singly, then in small groups, Patterson asked one why he was trembling so violently, and he said that his officer told him that the British cut all their prisoners' throats. Patterson laughed, and, after feeding him, proposed sending him back to show the Turks how well he had been treated. At that, Patterson recalled, "he cried bitterly that he did not want to return to his camp at any price, and begged to be kept by the British."[15] He was.

On August 26, 1918, thirteen Turks, an entire guard post, deserted. Patterson was about to order his own men to occupy it when a prisoner confided that their relief party would have already taken over the post.

Patterson was amused to think of the relief force's astonishment when they found the guard post empty.

Two nights later, a legion sergeant and six privates crept close to the Turkish trenches at the Umm-esh-Shert ford and spotted a Turkish sentry. Private Sapiashvili, a Caucasian Jew, walked casually toward him, pretending to be a Turk by speaking a few words in Turkish. Then he grabbed him by the throat and wrestled him to the ground. Despite a high wind, Turks in nearby trenches heard the scuffle and opened fire, hitting Private Marks. Meanwhile, Sapiashvili had disarmed his prisoner and taken him back to the legion camp. The rest of the patrol followed, including Private Gordon, who carried the wounded Marks under heavy Turkish fire. Private Marks had only recently joined the battalion and this clash was his first encounter with the Turks. He had previously fought in the British army in France and survived unharmed. But he died of his wounds that night, and was buried the next morning with his face toward Jerusalem, his grave within sight of buildings on the Mount of Olives.

At the end of August, Patterson and his men were invited to the Australian troops' headquarters four miles north of Jericho, where General Allenby was to inspect them. There, Allenby told Patterson, "By the way, I fear I cannot form your Jewish Brigade [a combination of several Jewish battalions which Patterson had expected to command with the rank of general]. For I have been notified by the War Office that there are no more Jewish troops coming out."[16] Patterson replied that he had recently heard from the officer commanding the Fortieth Jewish Battalion at Plymouth, in England, that his unit was about to leave for Palestine. Allenby was surprised to hear it but considered his information more recent and reliable than Patterson's. Two days later Chaytor told Patterson that his information was better than Allenby's. One of Chaytor's officers, just arrived from England, had reported that a strong Jewish battalion on the same ship with him had recently landed in Egypt.

The Fortieth Jewish Brigade led by Lieutenant Colonel Samuel arrived in Egypt in August 1918. It consisted largely of men ages eighteen to forty-five living in the United States, but not American citizens, and so not subject to the draft. However, they arrived too late to join the fight in Palestine.

On September 7, 1918, the first day of the Jewish New Year, at a parade after Shabbat, General Chaytor presented the military medals to Privates Sapiashvili and Gordon for their courage on patrol. Then, to the troops' delight, Chaytor ordered them to march past and salute not him but the two heroes.

The Thirty-ninth Battalion of the Jewish Legion commanded by the Australian Colonel Margolin, DSO, arrived in the Jordan Valley on September 15, 1918. At sundown, Erev Yom Yippur (on the eve of the Day of Atonement), Patterson's men and the Thirty-ninth, led by Margolin, marched together, singing "Over There" in Hebrew (as translated by legionnaire Morris Shiffman, who had been a Hebrew teacher in America). They then took up positions north of Jericho.

Soon after, General Allenby arrived at Patterson's headquarters to announce a big offensive for September 18, and asked if he was sure he could trust his men to fight. Patterson reassured him but advised Allenby that he was losing two hundred men to malaria every week and that the medical arrangements for their evacuation and treatment were inadequate. Allenby made a note of it.

Preparations for the major attack included an attempt to hoax the Turks into believing that Allenby had enormous forces at his disposal. As Patterson recalled,

> Parts of the Jordan Valley began to look very comical. Here and there would be a battery of artillery parked, or a cavalry regiment, with its horses tethered in neat and orderly array, in the most approved army style, but on closer inspection both horses and guns were found to be merely dummies. Great camps were pitched, but there was not a soldier in them; fires were lighted all over the place at dusk, as if a mighty army were bivouacked around, and every conceivable kind of bluff was put up to deceive the Turks.[17]

Allenby had hundreds of worn-out tents shipped from Egypt and pitched on the banks of the Jordan and five pontoon bridges flung across the river. He had captured Turkish cannons brought to the Jordan Valley to blast away at the Turkish troops in the Moab hills, and thousands of horse blankets thrown over bushes in the valley and tied up to look like horse lines.

Enemy-spotting planes flying over the Jordan River reported to Turkish headquarters that Allenby had two additional divisions at his command. And the British general made sure his lines were so carefully guarded that no German or Turkish spy got through to expose the hoax.

On the evening of September 23, Patterson was ordered to attack the next morning. He was also warned that horse-drawn wagons containing the legion's ammunition supply had disappeared. So he mounted his horse and eventually found wagon-wheel tracks, which he followed for almost ten miles. Then, to his astonishment, he saw the wagons moving north toward the enemy. Patterson caught up, and yelled at the sergeant in charge, a Welsh Christian, to turn the wagons around. Instead, the sergeant turned his own horse around and began to ride back to the legion's camp, "leaving his wagons still calmly proceeding in the opposite direction" (toward the enemy).[18] Patterson called him back, convincing him to halt the horse-drawn wagons and head them toward the legion's camp. His explanation for the sergeant's behavior was that the sun and endless sand had bewitched him. Fortunately, the wagons arrived in time for the predawn attack. Then, wading through water up to their chins, the legion crossed the Jordan and, after a ferocious battle, captured Umm-es-Shert. Patterson signaled this success to General Chaytor, who ordered mounted troops to cross the Jordan and to outflank the Turks.

While the legion defended the ford with their rifles and machine guns, the First Australian Horse Brigade kept moving for miles along a road lined with dead Turks and dead horses. Patterson found it curious that "the whole movement of the British Army in Palestine which swept the Turks out of the country was pivoted on the sons of Israel, who were once again fighting the enemy not far from the spot where their forefathers had crossed the Jordan under Joshua."[19]

Author Lowell Thomas confirmed in his *With Lawrence in Arabia:*

> The camouflage army of the Jordan was a complete success: There were only three battalions of able-bodied troops in that part of the Holy Land, two of which were made of newly arrived Jewish troops from the British Isles and the United States. If the Turks had known the truth they might have sent down one brigade, pushed up behind Allenby's lines, and recaptured Jerusalem! [Allenby's] sole object was to

hoodwink the Turks by luring them to the wrong place, the Jordan Valley, thus leaving a vulnerable stretch over near the Mediterranean. . . . He had transferred nearly all his infantry and cavalry there by night, and they remained concealed in the orange groves until the day of the real battle [on September 19], the battle that broke the backbone of the Ottoman Empire.[20]

On their way to Es Salt, the Jewish Legion had taken fifteen hundred prisoners and a lot of weapons but suffered only twenty casualties, although an additional twenty died of malaria, partly because British headquarters had moved all spare hospital beds and medical personnel from Jerusalem to Cairo (probably because the Turks had counterattacked and threatened to retake Jerusalem). After Patterson complained to London, Palestinian Jewish nurses in Palestine were allowed to serve the legion, but it was too late to save many of the men with malaria.

Jabotinsky, who had commanded a machine-gun unit in the fighting, praised the courage of his company in a letter to his wife, and described his own main exploit as requisitioning an "educated and impudent" Bedouin's ass, whose owner he caught looting ammunition. The man had demanded a receipt, and Jabotinsky's sergeant had suggested instead to punch him in the jaw. He thought it over and decided to grant the Arab's request. He then loaded the ass with the packs of some of the most exhausted men. Because there were more than fifty Cohens in the battalion and their initials included the entire alphabet except X, they decided to name the ass "Cohen X." In writing of this lighthearted incident in his book, Jabotinsky asked the pardon of all Jews named Cohen.[21]

It was almost impossible to breathe on the march toward Es Salt because the Turks burned the dry grass as they retreated. One after another, legionnaires would drop out of line, gasping for air and unable to continue. "Now they'll laugh at us—Jewish heroes!" Jabotinsky thought, almost ashamed, until he saw two tall, slim, athletic non-Jewish English sergeants who had been sent to replace malaria-stricken Jewish sergeants, "sitting against a rock with their eyes closed, gasping like fish on dry land."[22]

The legion had almost reached Es Salt when they were ordered back to the Jordan Valley. "This happens often with the English," Jabotinsky wrote. "First climb up, then down, with no reason for either. In such cases they usually quote Tennyson's famous line: 'Someone has blundered,' causing six hundred of a crack Guards' Regiment to die in the battle of Sevastopol."[23] Irishman Patterson assured Jabotinsky that this line was the most typically English line in the whole of English poetry—and also explained their present inexplicable order.

Back in the valley, the order made sense. They had to take charge of a half-starved, half-dead mob of nine hundred Turkish prisoners and two hundred Germans and Austrians. The thirsty Germans and Austrians lined up as ordered and, one after another, drank quietly and obediently from a large can of water. But the Turks fought each other for the first drink. So, before riding off on another task, Patterson ordered two sergeants and twelve men to make the Turks behave like the disciplined Germans. It proved difficult. In fighting for the first drink they had spilled a lot of the water, and after fifteen minutes fewer than twenty Turks had taken a few gulps. Returning on horseback, Patterson decided that there was only one solution: to make the Turks, like Gideon's heroes, drink from the stream. It meant an extra mile's walk for the exhausted men, but it solved the problem.

Another unit took over the prisoners, and Patterson's battalion joined the main British force heading for Es Salt in the hills of Moab, far beyond the Jordan River—believed to be the ancient Ramoth. Mounted New Zealanders attacked the strong defenses at Es Salt with such spirit that they destroyed the enemy resistance before the rearguard forces could go into action. As they fled from the scene, in their frantic effort to escape, the Turks left behind overturned cannons, wagons, and ammunition carts. An enormous gun the British named "Jericho Jane" because it used to fire into Jericho was in a ditch with dead men, horses, and bullocks lying nearby. Bedouins were already swarming around the carnage, stripping the corpses and looting guns, ammunition, and stores of all kinds. Patterson was disgusted, but because the Bedouins were allies was reluctant to get involved. He did, however, report them to General Chaytor, who wired back, "Stop the looting by these marauders."[24] Patterson and his men then did the best they could, to the extreme annoyance of the looters.

Chaytor also ordered Patterson to make Es Salt his new headquarters and to prepare for an enemy counterattack. So he pitched his tent near the swift-flowing Nimrin River to make plans, in the shade of a huge fig-laden tree, pleased to hear that the legion's victories left the road ahead clear for other British troops to attack and capture Amman on September 25, 1918. Es Salt was filthy and full of hundreds of sick and wounded soldiers the Turks had abandoned. Captain Salaman began to take care of some of them, and worked wonders.

When Colonel Margolin and his Thirty-ninth Battalion took over the defense of Es Salt, Patterson and his men headed for Amman, where they found Chaytor. Patterson congratulated him, because although outnumbered, he had routed the Fourth Turkish Army in four days of fighting.

On October 1, 1918, the day the British captured Damascus, Patterson was ordered to take his battalion to Jerusalem. En route he was moved by the sight of sick and starving Turkish prisoners "crawling at a snail's pace up the steep ascent from the Jordan Valley through the Judean wilderness. Many fell and died from sheer exhaustion."[25] Patterson's own men were hardly better off. Hundreds suffered from malaria, and arrived at their new camp in a downpour. It was about a mile from the southern walls of Jerusalem on the Hebron road, and the ground was completely soaked. Patterson himself was sick, but the new medical officer, Captain Haldin Davis, kept him going.

As there was no room for them in any hospital, the sick men lay on the ground with only a blanket apiece to protect them from the wet earth. They had no medical treatment except for what little Dr. Davis and their fellow legionnaires could do for them. Many died from malaria and pneumonia, and one man in a delirium fatally cut his throat. By this time the battalion of more than 1,000 was down to 6 officers and fewer than 150 men.

Some of the sick men were admitted to Jerusalem hospitals later in the month, but soon after Colonel Margolin and Captain Salaman rode into Patterson's camp to complain that the men were neglected and subjected to discrimination. To protest against this anti-Jewish policy, Patterson sent in his resignation. It wasn't accepted, and he guessed why: "Certain individuals at GHQ had no desire to see me land unmuzzled in England. I

19. American members of the Jewish Legion in Jerusalem, 1918. Courtesy of Dr. Oscar Kraines.

would at once let the authorities there know that their representatives in Palestine were not carrying out the declared policy of the Imperial Government, but, on the contrary, were doing their best to make of the Balfour Declaration a mere 'scrap of paper.'"[26] Patterson warned the "certain individuals" that if the anti-Jewish policy was not changed, he would contact the secretary of war and have the matter brought up in Parliament. British military headquarters quickly responded, inviting him to send a list of complaints and his recommendations to improve the lives of the Jewish battalions. He made five specific suggestions—none was adopted.

One evening, under the weather and depressed, Patterson sat in his candlelit tent and forced himself to compose a letter of condolences to the widow of Private Cross, missing for several days and believed killed. He advised her to steel herself to face the fact that she would never see her husband again. Then he gave it to an orderly to send on its way with other mail, and began to read a book. It was almost midnight when a ghostly white face appeared in his tent doorway. It couldn't be Private Cross: he was dead. But it looked exactly like him. Then, Patterson recalled, "A sepulchral voice said, 'Are you awake, sir?' And I began to wonder if it were a dream. When the figure approached the light I saw it was Cross. So I bounded up to give him such a welcome as one would give to a friend who had risen from the dead."[27] After his patrol, Cross bad been wounded in an ambush, and the Turks had taken him as a prisoner to Amman and then by train to Damascus. He was about to be sent farther north when the British captured the city. During the fighting he had managed to escape and eventually made his way to Patterson's tent. Patterson explained that he had mailed Cross's wife a "missing, believed killed letter" that evening and it was too late to retrieve it. The War Office would inevitably inform her. Cross saved the situation by cabling his wife.

Patterson was in his camp at Lod on October 31, 1918, when the Turks surrendered, which the British and their allies in Palestine celebrated by firing guns and rockets. Planes looped and rolled joyously over Patterson's troops, who were guarding thousands of Turkish prisoners and a captured ammunition depot. Less than two weeks later, on November 11, Germany surrendered.

At war's end there were 6,000 Jewish Legionnaires in British-occupied Palestine. The additional 2,000 in England waiting to be sent to Palestine, about half of them Americans or Canadians, were quickly demobilized. Those legionnaires already in Palestine were reorganized as the Judean Regiment, with the menorah as its emblem and the Hebrew word "Kadimah" (Forward) as its motto.

Shortly after, the Council of Jews in Jerusalem sent Patterson an illuminated parchment scroll thanking him for upholding the ideals expressed in the Balfour Declaration, and for having successfully led the Jewish battalion. General Chaytor told Patterson that the men of the Jewish Legion had played an important part in winning the battle for Damascus and were among the bravest he had ever commanded.

On December 11, 1918, three weeks before he died, Theodore Roosevelt wrote to Patterson, congratulating him for his leading role "in what was not only one of the most important but one of the most dramatic incidents in the whole war."

> To have the sons of Israel smite Ammon on the hip and thigh under your leadership is something worthwhile. As for my loss, [in the war] the death of my son Quentin was very bitter, but it would have been far more bitter if he had been a hand's breadth behind his friends in entering the war. Two of my other sons have been wounded, one of them crippled. The other wounded one has recovered and as Lieutenant Colonel is now commanding his regiment on the march toward the Rhine. Kermit is Captain of Artillery, having first served in Mesopotamia [now Iraq], and then under Pershing in the Argonne fight.

When General Chaytor learned that Patterson was working on an account of the Jewish campaign in Palestine, he wrote to him:

> I hope the history of the 38th Battalion is out by now. So few have heard of the Battalion's good work or of the very remarkable fact that in the operations that we hope have finally opened Palestine to the Jews, a Jewish force was fighting on the Jordan within a short distance of where their forefathers under Joshua first crossed into Palestine, and all who hear about it are anxious to hear more. I shall always be grateful to you and your Battalion for your good work while with me in the Jordan valley. The way you smashed up the Turkish rearguard when it tried to counterattack across the Jordan made our subsequent advance up the hills of Moab an easy matter.[28]

Before the end of the year, the British government sent Chaim Weizmann, head of the Zionist Commission, to Palestine to advise on the future development of the country in order to fulfill the Balfour Declaration. U.S. president Woodrow Wilson sent a group of Americans to the Versailles Peace Conference in February 1919 and adopted their unanimous recommendations to, first, establish a separate state of Palestine under a British mandate and to help and encourage Jews to live there and, second, to support the League of Nations policy in recognizing Palestine as a Jewish state as soon as it was a Jewish state in fact.

According to author William B. Ziff, the Jews had not anticipated the attitude of the British authorities in Palestine, "who were used to the languors of Timbucto [sic] and Belize, and suddenly found their snobbish hauteur deflated by even common Jewish working men who did not know the word 'native' as applied to themselves. . . . Colonel Josiah Wedgwood, a pro-Zionist Labor member of the British Parliament, characterized this type of Crown servant as 'the ordinary, narrow-minded, half-bred Englishman who feels about Jews just as his counterpart Herr Hitler does.'" Even the amiable and well-bred Sir Ronald Storrs, who became governor of Jerusalem, lost his sense of humor, complaining that the Jews "almost forget the difference between themselves and their employers. My first chauffeur was a Jew. He was an excellent driver, but it never occurred to him to brush me down after I got out of the car. I stood it for three months and then I engaged an Arab chauffeur in his stead."[29]

In the last year of the war, Jabotinsky had written to his wife that General Allenby had definitely decided to create a Jewish brigade and any day Patterson would be its general. But it was not to be. Colonel Patterson, in fact, was never promoted, despite his exceptional service in the war. True, he had frequently questioned or complained of the decisions of those individuals in power. But what more likely sabotaged his military career was being too outspokenly and enthusiastically pro-Zionist.

10

Patterson's Command of the Sinai, 1919–1920

SHORTLY AFTER THE WAR'S END, Patterson learned that General Bols was to be military governor of Palestine. Having known Bols for two years as General Allenby's chief of staff, he despised him as the most rabid anti-Semite he had ever met. So he caught the next train to Cairo, where Zionist leader Chaim Weizmann was staying, and asked if it was certain that Bols would be the military governor. When Weizmann confirmed the report, Patterson said that it would be a catastrophe, that Bols "will get every anti-Semite in the Colonial Service, from as far away as the Sudan and India, and will fill the administration with them." He warned Weizmann, "If you give him this much of a start, you will never see your National Home." Weizmann responded, wrote Patterson, "with a smile of superior knowledge and said, 'I fear you exaggerate, Colonel. I found General Bols a most charming gentleman. I have just had a two hours' conversation with him.'"[1]

Patterson was right; Weizmann had been bamboozled. As governor of Palestine for thirteen months, Bols packed his administration with anti-Semites who remained in office for years, permeating the Palestinian government with a spirit of antagonism to Zionism. Typical was General Arthur Money, head of the military administration, who complained of British prime minister Lloyd George's "hook-nosed friends," had government forms printed in English and Arabic and not in Hebrew, and refused to stand for "Hatikvah," the Jewish national anthem.[2]

Even in Poland or Russia, Jabotinsky had never encountered such a widespread atmosphere of hatred of the Jews as prevailed in the British army in Palestine. Fearing that this attitude would encourage Arab violence, he told U.S. Supreme Court Justice Louis Brandeis, an American Jew visiting Palestine, of his plan to create a Jewish defense force. Brandeis ridiculed the idea, saying that "anyone who envisages a pogrom in Palestine is dreaming wildly."

"Your honor may be an excellent judge," Jabotinsky replied, "but you cannot see what is going on under your nose—a sign that you lack even minimal political sense."[3]

Trying to remedy the situation, Jabotinsky wrote to General Allenby. After describing his war service, he continued:

> The common opinion is that you are an enemy of Zionism in general and of the Jewish Legion in particular. I will try to believe that this is not true, that things happen without your knowledge, that there is a misunderstanding, and that the situation can improve. In this hope, as the last attempt to stop a process which threatens to impair for ever Anglo-Jewish friendship throughout the world, I beg you to grant me a personal interview and permission to speak freely. This letter is entrusted to your chivalry.[4]

At the time Patterson knew nothing of the letter, but later understood it as a cri de coeur, because, all through his military service with the battalion, Jabotinsky did his utmost to allay the resentment felt by Jewish soldiers at the terrible treatment they received from the British military authorities on the spot, apparently adopted to make practical application of the Balfour Declaration impossible. Hostility to all things Jewish was so blatant that only those individuals who ignored the situation could fail to see the game. Jabotinsky saw that this policy would inevitably lead to outbreaks against the Jews, and naturally wanted to ward off such a calamity.

Patterson also realized how a letter from a lieutenant to the commander in chief would be treated. Red tape would "hold up its hands in holy horror at the audacity of it."

> But Jabotinsky's position was an exceptional one. Although pro-British to the core, he was not a British subject, and not used to the routine of British red tape. Members of the British Imperial War Cabinet had previously

thought it a good policy to hear his views [when he was a mere private]. They knew he had a very high place in the Zionist movement and was looked up to by Jews the world over as one of its most brilliant leaders. The fact was also known to the Egyptian Expeditionary Force, but when he sought an interview with the Commander in Chief . . . he was not only refused a hearing, but methods were immediately employed to strike him down, which I can only describe as despicable and un-English.[5]

As members of a peacetime army, the Jewish Legion moved to an isolated station at Rafah, where it was joined by Australian, New Zealand, Indian, and South African troops. Patterson was given command of the entire Sinai Desert to the south, Palestine to the north almost up to Bir Salem, and east beyond Beersheba to the Arabian Desert. His two big problems were the marauding Bedouins, who frequently smashed the 150-mile freshwater pipe from Egypt that ran alongside the railroad tracks to refresh themselves and their camels and tried to loot the military stores and an enormous ammunition depot in Rafah. It became an even greater problem when other troops were withdrawn to handle riots in Egypt and the Jewish Legionnaires were left on their own to protect the area. Still, they succeeded remarkably, and in good spirit until they received an order from GHQ that Jerusalem would be placed out of bounds to all Jewish members of the Jewish Legion from the fourteenth to the twenty-second of April. "Think of it!" Patterson wrote.

> Jewish soldiers for the first time in their lives in Palestine and barred from the Temple Wall of Jerusalem during Passover! Only a Jew can really understand what it meant to these men, and the strain it put on their discipline and loyalty. How provocative and insulting this order was will be better understood when it is realized that the majority of the population of Jerusalem is Jewish, and therefore there could have been no possible reason for excluding Jewish troops belonging to a British unit, while other British troops were freely admitted, more especially as the conduct of the Jewish soldiers was at all times exemplary. Not since the days of the Emperor Hadrian had such a humiliating decree been issued.[6]

Jerusalem being verboten, Patterson's response was to seek funds for a Passover celebration on the edge of the Sinai Desert. A Miss Berger, an American Zionist, and friends in England helped, especially Harry Friedenwald, acting chairman of the Zionist Commission in Britain. At his request Patterson read Friedenwald's letter to the troops at the seder service:

> The Commission is glad to be the means of aiding [the men] in celebrating Pesach, the Feast of Deliverance, and we trust that it will bring them all great joy. We have hopes now that our age-long prayers will soon be realized and it should be a source of pride and happiness to them to know that they have contributed by their courage and their sacrifice toward its fulfillment. The Commission speaks in the name of the Zionist Organization in expressing to them the thanks of the nation for the devoted services they have rendered, and are rendering, in the service of the liberty-loving nation, Great Britain, to which they have sworn fidelity, and to our people of Israel for whose future glory they have been willing to sacrifice their lives. The splendid part they have played and will continue to play, will ever be remembered as a bright spot in the long history of our ancient people.

With the contributions Patterson was able to provide unleavened bread and kosher meat and wine to some two thousand men. "It was a wonderful sight," he recalled, "when we all sat down together and sang the Hatikvah on the edge of the Sinai desert."[7]

Waiting to be demobilized, the men played cricket and soccer. When GHQ organized a boxing contest, the "Palestine Championship," to involve all the Allied troops in Palestine, Patterson equipped his best fighters with boxing gloves and punching bags and sent them with a trainer, Sergeant Goldberg, to El Arish, some thirty miles away on the Mediterranean shore. There, Patterson writes, "they raced, chase, boxed, bathed, danced and were generally licked into condition." Thousands watched the fights at Kantara, where the Jewish boxers beat all comers, walking away with five gold medals. Private Burack was heavyweight champion; Private Tankinoff welterweight, Private Cohen lightweight, Private Franks featherweight, and Private Goldfarb bantamweight. "Could anything be more fitting?" Patterson recalled. "Jewish soldiers as champions of Palestine."[8]

The wins made the team eligible for the great Cairo tournament, the championship for the whole of the Egyptian Expeditionary Force, which

20. Patterson when in command of the Sinai. Courtesy of Dr. Oscar Kraines.

meant competing against the best fighters among the British troops from Egypt and Syria, as well as Australian teams. For the first round held in Cairo on March 13, again watched by thousands, the Jewish fighters won almost every fight. In the championship's final round on March 15 (the Ides of March), they faced an Australian team. These bouts were great fights in which the Jews fought the Australians to a tie. But the judge, a British general who was also an Australian, disqualified the Jewish team on a technicality. As Patterson remarked, "I suppose it would not have been 'the right thing' for one Jewish Battalion to have defeated the whole of the Egyptian Expeditionary Force!"[9]

The Jews were unexpectedly outstanding in other competitions, too. Their cricket team, trained by Captain Pape, beat all comers except the Flying Corps. The soccer team were runners-up for the Palestine championship. However, no team beat the American and Palestinian Jews from the Fortieth Battalion at baseball.

The legion's concert party also excelled, and whenever Patterson announced that a violinist named Tchaikov would appear, a huge crowd assembled to hear him play. Sir Ronald Storrs was so impressed that he persuaded Patterson to let Tchaikov move to Jerusalem to be the director of its school of music.

In March 1919, Arabs attacked Jewish settlements, but the British did not protest or attempt to protect them. Many Legionnaires stole or "borrowed" weapons and rushed to drive off the Arabs. The British reaction was to start demobilizing legionnaires.

A month later Patterson was ordered to demobilize Jabotinsky immediately. When Patterson protested that he needed Jabotinsky's services, he was overruled. Leo Amery, now in the British Colonial Office, responded to a letter from Jabotinsky:

> I am very sorry indeed to hear from you that the military authorities in Palestine demobilized you in so summary and ungracious a fashion. I don't suppose that anything could be done now to re-mobilize you. But I think the least the War Office could do would be to show their recognition in some way or other of your services in the creation of the Jewish units, and I have written to urge this upon them. Meanwhile I know in the keenness of your cause you will be concentrating all your efforts on the future.[10]

Jabotinsky was offered the MBE (member of the British Empire), but he told Patterson he did not want to accept it. When Amery heard about it, he wrote to Jabotinsky:

> I can quite understand that you feel sore at the unsympathetic treatment which, I gather, you received from some of the military authorities you had to deal with. But after all I should like you to regard that as a transitory and incidental vexation, and not to let it obscure in your eyes the fact that the permanent view of your services held by the British government is that which is embodied in the decoration officially recommended by the War Office and approved by his Majesty the King. The

fact that I personally had some small part in ensuring, through General Macdonough, who was most sympathetic, makes me all the more anxious that you should not let your present feeling of annoyance persuade you to reject a distinction which it will always be a satisfaction to you in later life to have won.

Jabotinsky asked Patterson for his advice and sent him Amery's letter. Patterson wrote on the letter, which he returned, "My dear Jabotinsky, you see what Amery says. Do what you think best."[11] He accepted the decoration.

That summer of 1919 Patterson was given a brief leave, which he spent on a sightseeing trip to Lebanon and Syria. En route to Damascus at Baalbee railroad station, he spotted a beautiful young Syrian woman selling peaches. While waiting for his train, a dust storm developed, and when it was over he saw her lick the dust off every peach and then sell them to the incoming passengers. Patterson was off peaches for the rest of his trip, especially, as he noted, since none of the sellers was as attractive as the Syrian maiden.

Again in late October 1919, he visited places he had read about in the Old Testament—first the Sea of Galilee, glinting in brilliant sunshine, where he saw the spot where the Gabarene swine were said to have made their suicidal dash into the water, then to Tiberias, where the great Jewish religious philosopher, jurist, and physician Moses Maimonides is buried. He stayed at a small hotel where its German owner, Frau Grossmann, greeted him with a welcome cold beer, and, where, wandering outside, he met a Franciscan monk, Father Vendelene, a German "full of Christian charity and apparently resigned to the blow which had fallen upon his nation."[12] He had been the squadron leader of Prussian cavalry during the Franco-German War, before becoming an architect designing monasteries for Franciscans throughout the world. Then he became a monk himself. He showed Patterson a ruined synagogue near the hotel, reputed to have been built by the Roman centurion whom Jesus had healed. Patterson also met two vivacious nursing sisters on leave from Egypt in the hotel, and they joined him in a boat trip across the lake, during which one nurse, Sister Cook, who had a charming voice, burst into song. Briefly stuck on a sandbank, they watched young men atop wooden platforms use slingshots to scatter birds eating the maize in nearby fields.

The area's military governor had arranged for a mounted escort to show Patterson around. They were waiting for him when he landed: an Arab policeman under the command of a Jewish corporal who had served in the Fortieth Battalion of the Jewish Legion. Patterson noticed with pleasure that the two seemed on good terms. The nurses stayed on the boat, intending to continue on to Capernaum, where Patterson hoped to join them later. The three men were lost for a while in a dense, marshy oleander jungle when they spotted a herd of sleeping buffalo. They emerged bleeding, their clothes torn, at the entrance to a dark, rocky gorge below which Patterson saw the rushing water of the Jordan River.

Back at the lake, they met a Bedouin hunter who warned them that the thickets were alive with wild boars, and spoke of recently shooting a leopard on a nearby hillside. When Patterson asked what chance he would have of bagging a leopard, the hunter said that he would probably have to wait a month before he saw one.

On rejoining the nurses at Capernaum, Patterson was amused to see them flirting with Father Vendelene. The four of them traveled together to Migdal, where Mary Magdalene was born and where the Jewish manager of a fruit farm gave them tea under the shade of an enormous fig tree and gifts of oranges, pomegranates, bananas, and nuts.

Before he left Galilee, Patterson looked up Captain Trumpeldor, his second in command in Gallipoli, who had just returned to Palestine from Russia, and they had a long chat about old times. (Trumpeldor was killed by Arabs in Palestine on March 1, 1920, leading fellow Jews in defense of their village.)

Patterson paid for his pro-Jewish and pro-Zionist attitude and behavior, according to Jabotinsky, by being the only man in the British army who began the war as a lieutenant colonel and ended it without promotion or decorations. But he never expressed regrets for his decision. In fact, he was so impressed by the integrity and dedication of Zionists such as Jabotinsky and Weizmann, and by the courage of the Jewish Legionnaires, that he would devote the rest of his life to the cause of a Jewish homeland in Palestine.

11

Defending the Jewish Homeland,
1919–1930

AFTER THE ARMISTICE and an idyllic summer spent in Tel Aviv, Jabotinsky was reunited with his wife and son, Eri. They moved to Jerusalem to live in the second-floor apartment of an old three-story house on
what is now Shimon ben Shatah Street, near the General Post Office. The
same Sir Ronald Storrs who had fired his Jewish chauffeur for neglect-
ing to behave like a servant was a frequent visitor. Storrs, like Patterson,
regarded Jabotinsky as an exceptionally gallant officer and an extremely
cultivated gentleman. And Eri recalled that, as governor of Jerusalem,
Storrs had once visited him when he was ill and said, "When you are
well again, come to see me at Government House and I will show you
your country."[1]

Patterson, too, would become a frequent visitor when he needed his
friend's input for the military history and memoir he was working on,
With the Judeans in the Palestine Campaign. Patterson believed that Jabotinsky's years in Jerusalem were the happiest of his life, and regarded
his home as "the center of Palestine life at its best and brightest," where
the devoted husband and father enjoyed leading his family and friends
in singing Hebrew and Russian folk songs.[2] There Patterson met other
visitors, including legion colonels Margolin and Samuel; Dr. M. D. Eder, a
Zionist and a psychiatrist; doctors and nurses from the American Hadassah unit; Siegfried van Vriesland, treasurer of the Zionist Commission,
who lived on the top floor; and Moshe Sherok, a future Israeli prime minister, who lived in the ground-floor apartment.

Jabotinsky's home soon became a popular meeting place for other notable Zionists. Among them were Eliyahu Golomb, a future cofounder with Jabotinsky of the Haganah, the Jewish defense corps; Pinchas Rutenberg, about to win Winston Churchill's approval to harness the power of the Jordan and Yamuk rivers to electrify the entire country, with the exception of Jerusalem, which would be handled by a Greek contractor; and Ittamar Ben-Avi, son of Eliezer Ben-Yehuda, the legendary father of modern Hebrew.

Most of the British government in London still wholeheartedly supported the Balfour Declaration, especially the prime minister, Lloyd George; Winston Churchill, the secretary of war; and, of course, Balfour himself, the foreign secretary. So did the British press, especially the *Times* and the *Manchester Guardian*.

But it was a very different matter on the ground in Palestine. As Patterson had predicted, because they wanted to sabotage British policy and force their government to abandon the Zionists and renege on the Balfour Declaration, General Bols and his chief of staff, Colonel Waters-Taylor, together with General Palin, Colonel Vivian Gabriel, and Major Fitzroy Richard Somerset (later Lord Raglan), acting as agent provocateurs, made common cause with Arab protesters. Their methods and motives had the support of many petty British officials.

On the other, pro-Zionist, side, also in Palestine, energetically supporting the Balfour Declaration, were Colonel Patterson and Colonel Richard Meinertzhagen, the head of intelligence, officially known as the chief political officer. They were outnumbered, but not outwitted.

Historian Howard Sachar agrees with Patterson in characterizing most of the British administrators of Palestine, other than those men at the top, as "a somewhat unimaginative collection of lower-rung professional functionaries who had been assembled hurriedly from the British Army and the Egyptian civil service. Because their connections essentially were with Arabs, most of these officials were convinced that Moslem friendship alone should be the central preoccupation of the government's policy. The Jews sensed—indeed exaggerated—this combination of mediocrity and philo-Arabism."[3]

Continued Arab attacks on Jews in Palestine spurred Jabotinsky to invite Jewish youth groups to join the defense force known as the

Haganah. Units went hiking on Saturdays and holidays, often led by Jabotinsky. Sometimes they assembled as early as five in the morning, in the deserted playground of the Laemel School, to drill and to practice throwing hand grenades. According to Patterson, all this activity took place openly under the eyes of the British. Furthermore, he said, Jabotinsky's first act was to inform the authorities, including Sir Ronald Storrs, of the existence of the corps, its arming, and its purpose.

Elias Ginsburg, a former legionnaire in charge of training recruits, agreed that its existence was well known to the British authorities, and added that a few days before the Muslim festival of the prophet Moses, "regular military manoeuvres were staged by the Self-Defense Corps at the foot and on the slope of the Mount of Olives, the seat of Government, and British officers 'reviewed' our movements through field glasses."[4] What members of the Haganah did not do openly—none of the demobilized legionnaires having been allowed to keep their rifles and ammunition—was to buy arms from secret suppliers and hide them in their homes for use in an emergency.

In January 1920, after many extraordinary adventures and thirty-five years in the British army, fifty-three-year-old Colonel Patterson officially retired. Colonel Margolin took over command of the Jewish Legion, now reduced to four hundred men.

Patterson returned to England to rejoin his wife, Frances, and their eleven-year-old son Bryan, at Iver, Buckinghamshire, a bucolic spot west of London. Unofficially, he was as active as ever, helping the Zionist cause, and often returned to Jerusalem to discuss the country's future with Jabotinsky and various British officials.

In March 1920, Arab King Feisal, who had fought with Colonel T. E. Lawrence [of Arabia] against the Turks, proclaimed himself ruler of all of Syria, including Palestine. British Arabists supported his claim. Colonel Richard Meinertzhagen, who had planted agents to monitor the anti-Zionist activities of his own government, reported:

> Waters-Taylor approached these Arabs in early 1920 with the idea of organizing "anti-Jew riots" to impress on the Administration the unpopularity of the Zionist party. Both Storrs and Feisal were informed of this effort.
>
> Waters-Taylor saw Haj al Amin [the mufti of Jerusalem] on the Wednesday before Easter, 1920, and told him that he had a great opportunity at

Easter to show the world that the Arabs of Palestine would not tolerate Jewish domination in Palestine; that Zionism was unpopular with the Palestine Administration ... and if disturbances of sufficient violence occurred in Jerusalem at Easter, both General Bols and General Allenby would advocate the abandonment of the Jewish Home.[5]

The advice was taken. On April 4, 1920, Arab mobs attacked Jews in Jerusalem, looting, raping, and murdering. One British army officer and a group of unarmed British sailors on shore leave tried to hold back the mob, but were overwhelmed and had to retreat. A Haganah squad that had rushed to the Jaffa Gate to protect the Jews was kept at bay by Indian soldiers with mounted machine guns.

Patterson wondered why Storrs was not fired for his mishandling of the riot. Storrs had ordered the gates of the Old City to be closed for three days, well knowing, as Patterson wrote, that "inside fanatical mobs were murdering and raping a helpless and unarmed Jewish community. No assistance, neither military nor police, was allowed to enter the City to quell the murderers' outburst." Patterson's explanation for Storrs' survival was that, despite his mishandling of the riot, being the most astute and polished civil servant in Palestine, he "contrived to beguile the majority of the Jewish leaders."[6] In Britain, Winston Churchill regretted to report to the House of Commons that about 250 casualties occurred, of which nine-tenths were Jewish.

After the riot had been quelled, British military police searched Jabotinsky's home and arrested him. A military court gave him fifteen years at hard labor for possession of hidden weapons. The same sentence was imposed on two Arabs for raping two Jewish women. Other Arab agitators were held in Government House—not a prison—and released without trial. Jabotinsky's sentence, in addition, was to be followed by expulsion from Palestine.

The British arrested Haj Amin el Husseini, but he escaped to Damascus via Transjordan. He was sentenced to ten years in prison in absentia. But the following year he returned under an amnesty agreement. The new high commissioner, Herbert Samuel, accepted his promise to keep the peace, and made the monumental mistake of appointing him grand mufti of Jerusalem for life. (During World War II, he became an enthusiastic Hitler supporter.)

Heads shaved and wearing worn-out prison clothing, Jabotinsky and his comrades were locked in a large cell, where they slept on thin mattresses on the stone floor. After refusing prison food, they existed for a week on bread dipped in something that tasted like chopped grass. They made the most of the situation, though, by exchanging stories and giving lectures as if they were members of a club.

A week after their imprisonment, the police chief entered their cell and, to Jabotinsky's surprise, saluted him. Storrs followed him in and, without explanation, and with the police chief tagging on behind, led Jabotinsky to another cell twice the size of the first. This cell had a mattress on an iron bed, a table, and an oil lamp. After giving the place a critical glance, Storrs ordered it to be furnished with two chairs, a washbasin and stand, and a better dining table. Then he said that he was going to Jabotinsky's home, but would soon return.

He did, that evening, together with Yohana Jabotinsky, explaining that although it was against regulations, he felt that the place needed a woman's touch. Soon after, the police chief and several policemen joined the trio in the cell, carrying suitcases, a mirror, and the furniture Storrs had ordered. Someone completed what seemed like a house warming by bringing in a bottle of Rishon Le Zion wine. The still puzzled Jabotinsky asked about his imprisoned comrades, and Storrs promised that he would do his best for them, then said that he would return in an hour to drive Mrs. Jabotinsky home.

When the couple were alone together, Mrs. Jabotinsky laughed at Storrs' behavior, saying that the special treatment was because the British government had ordered him to treat her husband as a political prisoner, not as a criminal. "Still, he's a darling." She added, "He did almost all the packing and reminded me not to forget books and paper and to fill the fountain pen, and he himself proposed that I should come here."[7]

Early the next morning, Jabotinsky and his twenty comrades got back their civilian clothes and marched in formation to a railroad station, where, a large, cheering crowd awaited them. The Jabotinskys were allowed to travel together in a separate compartment—en route to Kantara. They also had lunch on the train with his guards—a British army officer, and Major Smoley, who had been second in command of the Thirty-ninth Battalion of the Jewish Legion.

The twenty-one prisoners spent only one night in Kantara, then were taken north to the fortress at Acre, the most secure prison in the country, surrounded by walls and encircled by a deep moat. Mrs. Jabotinsky did not accompany her husband there, but he was still given the VIP treatment, traveling in a first-class carriage. En route, at Lod, and at Haifa, large, cheering crowds greeted him and his fellow prisoners.

At a rally in London attended by thousands, Patterson protested Jabotinsky's imprisonment. Afterward, he told the Jewish Legion padre, Rabbi Falk, "It won't be long before we have old Jabo out and crowned with victory. I hope General Bols takes his place for, if anybody deserves penal servitude, it is that scoundrel."[8]

Outraged by Jabotinsky's treatment, Chaim Weizmann said that the British could just as well convict him (Weizmann) for organizing Jewish self-defense in Jerusalem. He conceded, though, that Jabotinsky was the more daring of the two: "Anyone meeting a lion on the street would run away, except Jabo, who would beckon it with his finger."[9]

In the British House of Commons, Lord Robert Cecil, the undersecretary of foreign affairs, protested Jabotinsky's long prison term. Calling the punishment vindictive, the *London Times* added, "Jabotinsky is well and honorably known in this country [and] has made journalistic attacks on the British administration of Palestine—a crime that may well seem to the objects of his criticism to merit a lengthy term of punishment."[10]

The protests worked. Allenby commuted Jabotinsky's sentence to one year at Fort Acre, with no hard labor, and he was not to be deported. The other Jews arrested with him had their imprisonment reduced to six months under similar conditions.

Interviewed by a *Jewish Chronicle* reporter, Patterson said, "After many years of soldiering in different parts of the world and of railway engineering in the wilds I'm going into mufti." Questioned about the Jewish Legion, he replied, "My boys, your boys, did well. They did better than you know. Their achievements are not sufficiently known."[11]

Now, the former bridge builder, lion hunter, author, and military commander was to begin his fifth career—as an active political advocate for the Zionist cause at home and abroad. The fighting Irishman launched the first missile in a battle of words with Lord Sydenham, chairman of the British Empire League. Patterson's article in the *London Evening Standard* on January 14, 1920, described Palestine as a sparsely populated, barren land in need of drainage and irrigation, with "room to spare, for many years to come for both Jew and Arab. . . . The hope of the Jewish people rests in the soil. . . . The barren hills must once again be terraced and planted with vine, fig and olive."[12]

Sydenham fired back in the *Spectator* that Jewish claims to the land were based on ancient conquest that lasted for only four centuries. And as the Arabs regarded Jerusalem as holy a city as Medina, they would doubtless vigorously claim it as theirs. Furthermore, he asserted that if Jerusalem came under Jewish control, it would arouse Muslim fanatics in Syria and India. Although he did not object to Jewish immigrants "of the right type," in his view the imminent creation of a Jewish state was out of the question.[13]

Patterson, in turn, disputed Sydenham's historical accuracy. Jewish occupation of the country, he wrote, had lasted for 730 years—from Joshua's conquest to the destruction of the Kingdom of Israel. (Although the Old Testament is not accepted as a historical document, many historians agree that the Jewish connection to the Land of Israel goes back at least 3,000 years.) Patterson also asked, naively in biographer Streeter's view, why the Muslims should fear a Jewish-controlled Jerusalem any more than a British one. And, finally, he called for Britain to honor the Balfour Declaration.

Historian Leonard Stein acts as referee, judging Patterson to be over-optimistic and Sydenham too pessimistic. Stein concludes that a Jewish homeland was possible only if its advocates used caution and restraint, treated non-Jewish farmers fairly, and respected the religious rights of Muslims and Christians.[14]

There were, of course, other proposals for the future of the former Ottoman Empire, including King Emil Faisal's claim, for example, to be the future king of Syria, Mesopotamia, and Palestine. This proposition was countered by Patterson in a speech to the Zionist Organization of the United Kingdom at the Aeolian Hall on New Bond Street. Then his "Hands off Palestine!" was greeted with cheers.[15] And when someone proposed a joint Arab-Jewish defense force in Palestine, Patterson responded in the *London Times* to say that recent deadly Arab attacks on Jews in Palestine had changed his view that the two peoples could work together.

That same year of 1920, many Zionists had high hopes when, as a result of the riot, the British government replaced Palestine's military with a civilian administration, and appointed as Palestine's high commissioner Sir Herbert Samuel, a Jew and former member of the British cabinet. Others feared that, to avoid appearing to favor his own race, he would support Arab interests. Patterson was among these pessimists. He had been disillusioned after meeting Samuel in Jerusalem soon after his appointment. They had discussed what the Irishman saw as "the great promise of the Jewish National Home." To Samuel, however, Patterson wrote, "the Zionist effort was not practical politics. . . . I went away feeling that I had spoken to a man with a blind eye. The man with the eye that was open looked upon the Prime Ministership of Great Britain. The blind eye was turned upon Palestine."[16]

Meanwhile, Mrs. Jabotinsky had moved into Haifa's Herzliya Hotel to be near her imprisoned husband. She was allowed to visit him twice a day in the Acre prison, where she also undertook motherly chores for the younger prisoners, mending their clothes and shopping for them in the nearby town. Jabotinsky gave the group talks on Herzl, Gorky, and Chekhov, and on current affairs, including Zionism, the troubles in Ireland, the mistreatment of blacks in America, and the weaknesses of his political rival, Chaim Weizmann. He also tutored a young man in English. They all exercised daily, played soccer, and entertained a flood of visitors. In the evenings, Jabotinsky worked on translating into Hebrew Dante's Inferno, Fitzgerald's Rubiyat of Omar Khayam, and several Conan Doyle stories. Still, it was a prison. And although the British soldiers guarding them were ordered to be polite, in case of trouble they were instructed to shoot at the troublemakers' extremities. There was no trouble.

After Jabotinsky's release in 1921, Patterson accompanied him to the Twelfth Zionist Conference in Carlsbad, Czechoslovakia, the first since the war. There, delegates confirmed Chaim Weizmann as president of the World Zionist Organization. They also passed a resolution that Zionism sought to live in harmony and mutual respect with the Arab people, and instructed the executive to achieve a sincere understanding with them.

But Jabotinsky was bitterly opposed to Weizmann's election, telling an old friend, Shlomo Gepstein:

Weizmann wants to follow his system, without a struggle, in an atmosphere of beautiful words and expressions of love. This means to concede, to retreat. He would like the English to regard him always with "quiet satisfaction." But we shall achieve this only if we show firmness in our views, if we don't stop pressing, if they have to regard us sometimes with "anxious dissatisfaction." . . . Today I had a long talk with Weizmann. It was pleasant and friendly. Each of us presented excellent arguments and proofs. But I felt intuitively that I can't go along with him: in fact, it is morally wrong to go his way, for that will lead us to abandonment of our principles.

He thinks that his is the way of the flexible architect of compromise who takes the realities into account, while mine in the method of a stubborn utopian. But I feel that his is the road to disavowal, to unwitting apostasy. I admit that my ways are difficult and stormy, but they will bring us more speedily to the Jewish State. Of course, Weizmann will be successful with solid, "respectable" people. But, after all, you and I never believed that the Jewish State would be built by a solid, sedate bourgeois.[17]

By April, the Jewish Legion, led by Colonel Margolin, was down to only thirty-two men. And as there was an urgent need for more and better police to keep the peace in Palestine, Margolin expected to be demobilized very soon to head a proposed joint Arab-Jewish defense force. The need became obvious on May 1, in Jaffa, the main port through which Jews entered the country, when Arabs set out to kill and maim Jews, rather than live with them in harmony and mutual respect. The brutal attacks were witnessed by writer Yitshaq Ben-Ami's horrified father. According to Ben-Ami:

An Arab friend of my father's saved him from almost certain death. As the mob surged down Boostros Street, Father's friend raced ahead of them, burst into the shop, shouted to Father to lower the shutters and ran with him to a friend's apartment across the street. Father looked down helplessly from an upper story as Jewish merchants and passersby were clubbed and stabbed to death. The mobs surrounded isolated Jewish houses, murdered those inside, mutilated their bodies, ransacked and burned their homes. The mobs raged for hours, until the Jews of Tel-Aviv could organize self-defense units. Finally, together with soldiers of the Jewish Battalion, they dispersed the mob and halted the massacres.[18]

Colonel Margolin's SOS to British Headquarters for arms to defend the Jaffa Jews had been turned down. So, with his approval, fellow legionnaires broke into the munitions depot,

> seized weapons, rushed to Jaffa where former Legionnaires joined them, and killed sixteen Arabs and drove off hundreds. The Arabs had killed twenty seven Jews and wounded 106.
>
> The British declared martial law, and Margolin submitted his resignation. High Commissioner Herbert Samuel gave him two choices: to face a court-martial for allowing Legionnaires to break into the munitions depot, or to leave Palestine immediately. Margolin chose to leave, and returned to Australia. The remaining thirty two Legionnaires were demobilized on May 31, 1921, marking the official end of the Jewish Legion and also of the plan for a joint Arab-Jewish defense force.[19]

That fall Patterson appeared as a speaker at London's Regent Street Polytechnic together with Colonel Josiah Wedgwood, a pro-Zionist Labor member of Parliament. Patterson assured his audience that a Jewish Palestine would not be a burden on British taxpayers, because Zionists had undertaken to pay for the country's security. Patterson also lunched in London with the king of Iraq, and soon after, armed with various letters of introduction, set off for Baghdad to obtain an oil concession—perhaps for the Zionist treasury, perhaps as a personal business venture.

By chance, Colonel Meinertzhagen, his fellow British Zionist, encountered Patterson in the Iraqi capital, and noted in his diary:

> Patterson was surprised and somewhat embarrassed to meet me in the residency this afternoon, as he is aware that I am aware of his lurid past [presumably referring to the controversial death of Audley Blyth on safari in East Africa, and Patterson's suspected romance with Ethel Blyth. The rumor about Patterson had persisted, despite his exoneration by the House of Lords]. He came out here to wrangle some oil concessions, but I was able to warn Percy Cox [Mesopotamia's high commissioner] against him. Patterson is a man who knows no fear, but who is unscrupulous to a degree. He is not a suitable person to trust with a concession in an Arab country.[20]

Biographer Patrick Streeter disagrees with the negative aspects of Meinertzhagen's evaluation, and so, from the available evidence, does this writer. "Patterson was totally determined rather than unscrupulous," says Streeter, "and his straight dealing stands out. He was very reliable with other people's money. As Dr. Weizmann's confidence bore out, Patterson's weakness was lack of commercial experience."[21]

On his return journey from Iraq, Patterson's plane had engine trouble and landed briefly in the Jordanian desert, where Bedouins found it a great curiosity. Biographer Streeter reports that while flying over Palestine, Patterson's thoughts were not of his failed business mission but of the history of the land below, the progress being made by Jewish colonists, and of the country's great potential. Instead of an oil concession, he came back with Babylonian tablets that he sent to the British Museum to be authenticated.

Both Weizmann and Jabotinsky continued to encourage Patterson to give pro-Zionist fund-raising speeches, especially in the United States, for little more than his expenses. He willingly did so. Some money collected was used to buy and ship arms secretly for the Haganah, the growing Jewish defense force. One such effort for the Palestine Foundation Fund began late in 1921, when Patterson sailed for New York on the SS *Aquitania* with Jabotinsky, Nahum Sokolow, Professor Otto Warburg, and Alexander Goldstein on a fund-raising trip throughout the United States. A reporter for the *New Palestine*, an American journal, sensed that with the appearance of the Patterson-Jabotinsky team, "an element of romance has come into the more or less prosaic lives of Jews. These two represent the aggressive and militant aspect of Jewish national restoration."[22]

On January 10, 1922, Patterson wrote from St. Louis to put a colleague, Barnard Stone, in the picture:

> We have arrived at St. Louis after a pleasant journey. . . . We were welcomed at a splendid banquet—really the best organized I have seen so far in the United States. I should say some 200 to 300 people were present and although Mr. Slonia tells me that the response was not as great as it should have been, yet on the whole I consider it was fairly satisfactory. I think it amounted to some $17,000 or $18,000—about one-third in cash.
>
> Then last night we had a Mass Meeting at the Odeon Theatre, at which about 1,000 people were present—not a very large number, certainly, considering that this city has a population of 50,000 or 60,000 Jews. A charge

was made for admission. But those who didn't come were not deterred so much by the price of admission as by the knowledge presumably that they would have to part with from $50 to $100 each if they put in an appearance. At all events, the response at the meeting was excellent. The audience so far as I could see was mostly men of not very great means, but they responded most generously and I think New York will get a check of some $6,000 from St. Louis with probably another $18,000 in pledges.

We have impressed upon the Keren Hayesod [Hebrew for Foundation Fund] officials here the absolute necessity of organizing a personal canvas of every Jew and Jewess in St. Louis. . . . I think Mr. Slonia has to be heartily congratulated on the great amount of publicity which he has induced in the local papers to give us and the movement generally. You will not see any record of my speeches because I was reserved each evening for the "star turn to hold the audience." So that I spoke after the collection when the reporters had all gone, but that is quite immaterial as far as I am concerned and I am only happy to think that the people did wait for me and so pay up for the Keren Hayesod.

I think St. Louis is backward in Jewish affairs. Even the young lady who is taking down this letter for me admits that she herself knew little until she was brought into the movement, but I think that "the Dry-Bones of Israel" in this city can be reawakened to new life. . . . The people are kindly and well-disposed and even the German Jews here will in time realize that they, too, can't stand apart—that they must help rebuild Israel.[23]

In another letter to Stone from Cincinnati on February 2, 1922, Patterson complained:

I wrote you last from Waco, and unfortunately found the town as dead as its name. The meeting was a fiasco—less than a hundred were present, the majority babies in arms. No attempt was made at any collection and we went on to other cities in Texas where things were not so bad. Mr. Freed is a very nice man, but is somewhat inexperienced at handling meetings. . . . In Houston, San Antonio, Galveston and Beaumont, there were results certainly, but nothing compared to what they ought to have been had the ground been prepared before our tour. . . . From Texas we went on to New Orleans, the community there for the first time in its history came together at a banquet presided over by Dr. Heller, a splendid man. . . . He is a follower of Justice Brandeis, but he helped us heart and soul and was mainly responsible for the success we achieved at New Orleans. I believe some $5,000 cash was collected and pledged to a fair extent, in addition. There was a luncheon yesterday and a mass meeting in the evening at which some $10,000 cash was raised.

I heard bad accounts of Cincinnati, but we had one of the finest meetings last night that I have so far attended in this country, and with Slonia to work this city up, I am sure it will go over the top with its hundred thousand dollars.[24]

Patterson summed up the tour in a letter to Chaim Weizmann, written from the Hotel Chuisca in Memphis on May 30, 1922:

After having traveled this great land of the stars and stripes and having met various shades and brands, both of the Orthodox and the Reformed element, I have come to the conclusion that the former are anxious to hear the message from Palestine, are anxious to help in rebuilding the old land, and are anxious to see it once more green and Jewish. But the Reformed Jews on the whole care for none of these things. Palestine is not yet fashionable enough for them; but you might possibly arouse their interest in the land of their Fathers, if you could arrange for a delegation composed of the Archbishop of Canterbury, Cardinal Gaspari and, say, Lord Rothschild!!

The one bright spot in Reformed Jewry in this country I found in Mobile. There they all came to hear the message and having heard it promised to do—and are doing—their duty. The Mobile Reformed Rabbi, Moses, and the president of the congregation, Mr. Leo Brown, are good Zionists and greatly helped Dr. Goldstein and myself during our stay in Mobile. It may be that this city will yet make history, for these Reformed Jews are veritable sheep. And it is just possible that they may follow the excellent lead given them by their Brethren in Mobile.

I had a very friendly chat with Justice Brandeis [of the U.S. Supreme Court] in Washington recently. I was quite frank in my talk with him and told him that I considered it a tragedy that he was not actively supporting the K.H. [Keren Hayesod] at this critical hour. He admitted that it was a tragedy. I asked him if he realized that if the K.H. failed, then practically everything Jewish in Palestine would fail also. When I pointed out that the organization to which he lends his support does nothing whatever for the unfortunate immigrant who arrives in Palestine, often starving and in rags, he said he did not wish to interfere in the special activities of the K.H. He said this, I thought, rather lamely. The purpose of my visit was merely to thank him for the great help he gave me at a critical time in Palestine, but he broached the subject of Zionism and then, of course, I had my chance and took full advantage of it. It was a very friendly talk and, of course, he said many things which I must not repeat. All this time he was saying these things I felt I was listening to the voice of Brandeis, but I felt the unseen hand was the hand of "Jacob." [The biblical Jacob is the traditional ancestor of the people of Israel.]

It was evident to me that not a great gulf exists between the two parties. I believe a bridge could be made.

On my asking Brandeis if he would be prepared to discuss the situation with a view to finding a basis of agreement, he told me he was prepared to sit around the table with anybody at any time. . . . I am confident that his heart is in the right place and if you could bring him back to the fold, it would mean much to the cause in this country.

The traveling and speaking day after day and night after night has been very trying, but on the whole considering the bad time, the split in the Zionist ranks, and the criminal apathy of the Reformed Jews, the results are not bad, and I trust you are not disappointed with the work of the delegation.

I hope you keep fit, and with kindest regards to you and Mrs. Weizmann.[25]

Patterson's conversation with Brandeis came a year after Albert Einstein had toured the United States with Weizmann to raise money for the Hebrew University.

[Einstein] had a ringside seat at the ongoing battle between Weizmann and Brandeis supporters who wanted their man to be leader of the World Zionist Organization. Vera [Weizmann's wife] recalled how at one meeting, when Brandeis explained "that Palestine was full of malaria and therefore it would be wrong to encourage emigration to Palestine until malaria had been eliminated, our much admired friend and magnificent orator, Schmara Levin, burst out ironically, 'Do you mean, Justice Brandeis, that the first immigrant should be allowed in when the last mosquito has left it?'"[26]

As well as a cautious approach, Brandeis wanted the Zionist organization to be backed by private, mostly American, money, rather than public funds. And to be a loose federation, autonomous in each country, rather than a centralized body, and consequently with no one in overall charge. Weizmann rejected both views, and won the argument. He remained president of the worldwide Zionist Organization.

Patterson understood that Brandeis was devoted to the Zionist cause, but resented the suggestion that he should resign from the U.S. Supreme Court to become its leader, and was unwilling to take any action that might question his prior loyalty to the United States. Although Patterson was willing to help any Zionist achieve his ultimate goal, he was committed to Jabotinsky's more dynamic approach.

Shooting for a worldwide total of twenty-five million pounds on behalf of the Palestine development fund, on their return from the United States, the Patterson-Jabotinsky team continued their fund-raising tour back in England. At meetings of Zionists in East London's Camberwell, and then in the West End, Patterson told them that any Jew unable to go to Palestine to help with reconstruction should send cash to support the effort. From London he traveled to Liverpool to speak to small gatherings in various Zionists' homes, raising in one home alone six hundred pounds. That summer, after more Arab riots in Palestine, Patterson mailed a letter to all former members of the Jewish Legion, inviting them to discuss the situation at a meeting in Bath Zion Hall in London's East End.

His opponent, Lord Sydenham, formerly a pro-Zionist who had joined the opposition, chose the House of Lords to express his new views, saying in June 1922: "Palestine is not the original home of the Jews. It was acquired by them after a ruthless conquest, and they never occupied the whole of it, which they now demand. The Jews have no more claim to Palestine than the descendants of the ancient Romans have to this country. The Romans occupied Britain nearly as long as the Israelites occupied Palestine, and they left behind them in this country far more valuable and useful work."[27] Sydenham's arguments were at odds with the facts, but, even so, in a vote after his speech, 60 peers were against the Balfour Declaration and only 29 supported it. Fortunately for the Zionists, on July 4, 1922, Winston Churchill supported the views of Chaim Weizmann and Patterson. So did most of the House of Commons, with 290 voting for the

Balfour Declaration and just 35 against, effectively quashing the House of Lords' negative vote.

On July 22 the League of Nations approved Britain's Mandate of Palestine, which meant, because of Parliament's acceptance of the Balfour Declaration, that the British were honor-bound to make the country the Jewish national home. Patterson was delighted. So was Meinertzhagen, who made this diary entry on July 22: "I am more pleased than I can say at the passing of the Mandate. It will once and for all convince the Arabs and their anti-Zionist friends that the Zionist policy has come to stay and that all their obstruction has been of no avail."[28]

Lord Sydenham again expressed his views on August 19, writing to the *London Times* that the government was pursuing "a policy of forcing by British bayonets a horde of aliens, some of them eminently undesirable, upon the original owners of the country."

Churchill took over from Patterson in responding by letter to Sydenham, reminding him of his previous support of the Zionists. He added:

It seems to me that before you take further part in this particular controversy you owe it to the public . . . to offer some explanation of the apparent discrepancy between these positions. In particular it would be interesting to know what has occurred in the interval to convert "the Jewish people" for whom you hoped to make Palestine "the national home" into "a horde of aliens." Your opinions as to the expediency of the policy of Zionism may no doubt quite naturally have turned a complete somersault in the last five years, but the relation of the Jewish race to Palestine has not altered in that period. Either, therefore, you were mistaken then in thinking that the Jews were entitled to regard Palestine as "the national home" or you are mistaken now in describing them as "a horde of aliens."

Sydenham replied, on August 19, that he had made a mistake in supporting the Balfour Declaration. He now believed that the Jews had no more claim to Palestine than the modern Italians to Britain, or the Moors to southern Spain, and he also believed that calling the Jewish immigrants "a horde of aliens" accurately described them.

Two days later, Churchill responded:

If the only reasons which have changed you from an ardent advocate into an active opponent are those set out in your letter, I cannot but feel that they are inadequate even when they are based on misconceptions.

1. The policy of His Majesty's Government has always been to bring in only "carefully selected immigrants gradually without grave injury to the inhabitants," or, I may add, any kind of injury to the inhabitants.

2. Lord Balfour's declaration did not arise from underhand methods of any kind, but from wide and deep arguments which have been clearly explained. No Jewish Government has been set up in Palestine, but only a British Government in which Jews as well as Arabs participate. A reference to the White Paper recently published should reassure you in this respect.

There is, however, one reason for a change of view which I am glad to see you do not give, namely, that it was an easy and popular thing to advocate a Zionist policy in the days of the Balfour declaration. And that it is a laborious and much criticized task to try to give honorable effect at the present time to the pledges which were given then. Still it seems to me that if a public man like yourself has mistakenly supported the pledge, he should, even if he has changed his mind, show a little forbearance and even consideration to those who are endeavouring to make it good. Might you not have left to others the task of inflicting censure and creating difficulties and reserved your distinguished controversial gifts for some topic upon which you have an unimpeachable record? To change your mind is one thing; to turn on those who have followed your previous advice is another.[29]

After that, Lord Sydenham faded from the picture.

If anything, Jabotinsky was energized by the opposition. He still believed that Patterson was the best man to lead a Jewish defense force, and in October 1922 he negotiated with British officials, hoping for their approval of such a force (in fact legitimating the Haganah) with an Irish commander. It was unfortunate timing. Patterson's book blasting the authorities, *With the Judeans in the Palestine Campaign,* had recently been published by Hutchinson. And an early concerned reader, the infamous General Bols, had complained to General Allenby of the attacks in it on himself and his staff. He decided not to make a public protest, though, for fear it might boost the book's sales. However, Bols asked Allenby to put in the official records Bols's rebuttal of the negative charges, in order to protect the careers of those individuals Patterson had excoriated. Allenby complied, although before Sir Herbert Greedy, the War Office's permanent secretary, filed away the rebuttal, he noted in a margin of the report that the War Department was not able to agree that the words in Patterson's book were untrue, a tepid but nonetheless telling confirmation of Patterson's complaints.

Instead of commanding a Jewish defense force in Palestine, Patterson spent the early days of 1923 with a delegation in Canada on another fund-raising tour for Keren Hayesod. While there, he was encouraged by a message from Israel Zangwill, a distinguished British Jew, novelist, playwright, and the creator of a movement to settle Jews within the British Empire. Zangwill described his friend Patterson as "a man of the simplest and most loveable character, imperturbable, breezy, hopeful and humorous, a crusader in a truly Christian spirit, whose aim is to restore Palestine not to Christendom, but to the only homeless people on earth. Colonel Patterson has written his name indelibly on the scroll of Jewish as well as British history."[30] At a banquet in Winnipeg alone the group raised $10,000.

Jabotinsky hoped to make more active use of Patterson's talents. With this ambition in mind, he approached Richard Meinertzhagen, now military adviser to Winston Churchill, the colonial secretary. Meinertzhagen was working on a proposal to create a multinational police force in Palestine to back up the regular police. Although having failed once on a similar proposal, Jabotinsky suggested Patterson as its commander. Why it again failed is explained by a note on a file by Sir Gerard Clauson, the Middle East Department's permanent undersecretary: "I do not think Colonel Patterson can very well be considered for any of these jobs, apart from other considerations he is too senior."[31] The other considerations surely included his pro-Jewish and pro-Zionist activities—and, perhaps, Meinertzhagen's reservations about him.

In 1925 Jabotinsky broke with the World Zionist Organization, which he found too timid, and formed the World Union of Zionist Revisionists. Its more ambitious goals included the establishment of a Jewish state to include Transjordan, the re-creation of the Jewish Legion, and the formation of a Jewish youth organization, a militant version of the Boy Scouts, to

21. Zionist leader Chaim Weizmann, who met Patterson in New York in 1926, when they were both working for the Zionist cause. Courtesy of the Library of
Congress Prints and Photographs Division, LC-DIG-
ggbain-36518.

be named Betar, in honor of Brit Joseph Trumpeldor. The Revisionists, as
they were known, would become a powerful organization in opposition
to David Ben-Gurion's Labor Party, with Jabotinsky himself Ben-Gurion's
most serious rival. Although Jabotinsky never became prime minister, his
heirs have included Prime Minister Menachem Begin and Prime Minister
Benjamin Netanyahu.

22. Jabotinsky and Patterson inspect Betar volunteers. Courtesy of Joan Travis.

In the periods between his frequent foreign travels Patterson lived with his wife and teenage son, Bryan, at Grove House in Iver, Buckinghamshire, near what is now Pinewood Film Studios. Millie Pope was their housekeeper, and their flowers and lawns were cared for by a gardener named Geary. Patterson and his family went on picnics in nearby Burnham Beeches with their neighbors, a Dr. MacDiarmid, his wife, and her sister. He played bridge and went to racetracks, where he was quite a successful gambler. At his Cavalry Club in Piccadilly he met his friends Colonel Collings-Wells, the brother of a World War I Victoria Cross winner, and Colonel Fleetwood-Wilson, also retired from the army and now working for the British Board of Film Censors.

But he was never at home for long. In 1926 he was off to New York City, where he met Chaim Weizmann, Leo Amery, and Dr. M. D. Eder. They all supported the idea of an all-volunteer defense force in Palestine with Patterson at its head, but nothing came of the plan. Early in 1927 Patterson was in Tulsa, Oklahoma, where he befriended a Jewish couple named Travis, originally from Lithuania, who were in the oil business. Many years later, they were to become an important part of his life. In 1928 and again in 1929 he and Jabotinsky toured Betar camps in Palestine. Jewish opponents who supported Weizmann's more moderate goals greeted them with catcalls. As militant Arabs threatened to kill them, they often traveled with an armed guard. And a murder of a Jewish politician, Chaim Arlosoroff, on the beach at Tel Aviv brought Patterson back to Palestine in the early thirties. Jabotinsky wanted him there as a witness at the controversial murder trial that, even today, is still remembered and discussed with passionate intensity.

12

Murder on a Tel Aviv Beach and
the Start of World War II,
1931–1939

RETIRED FROM THE BRITISH ARMY, Patterson had made enough money from his books and other enterprises to live modestly but comfortably in his Buckinghamshire home. The Pattersons' son, Bryan, was self-supporting, still working as a budding and eventually famous paleontologist at the Field Museum in Chicago. But after the big crash in 1929 and the increasing disablement through arthritis of his wife, Frances, Patterson was strapped for ready cash. It was urgent enough for him to set off, in 1931, for Jalisco, Mexico, looking for gold. Far from striking it rich from a mine he was developing, he had to ask his publisher, Sir Frederick Macmillan, to send twenty-five pounds to take care of Frances for a few weeks. Fortunately, his military pension came through, which saved him from financial disaster.

Patterson was still in Mexico on July 3, 1931, when Chaim Weizmann was under attack at the Seventeenth Zionist Congress in Basel, Switzerland. There, he declared that "the Arabs in Palestine must be convinced by deed as well as word, that whatever the numerical relationships of the two nations in Palestine, we on our part contemplate no political domination." Jabotinsky disagreed vehemently, insisting on a Jewish majority and a Jewish state in Palestine on both sides of the Jordan River. For him, it could hardly be a safe haven for threatened Jews if the Arabs were a majority.

Weizmann responded calmly to Jabotinsky's fierce outburst, underlining their radically different approach to the problem: "The walls of Jericho fell to the sounds of shouts and trumpets. I have never, however, heard of walls being raised by that means." American rabbi Stephen Wise, a Justice Brandeis ally, hit a nerve and destroyed Weizmann's calm demeanor when he scornfully accused him of sitting too long at English feasts.

Weizmann left the hall in a fury. Chaim Arlosoroff, his heir apparent and a rising star of the Labor (Mapai) Party, rose to his rescue. "You spoke in such a manner that it was much more than a speech," he said, addressing himself to a man no longer able to hear him. But he went on: "It was a great historic deed. And I am happy to feel that there is someone who will ... I hope soon, be able to continue the true and unsullied policy."[1] It didn't help, perhaps because it seemed too self-serving. Delegates continued to denounce Weizmann's commitment to full cooperation with the British. And a vote of censure, implying no confidence in his leadership, passed by 123 votes to 106. Jabotinsky's attempt to replace him failed. Bitterly disappointed, he, too, stormed out of the hall and, shouting, "This is not a Zionist congress!" tore up his delegate's card as he went, followed by fellow Revisionists.

The remaining delegates elected a new president, Nahum Sokolow. A journalist who spoke twelve languages, he was a friend of several prominent members of the British clergy, including the archbishop of Canterbury. But he could do nothing to reduce the animosity between the two major parties.

Patterson stayed loyal to Jabotinsky. And after his arrival home from Mexico he answered Jabotinsky's SOS. The survival of the Revisionist Party was at stake, its members having been charged with murdering a fellow Jew, Chaim Arlosoroff. Studying a report of the crime, Patterson deduced what Labor leaders were up to. Pinning the murder on Revisionists even before the trial looked like a political hatchet job. He showed the report to his friend and ally British politician Leo Amery. Amery sent it to the British colonial secretary, Sir Philip Cunliffe-Lister, noting that, in such a charged atmosphere, he did not envy the police or judges their task of finding the truth. Jabotinsky was in Poland, and at his request Patterson went to Palestine to monitor the trial, which threatened to weaken if not destroy the Revisionist Party. Jabotinsky knew that Patterson was familiar with British trials and could give him a fair account of this one, which some even compared with the momentous and malicious Dreyfus trial.

Shortly before his murder, Chaim Arlosoroff had been sent to Berlin on a mercy mission. As head of the Jewish Agency's political department, he hoped to save the lives of 550,000 German Jews. According to Levi Eshkol, a subsequent Mapai prime minister (1963–1969) and confidant of Ben-Gurion, Arlosoroff "was to examine two questions in particular: how serious Nazi persecution of the Jews was likely to become, and whether avoidance of Nazi persecution could not be contained with the need to increase the immigration of German Jews into Palestine. . . . It was already clear to him that Nazi persecution was likely to increase but that the tendency of German Jews would be to stay put, and hope for better days."[2]

Jabotinsky had responded to the persecution of German Jews by declaring a moral and economic boycott of the Nazis, and he and his followers were adamantly opposed, as he put it, to "trading with the enemy," whatever the motive. Nevertheless, Arlosoroff hoped to persuade Jabotinsky to end the boycott through a quid pro quo: ending the boycott if the Nazi government allowed German Jews to leave the country with their possessions.

Two days after Arlosoroff's return to Palestine, on the evening of June 16, 1933, as he and his wife, Sima, were walking on the beach at Tel Aviv, two men, one tall, one short, passed them twice. It made Sima Arlosoroff uneasy, and her husband remarked, "They are Jewish. Since when are you afraid of Jews?" On their third encounter, the tall man shone a flashlight in Arlosoroff's face and, speaking in Hebrew, asked him the time. When he replied, "Why are you bothering us?" the short man shot him in the stomach. The two men then disappeared into the moonless night. The dying man's wife cried out, "Jews have shot him!" But Arlosoroff, lying on the ground, said, "No, Sima, no," as she later reported.[3]

Passersby drove them both to the emergency room of a nearby hospital. Sima Arlosoroff briefly returned to their hotel to phone the police. Questioned by police captain Stafford, she accused Arabs of shooting her husband. Although anxious to rejoin him, she was persuaded by Stafford to stop en route to the hospital to indicate the crime scene. Arlosoroff was on the operating table when she arrived, and so she couldn't see him. Meanwhile, Stafford took her to the police station, where she was shown photographs of known Communists (bogeymen to the Western world in the 1930s). She failed to identify any, and early in the morning, back at the hospital, she was told that her husband was dead.

Patterson knew that the Palestinian police had recently failed to solve several high-profile crimes and were under strong pressure to solve this one. They circulated Sima Arlosoroff's description of the killer. An immigration official noticed that it fitted Avraham Stavsky, a Polish Jew who supported Jabotinsky's Revisionist Party and had been actively involved in bringing illegal immigrants into the country.

Bedouin trackers brought him in. Harry Rice, deputy inspector general of the Palestinian police, now in charge of the investigation, showed Sima Arlosoroff a photo of Stavsky and of nine other men. She picked out Stavsky. When he and several other men were lined up, she again indicated him. However, he had an alibi: at the time of the Tel Aviv shooting he was miles away in Jerusalem.

Another suspect, Zvi Rosenblatt, was arrested after a young woman, Rivka Feigin, who had been a fellow member of a Betar unit, stated that at a group meeting he had been chosen to murder Arlosoroff. But she had also accused her ex-husband of the same crime. And she had a shady past, having been dismissed from Jabotinsky's Betar organization for theft. She had later joined the rival Labor Party, Mapai, and lived in a Labor kibbutz. Her testimony left a lot to be desired.

A young Arab, Abdul Majid Buchari, in prison charged with another murder, also confessed to killing Arlosoroff, saying that he and a friend had intended to rape Sima Arlosoroff. The police found a revolver and bullets of the right make in his home, and thought they had solved the case, until he retracted his confession, claiming that Stavsky and Rosenblatt had bribed him to confess to the crime.

To add to the confusion, Arlosoroff's widow, Sima, gave the police conflicting information. Soon after her husband's death, she told several people that the killers were Arabs, then later that they were Jews. When first questioned, she said that the fatal bullet had traveled from left to right, but when the examining surgeon reported that it went from right to left, she agreed with him.

Jabotinsky's most vociferous political rival, David Ben-Gurion, head of the Labor Party, convinced that the murder was an act of political terror, stated his belief that Stavsky, a Revisionist, was the killer. So did Golda Meir, a future Labor prime minister, and most if not all other leading Labor Party members. "Arlosoroff represented moderation, caution, a balanced approach to world problems," she wrote in her autobiography, "and, of course, to our own, and his tragic death seemed the inevitable consequence of the kind of anti-socialist, right-wing militarism and violent chauvinism that was being advocated by the Revisionists."[4]

Jabotinsky was convinced that the two men were innocent and would be vindicated. He raised money for the defense from a wealthy South African, Michael Haskell, and hired as defense attorney Horace Samuel, a former Jewish Legion officer and a cousin of Sir Herbert Samuel, Palestine's first high commissioner.

Patterson attended the trial, which began in a stifling courtroom on April 23, 1934. Among the notes in his fourteen-page report for Jabotinsky were the following:

• A real hatred existed between many Labour [Mapai] and Revisionist supporters.

• When members of a faction, individuals often lose their judgment.

• Arlosoroff was a moderate Labour Leader and so an unlikely target for assassination.

• It was a moonless, dark night and Mrs. Arlosoroff, in an emotional state, was not in a good position to identify suspects.

• Stavsky's subsequent behaviour was not that of an assassin. He openly attended Arlosoroff's funeral. The day after the murder, he drew attention to himself by conducting an argument at the immigration office and he sent letters home to Poland, making arrangements for his family to join him. An assassin would have headed straight for the border.

• Rivka [a prosecution witness], while in Romania, had worked as a spy for the secret police.

• The police insisted on pursuing only one line of enquiry. This led up a blind alley but they refused to consider other possibilities.[5]

During the trial, Patterson lunched with an old Boer War friend, Sir Arthur Wauchope, the new pro-Zionist high commissioner for Palestine. They discussed Sima Arlosoroff's contradictory evidence, in which she had described the fatal bullet moving in opposite directions. The two men, firearm experts, agreed that bullets don't go around corners. But although Wauchope expected a miscarriage of justice, he was not in a position to interfere in the trial.

Rosenblatt was freed for lack of evidence, and on June 8, 1934, Stavsky was found guilty and sentenced to hang. However, on July 19, the Palestinian court of appeals overturned the decision on technicalities.

Another courtroom observer, Yitshaq Ben-Ami, concluded, like Patterson, that Labor was using the murder to defame the Jabotinsky movement. And he reported, "When Hitler had risen to power in 1933 . . . Jabotinsky's certainty of an approaching catastrophe dominated his thoughts and actions. But the harder he and his followers tried to be heard, the harder their 'brothers' in the Jewish establishment fought them and tried to silence them."[6]

Fifty-two years after the murder it was still a cause of animosity between the two parties, and in 1982 Menachem Begin, the first Revisionist prime minister, appointed a Judicial Court of Enquiry to reexamine the case. Finding no new evidence, their report was inconclusive. Then, in 2004, Anja Klabunde published a biography, titled *Magda Goebbels*. If the book is to be believed, Magda Quant, who married Nazi propaganda chief Joseph Goebbels in the 1920s, had previously been Arlosoroff's lover and an ardent Zionist. When he went on his controversial mission to Berlin, he was shocked to find that she had married this high-ranking Nazi official. Still, he tried to enlist her help in his mission. Instead, she warned him to leave Germany immediately, afraid, apparently, that they were both in great danger. The reader is left to assume that Goebbels discovered his wife's involvement with a Jew, feared that if it became known it would end his political career, and hired two hit men to kill him. It remains a mystery to this day.

After the trial, Patterson went from Palestine to South Africa, where there was a significant Jewish population, to raise funds for a group of former Jewish Legionnaires who hoped to create an agricultural village in

Palestine at Avihayil, north of Netanya. While fund-raising in Johannesburg, he accepted an invitation from nuns at a Yeoville convent school to talk about his lion-hunting adventures in East Africa. Harriet Schlosberg, then a fifteen-year-old student, some seventy years later still remembered how impressed she was by the charming visitor and his account of his many adventures.[7] He returned from a successful fund-raising tour, to be greeted on the outskirts of Avihayil by a mounted guard of legion veterans, and in the village itself by a group of children who had built a triumphant arch of tree branches.

The village of mostly wooden huts prospered, and a year later Patterson learned to his delight that its 120 inhabitants had dug a well, planted several hundred acres of thriving orange trees, and were building a reservoir. The money he had raised from generous South African Jews was slated for school buildings. On his future trips to Palestine, he often visited the village, which, today, has memorialized Patterson's dedication to the welfare of the Jewish people. It is, writes Patterson biographer Patrick Streeter, "a pleasant suburb of the bustling seaside town of Netanya. In the sixties a community hall and Jewish Legion Museum was built and there can be found a tableau illustrating the exploits of the Zion Mule Corps, Patterson's dress uniform together with his medals and sword, and a copy of the Lord Mayor's letter granting permission for the 38th Battalion of the Royal Fusiliers to march through the City of London in 1918 with fixed bayonets."[8]

Frequently on the move, Patterson was in England in April 1936 when Arabs killed eighteen Jews in Jaffa. He and Jabotinsky protested the murders at a public meeting in Whitechapel's Pavilion Theatre. As Patterson rose to speak there was a storm of applause, and again when he called General Louis Bols "an out and out anti-Semite who would leave no stone unturned to destroy, root and branch, the Jewish National Home." He concluded: "What was promised to the Jews [by the Balfour Declaration] must be given to them. Let the Arabs do what they like with their own countries, but Palestine, the whole of Palestine, is a Jewish country in which they must be able to work out their salvation."[9]

Spurred by the continued violence, the British government appointed a Royal Commission headed by Lord William Peel, former secretary of state for India, who was suffering from stomach cancer. They were charged with examining the problems in Palestine and suggesting solutions. Arriving in Palestine on November 11, 1936, Armistice Day, they were lodged at the King David Hotel and took evidence at the Palace Hotel, a building owned by the Supreme Muslim Council.

Chaim Weizmann was the first to give evidence: a masterful and moving performance that lasted three hours but to some there, Sir Mark Sykes among them, seemed only minutes. Weizmann spoke of Zionism as the crystallization of a long historical process of a continual Jewish movement of return to their native land. And he spoke of the six million European Jews whose existence depended on their emigration to Israel and the establishment of a Jewish state. He said that they not only needed and wanted a Jewish state but also had the desire and the ability, economic and cultural, to bring it about. He was "tactful enough to express gratitude towards Britain while criticizing the negative aspects of British administration. Forty other Jewish witnesses were heard, including Jabotinsky who urged Britain to explain the Balfour Declaration to the Arabs, to tell them that the huge Arab world could afford to allow Palestine to become a small Jewish state, and to give up the Mandate if she, Britain, could not discharge it."[10]

The sixty-year-old Patterson contributed his vituperative views in a fourteen-page letter in which he repeated his charge that the British administration in Palestine was deliberately sabotaging the Balfour Declaration and encouraging Arab violence. He detailed the vindictive treatment the Jewish Legion had endured—at the hands of the British—both during and after the war. And he accused General Louis Bols of "conspiring to have the Regiment wiped out by the Turks by placing it at 1,200 feet below sea level, at the hottest time of the year, at the bottom of the Jordan Valley in the jaws of the enemy's 4th Army." Although he claimed not to be prejudiced, he obviously was on this occasion, when he characterized Palestinian Arabs as "lazy, ignorant, terribly fanatical, and easily aroused by their astute leaders to murderous acts." He also stated that "the Turks had ruled Palestine through three or four powerful Arab families" who were now being "assisted by arms and gold from Italy."[11] It was news to a British official, who had questioned this assertion in a margin of Patterson's letter. Patterson concluded by recommending the dismissal of all anti-Jewish officials from the Palestine administration, revival of the Jewish Legion, and having the Foreign Office take over responsibility for Palestine from the Colonial Office.

The most important Arab witness, Husseini, the mufti of Jerusalem, charged that the Jews intended to destroy the Muslim holy places in Jerusalem and to rebuild the Temple of Solomon on their ruins. He stated that the Balfour Declaration was prejudicial in favor of the Jews, who were able to buy all the good land. He asserted that the Palestinian Arabs had been happier under Turkish than under British rule. He demanded that no more Jews be allowed to immigrate to Palestine, and insisted that Britain make Palestine an independent Arab nation with the same status as Iraq.

According to Ben-Gurion, the commission's report "cited the problems of the Jews in the Diaspora, the settlement work of the Jews, the eternal values that the Jewish people had created in the Land of Israel for all mankind and their determination to revive their ancient Homeland. The report contained the best description of Jewish settlement ever to appear." The report also stated that "the Arab community had received its fair share of benefits of Jewish immigration and settlement and that the obligations to the Arabs, as laid down in the Mandate, had therefore been fulfilled. The Arab economy . . . had not suffered in any way because of the National Home." The report also "pointed out that Emir Feisal, who had represented the Arabs at the Peace Conference, had agreed to the Balfour Declaration, and to a program of cooperation between the Arab states and Palestine." The land shortage in Palestine, the report concluded, was owing less to purchase by Jews than to the increase in the Arab population. "The Arab claims that Jews have obtained too large a proportion of the good land cannot be maintained. Much of the land now carrying orange groves was sand dunes or swamps and uncultivated when it was bought." Ben-Gurion believed that Weizmann's testimony "made an enormous impression on the Royal Commission and undoubtedly influenced its decision to propose the establishment of a Jewish State in a part, albeit a small part, of the Land of Israel."[12]

Colonel Meinertzhagen did not testify, but his view of the situation appeared in the *London Times* on February 7, 1938: "Much has been written

about injustice to the Arabs. There is nothing in the Jewish State which con-
flicts with Arab rights. And, moreover, be it remembered that the Arabs are
the only nation in the world with at least three kings and several sovereign
states. The Jews are a nation without a home."

Three days after Jabotinsky gave evidence before the Royal Commission he and Patterson attended a "Jewish Legion Dinner" at the Hotel
Commodore to celebrate the twentieth anniversary of the founding of
the Jewish Legion. Guests included Leopold Amery, former secretary of
state for the Colonial Office; Herbert Sidebotham, a *Times* editor; Lieutenant Colonel Fitzgerald Scott, former commander of the Fortieth Battalion;
Field Marshal Sir Philip Chetwode; Colonel Josiah Wedgwood; Lady Dug-
dale, a niece of Lord Balfour; and diplomats representing France, Poland,
Czechoslovakia, Romania, Latvia, and Estonia.

Because of irreconcilable differences, the commission recommended
the division of Palestine into autonomous Jewish and Arab states. The
smaller Jewish state would be in the North and West and the larger Arab
state, including the Negev, would be united with Transjordan in the South
and East.

Weizmann reluctantly accepted the proposal, for which his critics
called him a traitor and a British spy. Ben-Gurion also accepted the Peel
plan. But Golda Meir didn't. She thought that the two thousand square
miles to go to the Jews was ridiculously small. The Zionist Congress
accepted the proposal but with radical qualifications. The Palestinian
Arabs rejected the idea outright, as did Jabotinsky, Patterson, and his fellow Revisionists.

The British government and most of the British press accepted the Peel
Commission recommendations. But Lloyd George, who had been prime
minister at the time of the Balfour Declaration, published an article titled
"The Scandalous Report," calling the proposals a gross violation of the
promises given to the Jewish people. Heated debate followed in the House
of Commons during which critics complained that the Jews were not getting enough territory and denounced the removal of Jerusalem from the
Jewish state in favor of international control. The criticism and the escalat-
ing violence in Palestine caused the British government to withdraw its
approval of the report.

In 1937 Jabotinsky met with Robert Briscoe, later the first Jewish lord mayor of Dublin, and the only Jewish member of the Irish Republican Army, which had helped win freedom for his country from the British, seeking his advice on how it could be done in Palestine. That same year, Patterson went to Palestine, where he twice reviewed a parade of Irgun soldiers, the Revisionists' illegal military arm, once by moonlight. Although a newsreel was made of the daylight event, titled *Colonel Patterson in Palestine,* it was banned by the Colonial Film Censorship Board and never seen by the British or Palestinian public.

That year the Zionist leadership tried to persuade the two illegal Jewish armed groups, the Irgun and Haganah, to merge. Patterson urged Jabotinsky to agree, but he refused. Moshe Dayan, a future Israeli prime minister, was a member of the Haganah. Officially, he was a sergeant in the approved Jewish Settlement Police Force—thirteen hundred members of which, including him, were also in the Haganah. They used their legal right to carry firearms to acquire others illegally for use by the Haganah against marauding Arabs.

The Haganah followed a policy of restraint, which meant that they attacked only when provoked. So had the Irgun, under Jabotinsky's orders, once responding to young Irgun leaders eager to launch retaliatory terror attacks against the Arabs, "I can't see much heroism or public good in shooting from the rear an Arab peasant on a donkey carrying vegetables for sale in Tel Aviv." Jabotinsky changed his mind after Arabs murdered five Jewish workmen. And the Irgun then began a campaign of retaliatory terror. However, Jabotinsky was never reconciled to indiscriminate acts of terror. Menachem Begin, second in command of the Irgun under Jabotinsky, tried to persuade Dayan to join them, but Dayan remained loyal to the Haganah and Ben-Gurion, opposed to indiscriminate reprisals that might kill innocent Arabs.

While still in Palestine, Patterson, who apparently never met Ben-Gurion or Dayan, was hospitalized with a chest infection at Dr. Danziger's Hospital in Tel Aviv. Patterson advised one of his nurses, Ilse Michelsohn, a young Jewish refugee from Nazi Germany, to complete her training in a London hospital, and when she expressed an interest he began to teach her English. She found him to be an excellent patient, very courteous and, to her continental mind, wonderfully English. Soon after his return to England, Patterson talked the matron at St. Mary's Hospital in Paddington into accepting Ilse on her staff. He assured Ilse that if she came, his Buckinghamshire home would be a second home for her. When she wrote back, her first letter in English, he advised her to practice speaking English with someone who had a good accent. Thanks to Patterson's pressure on the Home Office to allow Ilse into Britain, she arrived in the spring of 1938, and quickly earned her nurse's diploma.

She spent every vacation from the hospital at his Iver home, where she was welcomed by both Pattersons, and on days off she often had lunch with Patterson at the Cavalry Club. His whole house, she remembered, was "full of his hunting trophies including elephant feet made into small stools, heads of crocodiles, tigers, lions, and tiger rugs. He became my guardian as I was not yet twenty-one. His wife, Frances, was a semi-invalid, a charming lady, and, I believe, one of England's first women lawyers. Weizmann and Jabotinsky were among their visitors. I met their son, Bryan and his wife, there, when Bryan was on vacation from his work as a lecturer at Chicago's Field Museum." The Pattersons taught her to play bridge, and she went on picnics with them and their neighbors. "Colonel Pat, as we used to call him, was one of the most remarkable people I ever met," she told this author. "He was a very outspoken man and not always popular with the powers that be. He was a leader of men, a truly great man, and a great friend of the Jewish people. He was brave, conscientious, resourceful, very fair, but he did not suffer fools gladly."[13]

Whatever country he was in, Patterson always had up-to-date information on the situation in Palestine from his many contacts. In May 1938 he heard that Colonial Secretary Malcolm MacDonald had charged the mufti of Jerusalem with being the head of an organization terrorizing and assassinating the British, Jews, and moderate Arabs. When British police tried to arrest him, he escaped to the sanctuary of the Temple Mount for several months, before escaping to Beirut disguised as a woman, and eventually reaching Berlin.

In the summer of 1938, Jabotinsky was in Warsaw, where he gave a tragically prophetic warning to Polish Jews that they faced an imminent catastrophe:

I know that you are not seeing this because you are immersed in your daily worries. Today, however, I demand your trust. . . . [L]isten to me in this eleventh hour: In the name of God . . . there is very little time. . . . And what else I would like to say to you in this day of Tisha B'Av: whoever of you will escape from the catastrophe, he or she will live to see the . . . rebirth and rise of a Jewish state. I don't know if I will be privileged to see it, my son will. I believe in this as I am sure that tomorrow morning the sun will rise.[14]

In September 1938 the world conference of Betar in Warsaw endorsed the militant stand of the charismatic leader of Poland's Betar, Menachem Begin. Addressing the conference, he declared, "We are standing on the threshold of the third phase of Zionism. After 'Practical Zionism' and 'Political Zionism, the time has come for 'Military Zionism.' Eventually, military and political concepts will emerge but . . . if we create our military strength, the salvation of the diaspora will come. The world is indifferent. . . . [I]ts conscience ignores what is happening to our people. The League of Nations is impotent. We cannot continue on this road. We want to fight! To win or die!"[15]

In a last-ditch effort to saved the lives of millions of Polish Jews he feared would otherwise be doomed, in December 1938 Jabotinsky sent an Irish Jew, Robert Briscoe, to Poland to negotiate with the Polish government. Briscoe's tricky task was to persuade the Polish government to ask the British government to hand over their mandate of Palestine to the Poles. Jabotinsky hoped that the Polish government would then agree to send all its unwanted Jews to Palestine. Told that such a move would be of financial benefit to the Poles, the foreign minister expressed interest in the idea. But it was vetoed when leading ultra-Orthodox, anti-Zionist rabbis vehemently opposed such a move on religious grounds.

Early in 1939, as war in Europe now seemed all but certain, Patterson crossed the Atlantic to join a Revisionist group to raise funds in the United States. The money would go to arm the Irgun, who planned to protect the illegal Jewish immigrants they intended to rescue, despite British opposition, from Europe, and transport them to Palestine. Among this group were Hiam Lubinsky, the ranking Irgun officer; Robert Briscoe, a Jewish member of the Irish Parliament and former member of the Irish

Republican Army; and Yitshaq Ben-Ami, a member of the Irgun since 1932. Ben-Ami recalled:

> I spent my first evening in America listening to Lubinsky and Patterson. Lubinsky held the floor with his bursting staccato, while the ramrod Patterson, once a lion hunter, patiently waited his opening to inject bits of wisdom. What they told us about their progress was not encouraging. . . . Two of the strongest Jewish organizations here, the American Jewish Committee and the Jewish Labor Committee, were . . . sometimes vehemently anti-Zionist. Most Zionist groups were under the autocratic rule of Jabotinsky's opponent, Stephen S. Wise. Those friendly to us, like Jacob de Haas and Justice Louis D. Brandeis, were in retirement or dead, so our warnings, exhortations and appeals were falling mostly on deaf ears.
>
> Our people had held several meetings in synagogues and private homes, espousing free immigration to Palestine for the Jews of Europe. Listening to Patterson, Briscoe and Lubinsky, some individuals were sincerely moved. They went back to their homes and offices, called their rabbis or heads of their fraternal lodges and asked if they should help us. Who are these people? they asked. Who is Jabotinsky? What is the Irgun? And the answer was always the same: "Don't touch them."[16]

Jabotinsky had asked Briscoe to try to interest President Franklin Roosevelt in a project to move at least a million Jews from eastern and central Europe to Palestine, but Briscoe was never able to reach the president.

Before returning from the United States to England, Patterson and Lubinsky formed the "American Friends for a Jewish Palestine," housed in a small office on Madison Avenue, with a small, dedicated staff, still hoping to win some support for the cause from the American people. Typical of publications by the American Friends was Patterson's *Appeal to American Jewry*, which read:

> On the Irgun the Jewish National Military Organization of Palestine, rests much of the responsibility for the protection of Jewish life and property today. Its service to Palestine Jewry in years past, has been inestimable and on many occasions when British security measures failed, it came to the rescue and saved many dangerous situations. The Irgun today is badly in need of financial assistance and I would urge you with all my heart that

American Jewry now come forward and provide generously for the wants of this invaluable force.[17]

These remarks were followed by:

Do not let the bloody Swastika Wave over Jerusalem!

Eight million Jews enslaved under the Hitler yoke place all their hopes for life and salvation in you—Free Americans! Deliver Jewry from slavery and extermination in Europe. Destroy the gates of the Ghetto, by THE FORMATION OF A JEWISH ARMY—which will battle alongside England and the Allies, to defend Palestine, Jewish honor, and the most sacred principles of democracy.

The Jewish Army will become a reality—if everyone does his duty.

Passivity is the cause of the Jewish national tragedy, therefore, become active and join the movement for a Jewish Army.

We await your helping hand! Call our office immediately![18]

The unremitting Arab attacks on Jewish settlements and businesses persuaded the British to consider curbing Jewish immigration to Palestine. In response, the Irgunists attacked Arab enterprises and buses. The British hanged one Irgunist for shooting at an Arab bus, and began to turn back the small ships headed for Palestine with Jewish refugees. When, in April 1939, the British refused to admit the ship *Assimi* with 170 refugees aboard, armed Irgunists threatened to use force to rescue them.

The British gave in on that occasion, and followed up with a conference in London, known as the St. James Conference, or the Round Table Conference, chaired by British prime minister Neville Chamberlain. After meeting separately with representatives of Iraq, Jordan, Egypt, and the Arabs of Palestine, with leaders of the Jewish Agency, including Weizmann and Ben-Gurion, and with British and American Jews, the British issued a white paper stating that only seventy-five thousand Jewish immigrants could enter Palestine during the next five years, that Jews would only be allowed to buy land representing 5 percent of the country, and that, after five years, a Palestinian—not a Jewish—state would be established. The last point implied, of course, that Arabs, then still in the majority, would be in control of the country.

Although the Conservative majority in the House of Commons approved of the white paper, the Labour and Liberal parties strongly opposed it, as did a few conservatives, among them Winston Churchill and Leopold Amery.

Patterson damned the white paper of May 1939, for proposing

> to turn over the whole of Palestine to the Arabs, to nullify the Balfour Dec-
> laration, to turn its provisions and promises upside down and to restrict
> even the civil rights of the Jewish population which will have to remain
> a minority for ever. The Jews are consoled, however, by the promise of a
> British "guarantee" of their status.
>
> The progressive subversion of the Jewish National Home denoted
> by the various riots was no freak of fate or history. It was the result of a
> deeply laid plan. In every outbreak of terror, high officials of the British
> Administration were implicated.

Patterson conceded that the British government had tried to live up to the Balfour Declaration but was hampered by the permanent officials of the Colonial Office. He did not accuse these officials of initiating anti-Zionist policies, but believed that they were pressed by the career men of the civil service to adopt these policies. He pictured members of the British cabinet as fighting a rearguard action for the Jewish homeland, slowly and reluctantly giving way to the anti-Zionists of the Colonial Office.

Of all postwar colonial secretaries, he wrote, only two, Lord Passfield and Mr. Cunliffe-Lister, were indifferent to Zionism.

> All others—Mr. Churchill, the Duke of Devonshire, Mr. Amery, Mr.
> Thomas, Mr. Ormsby-Gore, and Mr. Malcolm MacDonald—entered upon
> their functions with a definite friendliness toward the great task which
> they faced in Palestine. And yet, every single one of them, once in office,
> found himself obliged to yield to some extent to the insistence of the per-
> manent officials, and to introduce some additional obstacles to the path
> of the Jews.
>
> During the period of murder and outrage that ensued, the Mufti of
> Jerusalem was allowed to go through the country urging his fanatical
> followers to organize and defy the government of which he was a paid
> servant. Lawlessness reached such a pitch that many decent Arabs asked,
> "When will the government act?" The law-abiding Arabs suffered severely

alongside the Jews. Arab peasants were robbed. Arab shopkeepers were terrorized and responsible Arab leaders were murdered by paid assassins of the Mufti.

The Jews could, of course, have protected themselves if they had been allowed to do so. British officials would not allow this. And the Arabs knew it. The restraint shown by the Jews under the greatest provocation has been hailed as a splendid tribute to their steadiness and discipline; but it also acted as an incentive to the Arab terrorists who, according to the War Office figures, never numbered more than 1,500 at the height of the depredations.

The first Arab riots occurred in 1920. Following the outburst, the Jewish battalions were demobilized, and henceforth the Zionist settlers in their Homeland had to rely on Englishmen and Arabs for the protection of their threatened life and property.

The next outbreak occurred in 1921. The result of this tragic episode was the cutting of Transjordan from Palestine and the subjection of Jewish immigration to permanent restrictions despite the explicit undertaking to facilitate Jewish immigration into Palestine under the terms of the Balfour Declaration.

After the bloody massacres of 1929, a White Book was published by the British Government inaugurating restrictions on land settlement by Jews in the whole of Palestine. And this was put into effect despite the declaration by the Mandates Commission of the League of Nations that the responsibility for the riots lay with British officials. After the riots of 1933, the restrictions for the acquisition of land by Jews was further tightened.

Since the reign of terror which commenced in 1936, immigration has been curtailed to a minimum, in spite of maximum needs for a Jewish place of refuge.[19]

Irgunists responded to the new restrictions by planting a bomb in British headquarters, Jerusalem's Palace Hotel, and announced that the bombing was their declaration of war. The British then began arresting Irgunists, and the leaders went into hiding or abroad.

Meanwhile, Jabotinsky was doing his utmost, against fierce opposition, to save Europe's Jews from the tragedy he foresaw. His work spurred New York rabbi Stephen Wise to call him a "'traitor' for preaching 'evacuation,' from the ghettos of Europe. Davar, the Socialist-Zionist Daily in Palestine, said that by working with the Polish government on annual immigration quotas, Jabotinsky was 'joining hands with the . . . pogromizers of the Jews of Poland.' And even in the Passover services held in the great Tlomacka Synagogue in Warsaw in 1939, the Chief Rabbi, Moses Schorr, attacked Jabotinsky's call for mass immigration."[20]

Patterson had been at home on September 3, 1939, when Prime Minister Chamberlain made a radio announcement that Britain was at war with Germany. Shortly after, sirens howled a warning of an enemy air attack—a false alarm. Then Patterson's phone rang. It was Jabotinsky. He was in London. Could they meet?

13

World War II and a Recruiting Drive
for a Jewish Army,
1939–1944

THE HIGH-FLYING AIRCRAFT had been identified as friendly, and, when Patterson met Jabotinsky in London, the air-raid sirens had given a steady all-clear signal. There, they discussed their resurrected plan to raise an army of one hundred thousand Jews to fight the Nazis. Now that the Germans had invaded Poland where millions of Jews were at risk, it was even more urgent to create such a force. In the more pressing need to defeat the Germans, Jabotinsky was to restrain the Irgun from fighting the British in Palestine, although a faction led by Abraham Stern continued to attack them. (The British killed Stern in February 1942.)

During their London meeting, Patterson wondered if the British war secretary, Leslie Hore-Belisha, a Jew and Liberal who had modernized the British armed forces, would now have second thoughts about the value of a Jewish Army. The previous year, when war against an increasingly bellicose Nazi Germany seemed unavoidable, Patterson had presented Hore-Belisha with a proposal to train one hundred thousand Jewish soldiers, but he had rejected the idea.

On January 5, 1940, before Hore-Belisha could respond to the second appeal, Prime Minister Neville Chamberlain fired him, replacing him with another World War I veteran, Oliver Stanley. Patterson then wrote to Chamberlain who replied from Downing Street with a polite thanks but no thanks. The new war minister, Oliver Stanley had too many other things on his mind to consider it.

So Jabotinsky and Patterson began to lobby other government ministers with their plan. Meanwhile, Jabotinsky came up with another idea—a Jewish Intelligence Bureau. But that idea, too, was rejected, or put on the shelf. The British War Office did accept one Jabotinsky plan: to use reliable Irgun agents to sabotage German oil barges on the Danube. It proved a success.

Colonel Meinertzhagen described an even more daring Jabotinsky suggestion—to kill all the top Nazis: "The first step in this ambitious plot was to blow up some highly-placed Nazi in Munich, to whose funeral would flock all the other leading Nazis, including Hitler. The Jewish undertaker in Munich, a friend of Jabotinsky's, would transpose an equal weight of jellybombs in the coffin and as all the Nazis were gathered in grief round the grave, some 200 pounds of jellybombs would explode and blow them all to glory."[1] Unfortunately, the British Foreign Office didn't buy it.

Having failed to convince the British to recruit a volunteer Jewish Army, Patterson and Jabotinsky set about arousing American public opinion in favor of raising one in the United States. In March 1940, they addressed a responsive audience of more than five thousand in the Manhattan Center at Thirty-fourth Street and Eighth Avenue. Jabotinsky repeated his call for a Jewish state on both sides of the Jordan, with no restrictions on Jewish immigration. Patterson focused on the proposed Jewish fighting force with the same status as the newly formed military units of the Free French and the Poles in exile.

In an introduction to his 1940 book, *The Jewish War Fronts,* Jabotinsky explained in detail how a Jewish Army could lead to a safe homeland in Palestine for the oppressed Jewish people:

> A brutal enemy threatens Poland, the heart of Jewish world-dispersion for nearly a thousand years, where over three million Jews dwell in loyalty to the Polish land and Nation. France, all the world's fatherland of liberty, faces the same menace. England has decided to make that fight her own; and we Jews shall, besides, never forget that for twenty years, England has been our partner in Zion. The Jewish nation's place is therefore on all fronts where these countries fight for those very foundations of society whose Magna Carta is our Bible.[2]

There had been no positive response to his appeal when Oscar Kraines, of the Socialist Zionist organization Hashomer Hatzair (Young Watchmen), interviewed Jabotinsky in his small Manhattan brownstone apartment on May 7, 1940. Jabotinsky said that he was expecting Patterson to join him to discuss the formation of a new Jewish Legion, not only to fight the Germans but to rescue Jewish refugees and get them safely into British-mandated Palestine. (See Appendix A for what was probably Jabotinsky's last interview.)

What is not well known is that on May 23, 1940, thirteen days after replacing Chamberlain as prime minister, Winston Churchill instructed Lord Lloyd, the colonial secretary, to withdraw British troops from Palestine and to arm and organize the Jews there for their defense as speedily as possible. He assured his advisers, "We can always prevent them from attacking the Arabs by our sea power, which cuts them off from the outer world, and by other friendly influences. On the other hand we cannot have them unarmed when the troops leave, as leave they must at a very early date."[3]

That same day, as Nazi planes and tanks threatened British and French forces with a devastating defeat, driving some four hundred thousand of them toward the seaside town of Dunkirk, from which there was no apparent means of escape, Churchill repeated the order, and again on June 2. Four days later, he complained of military opposition to his order and at the end of June 1940 of "difficulties" with two ministers, especially Lord Lloyd, whom Patterson knew to be anti-Zionist and pro-Arab. Faced with Dunkirk and obstructive ministers, Churchill failed to enforce his order.

About this time a new group joined the Patterson-Jabotinsky team to discuss the possibility of a Jewish Army with Lord Lothian, the pro-Zionist British ambassador to the United States (formerly, as Philip Kerr, he had been Lloyd George's secretary). Among the group were Dr. Benjamin Akzin, Dr. Ben-Zion Netanyahu (father of a future Israeli prime minister), and Elias Ginsburg, who had briefly shared a Jerusalem jail cell with Jabotinsky. They met on the fateful day of May 28, 1940, as the British began evacuating Allied troops from Dunkirk in an almost miraculous rescue operation. Lothian confided to the group that four influential members of the British war cabinet—Churchill, Amery, Duff-Cooper, and Sinclair— favored a Jewish Army. During their conversation Patterson described how such an army could be created, with which Lothian agreed. He cabled his approval to London with the suggestion that the British government announce its support of the plan, and arranged for Dr. Akzin to discuss details with the British military and air attachés in Washington. Soon after, Akzin met the British air attaché, who said that there already were a large number of Jewish airmen in the Royal Air Force and suggested that some of them could form the nucleus of a Jewish Air Force. Informed of the prospect of a Jewish Army, the Canadian government offered to open recruiting offices in Canada.

On June 7, 1940, Patterson again saw Lord Lothian, who agreed that as well as its military value, a Jewish Army would have a positive effect on American public opinion, The next day, Patterson wrote to a friend in Argentina that Lord Lothian not only "began to understand that Weizmann might be a Jewish edition of a Chamberlainite and an appeaser, and that it is no use relying on him for the formation of the army."[4] In fact, Weizmann would eventually discuss the Jewish Legion project with Churchill, who said he would support it. But other priorities delayed its adoption.

Patterson was in New York when Churchill replaced Chamberlain, and he expressed his delight in a note to Ilse Michelsohn, in London, on June 8, 1940: "I expect you are having plenty of nursing to do these days. Now that England has got rid of Chamberlain and the other defeatists she will really wake up and smash Hitler and the Nazis to pieces—this is quite certain. [He underlined "this is quite certain" twice.] Write and let me know what is happening. Yours sincerely, J. H. Patterson. P.S. Thank the good Lord that we have Winston Churchill."[5]

However, Churchill did not immediately live up to Patterson's expectations. When he and Jabotinsky cabled Churchill that the idea of a Jewish Army had aroused great interest in the United States and that he should clinch matters by announcing its creation, Churchill, with more pressing matters on his mind, sent a negative reply. Patterson couldn't believe it. "Can it be possible," he wrote to Lothian, "that the Cabinet is so blind that—at the moment—it deliberately turns down the offer of an American Jewish Army?"

Does he [Churchill] not realize that such a formation born on these shores (and trained in Canada), could have brought thousands of non-Jews also to its ranks and would have aroused a flame of enthusiasm throughout this country so fierce that it could have burnt to silence both Isolationists and Fifth Column men? . . .

During the last war when our fortunes were at a low ebb, Mr. Lloyd George had the brilliant idea of bringing the Jewish people to our side by creating a Jewish Legion and solemnly promising Palestine as their national homeland. On 6th of March last, Mr. Chamberlain did just the opposite. He forced an act through Parliament (Mr. Churchill opposing him) devouring Israel's heritage. Chamberlain paid no heed either to England's honour or the Bible's ominous warnings—you will find it in the second chapter of Jeremiah and the third verse, "all that devour Israel shall offend: evil shall come upon them saith the Lord." Lord Lloyd and his pro-Nazi minions in the Colonial Office have had their way and defeated the Jewish army scheme. [Lord Lloyd, the British colonial secretary, responsible for Palestine, was anti-Zionist and a pro-Arab supporter of Oswald Mosley's British Union of Fascists, at whose meetings he lectured.] But alas they have also brought England another step nearer her doom. . . .

You may rest assured if England continues her anti-Jewish policy, England will be destroyed. I have seen this coming for years and have fought against it tooth and nail because I loved England and hated to see her betrayed by a gang of pro-Nazi, neo-pagan permanent officials. . . . They, together with the brainless, spineless MacDonald's, Baldwins, and Chamberlains, have led her into the present perilous situation. . . .

Don't be afraid to tell Churchill. He is strong. A Jewish army and a Jewish Palestine would be of immense service to England. . . . The fate of England may be in your hands. Make use of every lever that will help. Please make no mistake—one Jewish mechanized division would be worth more than all the Arabs in the Near East.[6]

Afraid that Lothian might hesitate to send Churchill such an incendiary letter, Patterson made sure he got it, by airmailing a copy to the man now in charge of Britain's destiny.

In fact, Churchill was all for an army of the Jews in Palestine, complaining in *Their Finest Hour* of the "anti-Jewish policy which has been persisted in for years."

Should the war go heavily into Egypt, all [our] troops will have to be withdrawn and the position of the Jewish colonists will be one of the greatest danger. . . . If the Jews were properly armed our forces would become available, and there would be no danger of the Jews attacking the Arabs, because they are entirely dependent upon us and upon our command of the seas. I think it is little less than a scandal that at a time when we are fighting for our lives these very large forces should be immobilized in support of a policy which commends itself only to a section of the Conservative Party.

Among those opposed to his plan to bring the troops home from Palestine and to arm the Jewish colonists were two old friends, Leo Amery, at the India Office, and the secretary of state for the colonies, Lord Lloyd, "who was a convinced anti-Zionist and pro-Arab."[7]

On June 19, 1940, Patterson joined Jabotinsky for a second mass rally at New York's Manhattan Center, where Jabotinsky spoke of a Jewish Army of at least one hundred thousand men from all over the world to fight under British command, wherever needed. At the rally, Patterson declared: "If I were a Jew, nothing would give me greater pleasure than to show the German criminals that the Jews of today are capable of fighting just as their forefathers were, when in seven years of bitter warfare they shook the mighty Roman Empire to its very foundations." U.S. Senator Claude Pepper of Florida and Yale's president, Charles Seymour, among others, sent telegrams of support. And more than six thousand dollars was contributed to finance the recruiting drive. Afterward, Patterson and Jabotinsky cabled Alfred Duff-Cooper, the minister of information in Churchill's government, that the rally was a magnificent success, and the Canadian government had promised that with the British government's consent, "transit training camps [for a Jewish Army] would be allowed in Canada."[8]

A recruiting office was opened in Ottawa, Canada, where Jews and non-Jews volunteered to join the prospective Jewish Army. Among them were scores of German refugees; a veteran World War I German pilot; men with military training from Austria, Poland, Lithuania, Russia, and France, now living in the United States; American military officers; a British sergeant major; a judge from Los Angeles; and a journalist from St. Louis. That summer of 1940, Jabotinsky wrote to his wife, Yohana, that Patterson was at his side and a pillar of strength.

But he was not at his side on August 3, 1940, when the sixty-year-old commander of the Betar organization visited the Betar Camp at Hunter in the Catskills of New York to inspect a parade of young recruits. Jabotinsky's impassioned attempts to rescue his people had taken its toll. On returning to his room, he had a fatal heart attack. Unknown to Jabotinsky, the day he died his son, Eri, had been freed from a British prison in Palestine, where he had been held for smuggling in Jewish refugees.

Irishman Patterson, a Protestant, and Jabotinsky, a Russian Jew, had been close friends and political allies for twenty-four years, united by their mutual admiration, concern for the fate of the Jews, and determination to secure a Jewish homeland. Learning of Jabotinsky's death, Patterson wrote: "Vladimir Jabotinsky's last walk on earth was between the lines of young Betraim who awaited his arrival in Camp Betar in Hunter, New York. . . . I was not with him during the last hours of his life. But when I heard of it, I could not help saying to myself that if Jabotinsky were to choose the setting for his death, it would have been something after this manner, among his faithful young followers of Betar."[9]

To honor Jabotinsky all Tel Aviv's public buildings were draped in black. Israel's chief rabbi Hertzog called him "a miraculous personality." The Zionists Executive and the Weizmanns sent messages of condolence. The newspaper *Haboker* reported that "an eagle has fallen," and an opposition paper, *Davar,* that "the highly gifted violin that once seemed destined to play the first role in the orchestra of the Jewish revival has suddenly been shattered." Another opposition paper, *Ha'aretz,* conceded that "the whole House of Israel will mourn this highly gifted son. The history of the Zionist movement would be unwriteable without him."

Pallbearers included Patterson; author John Gunther; James McDonald, former high commissioner for refugees at the League of Nations and later the first American ambassador to Israel; book publisher William Ziff; and City College's Benjamin Akzin, later head of the Hebrew University Law School. Tens of thousands of New Yorkers lined the streets as the hearse moved through the Yiddish theater section of Second Avenue, and fifty cars and eight buses accompanied the hearse to the New Montefiore Cemetery at Farmingdale, Long Island.

Jabotinsky had written of Patterson that "in troubled time, he would smile the same Irish smile and one would at once forget generals, malaria and the enemy guns. It was the smile of a man who believes in the ultimate triumphs of inflexible determination [a belief Jabotinsky shared]. He would lift a glass and say 'It will be all right in the end. The Jews are a great people. Here's to trouble.' He believed that troubles were the essence of life, the mainspring of all progress."[10]

Patterson, now seventy-four, continued their campaign, speaking to mostly Jewish audiences in Buenos Aires, Uruguay, Chile, Brazil, Peru, as well as in Chicago and Blythe. He decided not to return to Britain, being too old to take an active part in the British war effort in any official capacity. So he sent for his wife, Frances, to join him in Chicago, where their son, Bryan, now a distinguished paleontologist, and his wife, were living. From there, Mrs. Patterson wrote to their friend Ilse Michelsohn on November 13, 1941: "I should love to have had you with me on the journey out here, but on the whole I got on wonderfully well and was very lucky to get here safely. The sea was rough and one big wave threw me over flat on my back!! There were lots of refugees on the ship. My good husband met me on arrival and brought me here."[11]

In Washington, D.C, addressing a conference of the Committee for a Jewish Army, the following month, Patterson said, "Mr. Churchill has blown a fresh breeze through Westminster. He bears a terrific load. Our hearts go out to him and we pray that like the great law-giver of old, his arm be supported until the battle is won."[12]

After a brief stay in Chicago, the Pattersons moved to a cottage at 1030 Coast Boulevard, in La Jolla, California. From there Patterson continued working for the Zionist cause. He kept in touch with his friends in Britain, especially Leo Amery, now secretary of state for India, who informed him that both the House of Commons and Lambeth Palace had been bombed. He had hardly settled into his new home when, in early December 1941, Patterson agreed to be cochairman with Pierre Van Passen of the "Committee for a Jewish Army for Stateless and Palestinian Jews."

Dutch-born Van Passen was a Christian Zionist whose book *Days of Our Lives* had described the 1919 pogrom against the Jews in Hebron. The group's first public announcement, in a full-page ad in the *New York Times* for January 5, 1942, was headed "Jews Fight for the Right to Fight." There were 133 signatures, among them those of the committee, three U.S.

senators, fourteen U.S. congressmen, and, among others, Louis Brom-
field, Melvyn Douglas, Bruno Frank, Waldo Frank, Ben Hecht, Reinhold
Niebuhr, Abraham I. Sachar, Lowell Thomas, and Paul Tillich, as well as
Jabotinsky's son, Eri. The ad was republished in the *New York Sun, Washington Post, Philadelphia Record, Philadelphia Evening Bulletin, Yiddish Forward,* and other newspapers.

Writer Ben-Ami, an active supporter of the committee, explained why
at the time the idea of a Jewish Army aroused less than massive public
support:

> The reports about the Nazis' attacks on Jews were hidden away as small
> news items in the back pages with the religious news, next to the obituar-
> ies, as if Hitler himself had chosen the location. Since 1933, owing to the
> Nazis' worldwide propaganda, the word "Jew" connoted the lowest spe-
> cies of animals, creatures that only knew persecution and deserved no
> better than pity. The non-Jew world was tired of reading about their plight:
> it was not news anymore. The only place Jews were mentioned loud and
> clear was in the German-American bund meetings, by Father Coughlin,
> Joe McWilliams and other anti-Semites. In good company, the word "Jew"
> was spoken quietly, the way it had been in Vienna in early 1938.[13]

On December 7, 1941, after the Japanese attack on Pearl Harbor, the
United States joined the Allies. Three months later, on March 6, 1942,
after Malaya and Singapore had fallen to Japanese troops, an FBI agent
sent a strictly confidential memo to Director Hoover, headed "Efforts
of the Zionists to Arm the Jews in Palestine," which noted Patterson's
speech at a fund-raising meeting in a Hollywood studio. The meeting,
which attracted, among many other celebrities, Charlie Chaplin and gossip columnist Hedda Hopper, had been organized by Hillel Kook and
Ben Hecht. Kook used the pseudonym Peter Bergson so as not to embar-
rass his uncle, the chief rabbi of Jerusalem, or endanger his family, who
were living in British-mandated Palestine. Bergson, who had represented
the Irgun in Poland, had cofounded the Committee for a Jewish Army.
The first page of the FBI memo to Hoover reproduces a telegram sent to
movie big shots Ben Hecht, David O. Selznick, Martin Quigley, and Nun-
ally Johnson. It reads:

This . . . is your pass to hear Senator PEPPER, Colonel PATTERSON, of the British Army, and other experts speak on a matter of crucial importance to Allied victories in the Near East. Two hundred thousand able bodied men are clamoring to bear arms for the Allied cause. They are frozen battalions. They are to date denied their place on the battlefield. They will receive these arms if the carefully selected group that has been invited to this meeting can be convinced that the cause already championed by Secretary of War STIMSON, Secretary of Navy KNOX, Rear Admiral JARNELL, and many Senators and Congressmen is right. If the facts that the speakers will present justify our becoming champions of the warriors without arms, we may be a great help in averting the danger, if Egypt, Syria, and Palestine will go the way of Malaya and Singapore. Let us know whether you can be at Twentieth Century Fox Studios at 8:30 P.M., Tuesday, the twenty-fourth. Phone MARION HAYMAN, Gladstone 1131. Space is limited, and we don't want to waste seats.

The memo reported that an informant had advised the FBI that "this meeting was part of the Zionist movement . . . the international idea that the Jews should be allowed to fight as a battalion on the battlefield. The British Government has opposed this because of the Arab question."[14]

On February 25, 1942, a special agent spoke to another informant, who described the meeting as an attempt to get Congress "to advocate arming the Jews in Jerusalem, so they could fight against the Axis."

However . . . after talks by Senator PEPPER and several others, an individual identified as Colonel JOHN HENRY PATTERSON, a retired British Army Officer, got up and instead of . . . telling what wonderful soldiers the Jews would make. . . . He told how the [British] Government had broken its promises on numerous occasions, and then knocked the Jews as well. At this point, DAVID O. SELZNIC [sic] got up . . . remarked that . . . they were confusing the issue, and sat down. HARRY WARNER, then got up and said that he did not plan to attend any meeting if it was going to divulge [sic] into an attack against a friendly country . . . wondered if PATTERSON might not be one of the Irishmen who was trying to foment disunity between this country and England. . . . [The informant] stated that one PETER BERGSON . . . [was] touring the country trying to interest the Americans to request the British to arm the 200,000 Jews in Palestine. . . . He recalled that an editorial had appeared in the New York Times against the movement. . . .

[W]ith reference to Major [sic] PATTERSON, he stated that he was an ex-British Army Officer who talked along lines that it was a mistake for the English not to arm the Jews in Palestine. . . . SELZNIC, although his name appeared on the invitation, disclaimed any part of the movement. . . . [The informant] said, as he understood it, PATTERSON was not pro-Axis, but just disgusted with the way England was running the present war.[15]

After the meeting an article in the *Hollywood Reporter* suggested that the movie industry should avoid controversial subjects, "and particularly should not allow any meetings to be held on property owned by various companies which were of a political nature . . . that . . . meetings on movie property, involving prominent figures in the industry, with a discussion of relationships between England and the United States, might have unhealthy repercussions."[16]

Patterson biographer Patrick Streeter gives a more discerning and colorful account of the event, reporting how Senator Pepper gave a low-key speech, stressing the fine traditions of Jewish culture, followed by Patterson, who was greeted by cheers.

[Patterson] looked splendid in his uniform and decorations, standing tall and dignified. . . . He was addressing a conservative American audience who were very pro-British. But Patterson launched forth on an anti-British tirade, highlighting her anti-Semitism and the failure to honour the Balfour Declaration. The speech went down like a lead balloon. . . . Boos and catcalls came from the audience. Sam Goldwyn stood and shouted "Sit Down! Sit Down!" People headed for the door and one phoned the FBI to say there were goings on at Twentieth Century Fox and that Patterson was probably a Nazi agent. Hecht and Bergson sat uncomfortably in their seats, while Selznick fumed. But Patterson continued unabashed and finally sat down in dead silence. Both Bergson and Hecht were among the subsequent speakers and they did their best to salvage the evening.[17]

Ben Hecht recalled in his autobiography that actor "Burgess Meredith spoke in favor of the Jewish army, and then Peter Bergson, and Miriam Heyman, and I."

Out of the oratorical free-for-all that started up in the audience after I had done talking, the voice of Hedda Hopper, the movie columnist, sounded.

"We're here to contribute to a cause," Miss Hopper said firmly. "I'll start the contributions with a check for three hundred dollars." Whereupon, despite the shock of Colonel Patterson's speech, and the confused objectives offered by Pepper, Bergson and myself, a wave of largess swept over the audience.

A hundred thousand dollars was pledged but only nine thousand collected. Hecht thought it strange "that the cause of justice to the Jews should burn so brightly in the heart of a Britisher who was no Jew—Colonel Patterson."

> It was odd, also, that this Britisher with a lifetime record of service in his country's armies should attack his own people when they were fighting so desperately. Then the thought came to me that it was on his unprejudiced sense of justice that the greatness of the England I admired was founded. There had always been British intrigue and hypocrisy in their dealings with the lands they occupied. But there had always been voices like this to keep justice a part of the Anglo-Saxon record—Patterson, Pitt, Burke.[18]

Even so, Patterson had made a serious miscalculation. As Hecht noted, it had been the wrong time and place to attack Britain, fighting for its life—alone, against a monstrous regime—and regarded as heroic by most of the Hollywood community. Fortunately, the controversial meeting got little if any press coverage, and the work of the Committee for a Jewish Army began to win over American politicians, many if not most of them non-Jews.

British members of the House of Lords headed by Lord Strabolgi also supported the call for a Jewish Army, especially after June 1942, when Tobruk fell and German general Erwin Rommel's victorious North African troops threatened Palestine.

Isaiah Berlin, a British Jew and an academic, working in the British Embassy in Washington, D.C., reported to Churchill that "the simplicity and humanity of the demand that Jews fight as Jews has many allies in the States. The British Government's arguments against a Jewish fighting force had been rebutted too often in the Zionist press to retain any plausibility." When Berlin was asked to comment on secret British intelligence assessments of the Jewish underground activity in Palestine, he replied that the assessments were both "anti-Semitic and nonsensical," because they stated that "on the one hand the Jews must not be allowed to form a Jewish Brigade to fight on the side of the Allies because they were hopeless fighters, and on the other, they must not be armed, lest they turn their guns against the British."[19]

But Churchill found a new excuse for delay—the British lacked the equipment for a Jewish Army. True or not, it was a response that added to Patterson's growing disillusionment with the British leader. If anything, it energized his own active concern for the Jewish people. He was founder of the American Friends of a Jewish Palestine, chairman and military adviser of the Committee to Save the Jewish People of Europe, chairman of the American Resettlement Committee for Uprooted European Jewry, president of the New Zionist League of America, supporter of the Emergency Committee to Save the Jewish People of Europe, and a member of both the Jabotinsky Publications Committee and the American Palestine Jewish League.

On his seventy-fifth birthday on November 10, 1942, Jewish groups and individuals in Palestine, England, Argentine, and several U.S. cities sent him friendly greetings. Joe Mirelman forwarded a thousand dollars collected from Patterson's friends in Buenos Aires, from which Patterson sent one hundred dollars to Eliahu Ben-Horin for Zionist causes. Ben-Horin, in turn, sent it to the Jabotinsky Publications Committee, which translated and distributed Jabotinsky's writings. Patterson's fellow Zionist and friend Ben-Zion Netanyahu, editor of the magazine *Zionews*, proposed to celebrate Patterson's birthday by dedicating a special issue to the Irishman. Patterson's counterproposal was to highlight Britain's failure to honor its pledges. Not to be deterred, Netanyahu put a portrait of Patterson on the cover and described him in an editorial as "the fighting Irishman who gave up the best of his life for the redemption of the Jewish people— an outstanding example of . . . a righteous man of the world." Journalist Ben-Horin wrote, "No other Gentile, except perhaps Josiah Wedgwood [a British member of Parliament], has demonstrated the same measure of faithfulness and devotion to the Zionist cause." Patterson wrote for his birthday issue that he was ready to take up arms again.[20]

Two weeks later, on November 25, 1942, one of the first horrifying accounts of the Holocaust, headed "Two Million Jews Slain," appeared in the *Washington Post*. It was easy to miss—as it was published on page 6. The source was World Jewish Congress chairman Rabbi Stephen Wise, who had been informed by the U.S. State Department that the Nazis were planning to annihilate all of Europe's Jews.[21] Patterson's committee responded by publishing a two-page spread in the *New York Times* and papers throughout the country, titled "Proclamation of the Moral Rights of Stateless and Palestine Jews." It read in part:

> We shall no longer witness with pity alone, and with passive sympathy, the calculated extermination of the ancient Jewish people by the barbarous Nazis.
>
> We recognize the right of these Jews to return to their place among the free peoples of the earth, so that the remnants of tortured Israel . . . may take up life as a free people . . . to fight as present fellow partners in the war. . . . Hundreds of thousands of Jews have perished as helpless martyrs in the war which Hitler is waging on Christian civilization. . . . No other people have suffered, comparatively, so much loss of life.[22]

Alongside the proclamation was the drawing of a Jewish fighter on a battlefield, holding the body of an old bearded Jew in his arms. It was signed by more than three thousand notable Americans and European exiles, among them Sholem Asch, Taylor Caldwell, Aaron Copland, Melvyn Douglas, Herbert Hoover, Clare Boothe Luce, Eugene O'Neill, and Bruno Walter. When neither the British nor the American governments was moved to action, Patterson's committee began to prepare a huge pageant, created largely by Ben Hecht, to take place in Manhattan's Madison Square Garden, titled *We Will Never Die* and dedicated to the two million Jews already slaughtered by the Nazis.

Meanwhile, Peter Bergson offered Patterson one thousand dollars to be military adviser to the Committee for a Jewish Army, reminding Patterson that seven years previously Bergson had proudly paraded with the Irgun when the Irishman had reviewed them. Patterson accepted the post but not the money, explaining that he never wanted his opponents to be able to accuse him of being in the pay of the Jews.

March 9, 1943, a month later, was the first night of the pageant to bring the plight of the Jews to public notice. It drew a record audience of some forty thousand, after which the pageant toured the country, ending in Washington, D.C., where it was seen by President Franklin Roosevelt's wife, Eleanor, six U.S. Supreme Court justices, and some three hundred congressmen and senators. But still neither the British nor the American government was moved to rescue the endangered Jews in Europe, or to support a Jewish Army to help in that effort.

In September, Patterson came to the support of a friend and fellow Zionist, Eliahu Ben-Horin, whose *The Middle East Crossroads of History* had been given a pasting in the *New York Times Book Review* by Princeton professor of Semitic literature Philip Hitti. In his letter to the editor Patterson characterized Hitti as an anti-Zionist Syrian-born Arab "and a vehement protagonist of pan-Arabism."

> Mr. Hitti is especially concerned to refute Ben-Horin's appraisal of the Arabs' role in World Wars 1 and 2. I can, however, vouch for the fact that the Palestine Arabs never lifted a finger to help the Allies. On the contrary, they hindered us whenever they safely could, by looting from our lines and carrying information to the enemy. The Arabs outside, under Feisal, and Lawrence [of Arabia], gave a somewhat nebulous support for our extreme right flank far beyond the Jordan, but, according to Lawrence himself, even this assistance was but sporadic and only obtained by heavy payments in gold—millions of pounds sterling—to the Arab Sheiks. The Jews, on the contrary, gave thousands of their men, and millions of their money to help the Allied cause to victory.

Patterson pointed out that in the present world war, the Arabs throughout the Middle East had refrained from giving any assistance to the Allies.

> On the contrary, they have endeavored to further a Nazi victory and have even openly exulted over the prospect of stabbing England in the back the moment it was safe enough. Of course, your reviewer gives quite a different picture—but unfortunately not a true one. . . .
> Mr. Hitti writes of Pan-Arabism and political Pan-Islamism as being neither a myth nor a bogy. . . . My own views correspond with those of

the late Colonel Lawrence, whose well-known writings clearly testify that Pan-Arabism and Pan-Islamism are mere moonshine. The same view is held by the great lover of the Arabs—the late Miss Gertrude Bell, who, when I was in Baghdad, was advisor to the Iraq Government. In writing on Mr. Hitti's own homeland in her book, "The Desert and the Sown," she states: "Of what value are the Pan-Arabic associations and the inflammatory leaflets that they issue from foreign printing presses? The answer is easy. They are worth nothing at all. There is no nation of Arabs. The Syrian country is inhabited by Arab-speaking races all eager to be at each others throats." Again, your reviewer endeavors to ridicule the idea that the Arab is ruled by political cliques, but in Palestine this certainly is the case. Has Mr. Hitti never heard that the notorious ex-Mufti of Jerusalem and his gang of cut-throats murdered hundreds and hundreds of law-abiding Palestine Arabs because they refused to come under his criminal banner and massacre unoffending Jews? Political self-seeking Effendis have for centuries been responsible for keeping the miserable fellah in a state of perpetual serfdom and abject poverty.

Where Mr. Hitti's antagonism to the book becomes overtly open is in connection with Ben-Horin's advocacy of several transfers of population, resulting in a concentration of Christians in Lebanon, of Jews in Palestine and Transjordan, and of Moslems (from Palestine and the Lebanon) into under-populated Iraq. [This idea led to President Herbert Hoover's transfer plan of 1945.]

Patterson, the ardent Zionist, "could not refrain from smiling at Mr. Hitti's 'strongest' argument against the plan—namely, that the Arabs got Palestine 'as a gift from Allah that cannot be relinquished without compromising their faith.' Is Mr. Hitti ignorant of the fact that this same Allah gave Palestine to the Jews 2,000 years before the Moslem faith was revealed to the Arabs?"[23]

In response, Professor Hitti stated that Colonel Patterson "raises no questions that were not adequately treated in my review—every word of which stands—and contests no correction of any of the few historical and geographical mistakes listed in that review by way of illustrating the scholarship of the book's author. . . . [T]o a student of Oriental affairs, even in their elementary stage, the pages of the book abound in historical, geographical, and other varieties of mistakes." He denied that he was "a vehement protagonist of Pan-Arabism" a subject of which I treated but once, and that objectively and detachedly in a learned journal "The American Historical Review," July issue: [which] the American Historical Association, at whose request the paper was prepared, is reprinting it in a special volume and in which there is the only reference I ever made in writing to Zionism. But what I may or may not be is irrelevant to the merits or demerits of Mr. Ben-Horin's work, which as recent developments seem to indicate, must have been intended as a spearhead to a highly-financed nationwide propaganda campaign.[24]

Strangely, Professor Hitti did not attempt to rebut any of Patterson's comments about the behavior of the Arabs in both world wars, the ex-mufti's activities, or to which people God first promised Palestine.

Later that year Patterson sent an optimistic telegram to Betar on the group's twentieth anniversary, praising Churchill as "our grim and steadfast Prime Minister," and quoting Churchill's confident prediction: "Assuredly on the day of victory, the Jew's suffering and his part in the struggle will not be forgotten. Help is coming: mighty forces are arming on your behalf. Have faith. Have hope. Deliverance is sure."[25] Churchill had reason for his optimism. Led by the American general Dwight Eisenhower, an Allied invasion—the greatest in history—to liberate Europe from Nazi occupation was under way.

14

Victory,
1944–1948

LIVING IN CALIFORNIA in 1944 with his ailing wife, Patterson had mixed emotions about the progress of the war: buoyed by the successful Allied D-day landings, but incensed by reports of British efforts to keep Jewish refugees out of Palestine—and even return those Jews they caught to camps in Germany. To Patterson the unwavering Zionist, Palestine was their country, revealed in the Bible and promised to them by the British government. Palestinian Jews had helped to free it from the Turks in World War I, under his command. And now tens of thousands of their children were fighting with the Allies. What more must they do to reclaim their ancient homeland?

In the late summer of 1944, thirty-seven Jews in the British forces—all volunteers—parachuted behind enemy lines, hoping to join partisans in Europe and to radio enemy positions back to London. They were also expected to lead escaping Allied troops and threatened Jews to safety. Among them was a woman poet, Hannah Sennes. Soon after landing in Slovakia and crossing the border into her native Hungary, she was betrayed to the Nazis. The Gestapo tortured her in a Budapest prison, but she did not divulge her mission or her secret radio code. In the winter of 1944, like seven of her fellow paratroopers who were also captured, she was executed by a firing squad. Ten others who escaped capture joined the resistance in France, Austria, Bulgaria, and northern Italy.

Even had the Haganah, the Irgun, and the Stern gang known of such small-scale and often doomed British attempts to rescue European

Jews, they were too incensed by the British policy to give them credit for anything. The British were denying Jewish refugees a safe haven in Palestine, causing the deaths of hundreds of other European Jews trying to reach Palestine in dilapidated ships that eventually sank, or forcing others who reached Palestine to return to the horrors and desolation of Europe.

The Haganah devised a plan to defeat or at least draw attention to this heartless policy. When a ship, the *Patria*, arrived at the Palestinian shore loaded with illegal immigrants, the Haganah decided to prevent its return to Europe by disabling it with a bomb. But someone miscalculated, and the explosion killed 259 aboard. At least part of the plan worked: the British were blamed for the disaster, and High Commissioner Sir Harold McMichael felt bound to allow the survivors to enter the country. But he warned that all future illegal Jewish immigrants would be sent to holding camps on the island of Mauritius, to be returned after the war to their respective countries of origin. As Irgun leader Menachem Begin, Jabotinsky's political heir, saw it, the British administration in Palestine "hands our brothers over to Hitler." The response of this equally dedicated Zionist—a tough survivor of Soviet prison camps—was to declare war on the British in Palestine. "A war to the end. [And] this is our demand: immediate transfer of power in Eretz Israel to a provisional Hebrew government. We shall fight. Every Jew in the homeland will fight. The God of Israel, the Lord of Hosts, will aid us. There will be no retreat. Freedom—or death."[1] Many Palestinian Jews not only rejected Begin's battle cry: by 1945 some fifty-two thousand of them were volunteers in the British armed forces. Jewish commando units under British command also fought in Libya and Ethiopia and were involved in the seizing of Syria and Lebanon from the Vichy French, among them Moshe Dayan.

In Palestine itself, the Haganah kept its agreement to cooperate with the British during the war against Hitler. Its members even exposed the illegal Irgun and Stern gang "freedom fighters," who then faced prison and sometimes execution. Despite their small numbers these underground fighters inflicted considerable mayhem: blowing up British immigration and income tax offices in Jerusalem, Tel Aviv, and Haifa, and killing several policemen.

When the Stern gang's attempt to assassinate Sir Harold McMichael, the British high commissioner in Palestine, killed only his aide de camp, they chose another target. Two young Stern gang fighters, Eliahu Hakin and Eliahu Bet-Zouri, set their sights on Lord Moyne, British minister of state in Cairo. A pro-Arab, anti-Zionist, he opposed a Jewish Army, and was a leading exponent of the current British policy in Palestine. He had once shocked Ben-Gurion by suggesting that, after the British had defeated the Germans, instead of Palestine the Jews could settle in East Prussia. The two assassins fatally shot Moyne outside his house on November 6, 1944, then tried to escape on bicycles. They were caught and eventually hanged.

Churchill was so distressed by his friend's murder that the Zionists almost lost one of their most powerful and staunch supporters. He told a shocked House of Commons: "If our dreams for Zionism are to end in the smoke of the assassin's pistol, if our labours for the future are to produce a new set of gangsters worthy of Nazi Germany, then many like myself will have to consider the position we have maintained so consistently and so long. If there is to be any hope of a possible and successful future in Zionism, all these wicked activities must cease and those responsible for them must be destroyed root and branch."[2]

Ever loyal to the cause, Patterson countered Churchill's comments in a full-page ad in the *New York Post*. His "Challenge to Churchill" reads in part: "The British Prime Minister's recent tirade, bluntly threatening the liquidation of Zionism unless the Jews crush the 'Terrorist gangs' compels me to bring to the attention of the American people some of the cardinal facts which are directly related to the tragedy of Palestine and the Jews. . . . I deeply regret to note that facts speak louder than words. Speak louder, clearly and overwhelmingly against Britain's rule in Palestine. I also wish to state that Mr. Churchill shares in this responsibility." Patterson went on to accuse Churchill of driving the first nail into the Zionist coffin by excluding Transjordan from the proposed Jewish homeland and giving it to Arabs. He characterized Britain's mandate as "one long outrage," and predicted that reprisals were inevitable. He concluded, "Before it is too late I appeal to Britain, as I appeal to America: make good the pledges given by God and men to the people of Israel."[3]

Reading the ad in the *New York Post*, a former corporal in the Zion Mule Corps, Nehemiah Yehuda, living in Brooklyn, grabbed his pen to tell Patterson that his time in the Dardanelles with the Mule Corps had been one of the most exciting times of his life, adding, "Palestine was and is ours. God give you strength for years to come to enjoy a Jewish Commonwealth in Eretz Israel."[4]

During the last months of the war, the British War Office finally adopted Patterson's views, approving the formation of a Jewish Infantry Brigade. It was commanded by a Canadian-born Jew, Brigadier Benjamin, with the Star of David as its flag. More than five thousand men volunteered for the brigade, and in early March 1945, flanked by Free Italian and Polish units, went into action against the Germans on the Italian front, south of the Senio River. Charging with fixed bayonets, they sent an elite German parachute division into a hasty retreat. Those Germans who surrendered were dismayed to find that they had been captured by Jews, some with relatives who had been victims of Nazi atrocities.

On April 9, the Jewish Infantry Brigade held a bridgehead on the far bank of the Senio River, near Bologna, against fierce resistance, then went on the attack. Thirty Jews were killed in the fighting, and seventy were wounded. Twenty-one officers and enlisted men were decorated for bravery, and seventy-eight were mentioned in dispatches. American general Mark Clark congratulated Brigadier Benjamin and his men for their part in the offensive around Lake Comacchio and south of Route 9 that forced the Germans into unconditional surrender.

By the spring of 1945, although the end of the war was in sight, it was hardly a time of rejoicing for the Pattersons. Frances was suffering from crippling arthritis, and John Henry was having heart trouble. Although he constantly worried about his wife, he wrote to his friend Netanyahu that he never let his own difficulties depress him. And, despite his ill-health, he traveled to Manhattan to speak at a dinner held by the New Zionist Organization at the Commodore Hotel, where President Woodrow Wilson's navy secretary, Josephus Daniels, was the chief speaker. The New Zionist Organization paid for a nurse to care for Frances while Patterson was away, and although he was not getting his army pension—because of wartime postal delays—he accepted only his expenses.

The day after his arrival, on March 12, Patterson wrote to his wife in La Jolla:

> I arrived here safely last evening at 6 p.m. Had a good trip. I saw Bea and Alan [their daughter-in-law and grandson] at Chicago. They dined with me and both looked well and cheerful. Alan is quite a nice child, well behaved and good-looking. . . . I was met by the Zionists at Chicago and here in New York. They are looking after me A.1. I am to speak over the radio on the 18th but do not know if they will hear me in California. . . . Hope all goes well with you. . . . Love to your brave self.

While in Manhattan he also spoke on Radio WHN, stressing that an international conference under way on the postwar settlement should include a Jewish representative. On that same trip Patterson joined Jabotinsky's widow, Yohana, at a reunion lunch of the Jewish Legion at the Commodore Hotel on April 6, 1945. He was still in Manhattan when his wife fell in their La Jolla home and was unable to get up. For some inexplicable reason the nurse did not find her for thirty-six hours. Frances was hospitalized with pneumonia.

Both Pattersons had been anxiously awaiting news of their soldier son, Bryan, who had been reported missing during the Battle of the Bulge. As Frances began to recover from her illness, there was good news. Bryan was safe, as a prisoner of war. Showing that he was his father's son, he had made two escape attempts.

After Germany's defeat there was still a food shortage in Britain, and Patterson sent food parcels to several of his friends there: the Needhams of Worthing got a box of fruit, the MacDiarminds dates, the Collings-Wells a cake, the Fleetwood-Wilsons candies for their children. Parcels of food went to "Brownie," a Cavalry Club employee, and to Millie Pope, his housekeeper at Iver.

With Churchill's Conservative government defeated and Clement Attlee's Labour Party in office, its blunt-spoken, heavyweight foreign secretary, Ernest Bevin, gave his controversial interpretation of the Balfour Declaration. He insisted that it did not promise the Jews a state in Palestine, but merely a homeland, which meant, of course, that if he had his way this "homeland" would inevitably have a permanent Jewish minority dominated by Arabs. Incensed, Ben-Zion Netanyahu asked Patterson to use his "craft, skill and fiery indignation" to persuade the new British government that the Jews were entitled to use all means of warfare to fight for their liberty.[5] Patterson's health was failing, but he willingly obliged, traveling to make speeches to attract more to the cause, and to energize supporters, working at times close to exhaustion.

The following year, Ben-Zion Netanyahu's wife, Celia, gave birth to a son they named Jonathan, after Patterson. Invited to be his godfather, he gave the infant a silver cup inscribed, "To my darling godson, Jonathan, from your godfather, John Henry Patterson." (Jonathan was killed at Entebbe, Uganda, as a thirty-one-year-old lieutenant colonel in the Israeli Army while leading a successful raid on July 4, 1976, to rescue Jewish hostages. Jonathan's brother, Benjamin, became the ninth prime minister of Israel, serving from 1996 to 1999).

What Patterson probably never knew—but would have thrilled him had he known—was the activity of the Jewish Infantry Brigade in southern Europe after the war. As its troops moved through various northern Italian cities, the local Italian Jews, spotting the Magen David on the soldiers' vehicles and uniforms, greeted them with astonishment, pride, and delight.

Nothing matched the emotional response they got from thousands of concentration-camp survivors on the Italian-Austrian border. A brigade member, Hanoch Bartov, recalled, "This is something which I think if I live a thousand years I will not be able to forget, because their reaction was as if they saw the Messiah. First of all they didn't believe, then they started to physically touch us, if we are real." A concentration-camp survivor, Lisa Derman, said, "We cried. We screamed. We jumped. We kissed one another. Can you imagine, from the ghettos and the fires, to see Jewish soldiers?"[6]

After sharing their food, clothing, and bedding with some of the destitute remnants of European Jewry, the brigade set about saving their lives. Knowing that Allied commanders intended to ship them back to their former homelands, where hundreds were still being killed in renewed anti-Semitic pogroms, members of the brigade—who were also undercover members of the Haganah—contacted Zionist activists and devised an ingenious plan to rescue as many Jews as possible. Commandeering their own well-armed trucks and other vehicles, they put the survivors in British army uniforms, gave them false identity papers, bribed border guards, and drove the refugees to secret staging posts in Italy. There, boats were waiting to brave the blockade and take them to Palestine. At first, British and Commonwealth troops and their commanders helped, too, by looking the other way. The British Jewish Relief Committee and the American Joint Distribution Committee in Rome, also trying to help the refugees, were overwhelmed by the thousands needing assistance.

Some members of the Jewish Brigade went AWOL to hunt down SS Nazis and their collaborators responsible for atrocities in the camps. As one brigade officer explained, "Our kith and kin had been slaughtered and revenge was very much in the air. It was the SS men we wanted to get our hands on. The higher the rank the better. The SS covered their indelible identification with plaster and bandages, but they were found. Our fellows stopped Germans and made them lift their shirts and then . . . "[7] He had no need to elaborate. They eventually killed more than two hundred men.

A third group smuggled into Palestine arms and ammunition, stolen from military depots throughout Europe. As the British continued to forcibly prevent Jews from entering Palestine, leaders of the Haganah, the Irgun, and the Stern gang agreed to protest through joint military operations, at least for a time. They sank two police boats, bombed railroad tracks and trains, and blew up police headquarters in Haifa and Jerusalem. Their bombing of British headquarters at the King David Hotel on July 22, 1946, after a phoned-in warning, killed ninety-one and injured forty-one, among them former members of the Jewish Legion.

At midnight on October 30, 1946, three young members of the Irgun packed two suitcases with explosives, took a taxi to the British Embassy in Rome, set the time fuses to give them plenty of time to get away, and left the cases in the main entrance. The early-morning explosions demolished the central part of the building and injured two Italians walking home from a nearby nightclub.

Patterson had been unable to follow the news about Palestine. Bedridden with pneumonia that almost killed him, he was out of action for several months in a California hospital. Meanwhile, his wife, Frances, had been moved to a nursing home. Their son, Bryan, freed from a prisoner-of-war camp, had rejoined his wife, Beatrice, and son, Alan, in Chicago and resumed his career. Despite the lack of a university degree he eventually became a professor of vertebrate paleontology at Harvard. A friendly man with a good sense of humor, he was to have a brilliant career as a paleontologist, internationally recognized, traveling throughout the United States, South America, Asia, and—in the steps of his father—Kenya, for his groundbreaking work.

When the seventy-seven-year-old Patterson recovered from pneumonia, he was too frail to care for himself, and his longtime Zionist friends Mr. and Mrs. Marion Travis invited him to stay in their Bel Air mansion. From there he wrote to Netanyahu, "I was for months with Nurses and Doctors, night and day, and only for the care I got from Mr. and Mrs. Travis, I would now be down among the dead men."[8]

Asked by the editor of the *South African Jewish Herald* to send a message for the 1946 New Year issue, he replied that the Irgun's enemies were not in the Holy Land but in Britain's Whitehall. Citing Ireland's successful fight for freedom as an example, he suggested that firepower should be directed at British bureaucrats. Netanyahu was so pleased with this response that he sent copies to London's *Jewish Standard*, South America's *Idea Sionista*, and New Zionist papers in Italy and China. Patterson biographer Patrick Streeter remarks that as Patterson got older, the wilder were his statements. But his proposal to attack bureaucrats was in line with his long-held beliefs that some British officials were traitors for trying to subvert the Balfour Declaration and that attacking them would be a patriotic act.

When this writer asked Patterson's daughter-in-law, Beatrice, if Patterson ever acknowledged that as a British officer, he had divided loyalties, she replied, "Of course."

"I take it then," I said, "that he felt more loyalty for the Irish and Jewish freedom fighters than for the British establishment opposed to them."

"I think he was more for the little man," she said. "The common man."[9]

Patterson had once clearly explained his views when he blasted British bureaucrats as "a blind junta in the Colonial Office in London, nourished by anti-Jewish prejudices," working for "the most inept government Britain had since 1776 [the year that the British lost America]."

I am speaking from intimate knowledge going back to 1918 when I say that the policy of sabotaging the Jewish National Home, of rousing Arab terror, of flaunting an Arab nationalist cause in Palestine, was deliberate on the part of certain key British officials misusing their position to deceive their own government and people. The chief responsibility for the Palestine betrayal lies squarely on the shoulders of British officials who in betraying the Jews also betrayed the British people.

The Jewish aid to the British Empire was indeed responsible for the charter of Jewish nationhood in their ancient homeland which was embodied in the famous Balfour Declaration issued in 1917. At that time we were in dire peril on all fronts. Lord Balfour, Lloyd George and others, with a blare of trumpets, blazoned forth to the people of Israel the world over the promise of the restoration of a Jewish state in Palestine. The Jews responded nobly to the dazzling bait. A Jewish Legion was soon fighting in Palestine under Allenby. Jewish soldiers died in Palestine in the belief that they gave their lives so that Israel might live once again in the land of their forefathers.

Again and again I witnessed these gallant men of Zion going to their death singing joyously. They said they were glad to die for England because she had promised to help them rebuild their old homeland. These Jewish soldiers lie side by side with their British comrades in the great military cemeteries throughout Palestine, but no Arab will be found there. For no Palestinian Arab lifted a finger during the war to drive out the Turkish oppressors.

During the war, when Jewish soldiers gave their lives to liberate Palestine, the Arabs of Palestine fought and spied for our enemies and their taskmasters, for the Turks. They murdered and looted in our back areas where they could do so with safety for themselves. The fellaheen [peasants] of the Holy Land did not know of such a thing as Arab nationalism and when Colonel Lawrence, aided by millions in gold, induced the Arabs of the Hedjaz to revolt against the Turks by holding out hopes for future Arab independence, the Arabs of Palestine remained quite indifferent to this temptation. It meant nothing to them.

Similarly, the Arab leaders in the surrounding territories accepted as a matter of course that Palestine should become the National Home of the Jews. Faced with the hope of independence over a huge expanse of territory, over 1,150,000 square miles, with a population of 10 to 14 million people (or, if Egypt be included in the calculation, territory of 1,500,000 square miles and a population of 24 to 28 million people), the fate of Palestine did not bother them. They never considered it an Arab country properly speaking. This attitude was made more natural by the traditional contempt with which the desert Arab looked upon the fellaheen of Palestine, whom he did not consider as of the same racial stock.

More than once I have had the pleasure of meeting the late King Feisal, the great spokesman for the Arabs in the Western world, and the son of King Hussein of the Hejaz. He was a noble soul, kind and patient, just. We spoke of Palestine, and he expressed his pleasure that the Jewish people were returning to it and prospering in their own homeland. Never did King Feisal drop a hint to me that the Jews were poaching on Arab rights in Palestine.[10]

The Irgun needed no encouragement from Patterson to continue their attacks. On March 1, 1946, its members bombed a British officers club in Palestine, killing 20 and wounding 30. That same month, the Stern gang destroyed two trains, robbed a Tel Aviv bank, and set thirty thousand tons of oil ablaze at a Haifa refinery. The most spectacular event was the attack on Acre prison, which held hundreds of underground fighters and was believed to be impregnable. On April 16, 1947, several Irgun fighters were hanged there. Less than three weeks later, the Irgun fought their way in and freed 251 inmates—131 Arabs and 120 Jews.

Though Patterson was seriously ill, he followed the news of the fighting in Palestine on the radio and in the newspapers. Because he was not receiving his military pension regularly, Marion Travis and his wife took care of his finances, and he agreed to leave them the royalties on his books and other properties. The Travises had once divorced, and although Patterson was not the cause, during that time Mrs. Travis and Patterson had an affair. But when she and her ex-husband remarried after four or five years, deeply appreciative of the work Patterson had done and was still doing for the Zionist cause, the couple allowed Mrs. Travis's wheelchair-bound former lover to stay in their house, where both treated him like a close friend. As the Travises' daughter Elaine Bloomberg told the author:

Patterson was very ill the last few years of his life and my parents were very, very kind to him, and I always felt it was ironic that my father was taking care of him in those years. I thought my parents were very gracious to him and especially in the circumstance.

They treated him beautifully. My brother, Roy, had just married an English girl and they were honeymooning at the house. And she had to get up every morning to make sure he had his breakfast tea served just the way he wanted it. He was very particular. He had a wheelchair and the little granddaughters would go up to him and say, "When are you going to your next experience?" Death had been presented to them as "the next experience." And I can remember one of the grandchildren taking a ride in his wheelchair. So he was very much in the center of the family.

The Travises' other daughter, Ava Zimmerman, said: "They wanted to befriend him because he had done a lot for the Jewish people." The Travises' son, Roy, concurred:

He was a great friend of our family while we were living in Tulsa, Oklahoma, from about 1929. My father was involved in the production of petroleum. They probably first met when Patterson was lecturing for the Zionist cause. My father was an ardent Zionist for as long as I can remember and continued to be so to the end of his life. Patterson revered Jabotinsky, who was one of his soldiers. He had a great deal of affection and esteem for that wing of the Zionist party—rather far right.

Patterson was my godfather. That means that he held me at the time of my circumcision, which is a signal honor from the point of view of a Jewish family towards a non-Jew. It suggests the great feeling of warmth that my family had for him. There was a problem he had in getting his retirement pay and my father made it possible for him and his wife to live in California. I think my father gave him a monthly income of several hundred dollars.

He was devoted to the Old Testament and I recall conversations with him in which he spoke of his great affection for the patriarchs. He was moved by that whole story of Abraham, Isaac, and Jacob and was aware of the connection between the Zionist dream and the Old Testament and aspirations for a permanent land. Just before I went into the army in World War II and after I got out we touched on religious questions. He said that for him the most convincing religion was Buddhism.

He spoke about attending a banquet Queen Victoria had given, and at some point in the conversation he heard her say, "We are not amused."

He also mentioned, speaking in a slight Irish brogue something like George Bernard Shaw's, of being in charge of some Irish Catholic troops during the Boer War, and when he was leading them into the church, the priest said, "I thought you were a Protestant." And Patterson replied, to the priest's amusement, "I always march into danger with my men."

Roy's sister-in-law, Joan, added: "He gave me a lovely gold pin for my engagement to Arnold. He was very kind and generous in that way. He was thin as a rail, because of his illness, and had had a romantic life in every sense of the word."

Roy continued:

He thought the British policy in Palestine was benighted. But he had an imperialistic attitude towards the British presence in India. He felt that was an entirely different situation from that of Palestine. And he felt that the minute the British got out of India there would be war, and of course, he was right. That obviously happened in Palestine as well.

In his last year he had a serious heart condition and was thoroughly depressed about the way the world was going. He was still avidly interested in world affairs and took a very dim view of the United Nations and the veto powers of the Security Council and the notion that any member could veto any action.

I can remember him saying, "My life is over. You can have it." Meaning, you can have the world.

He was a charismatic and very interesting man, whose ardent and courageous espousal of the Zionist cause—and his contribution to the birth of Israel—was at some real cost to his advancement in the British army.[11]

The birth of Israel was two years away when, on June 29, 1946, in order to stop the fighting between Arabs and Jews and by both against the British in Palestine, a general curfew was imposed. Tanks and armed cars filled Palestinian streets, homes were ransacked for arms, and Jews suspected of terrorism or of being illegal immigrants were arrested and taken to detention camps, where, according to author Dan Kurznan, "some were beaten, tortured, even killed."[12] Almost all the Jewish leaders were arrested, except Weizmann, who was out of the country.

On July 11, 1947, the ship *Exodus*, with Haganah commandos in control, set sail from southern France with 4,515 refugees, including 655 children bound for Palestine. A week later it had almost reached Gaza when British sailors boarded it, and in the ensuing fight 2 passengers and a crewman died and 30 people were injured. After the *Exodus* had been towed to Haifa, British Foreign Secretary Ernest Bevin ordered the refugees to be returned in three ships to their original point of departure. When the French refused to remove the passengers by force, Bevin sent the refugees on to the British occupation zone in Germany, where they were taken to holding camps.

Patterson protested this action in a letter to President Harry Truman on August 15, 1946:

> As the British Commanding Officer of the Jewish Troops who took part in freeing Palestine from the Turks in World War I, under Allenby, my conscience will not allow me to remain silent when I read the accounts of the bestial brutalities perpetrated upon the Jewish immigrants now trying to enter their own homeland.
>
> The Jewish troops under my command played no small part in winning Palestine from the Turks and I would like to bring to your notice, Mr. President, that not a single Palestinian Arab raised a finger to throw off the Turkish yoke. At the end of the war I was in command of a large area of Palestine and Egypt, peopled almost entirely by Arabs. My only troops to garrison this area were Jewish troops, yet, although the Arabs all knew that the soldiers were Jewish, there was never the slightest incident or friction to mar the good feeling between both peoples. There would never have been hostility between Jews and Arabs in Palestine had it not been carefully and criminally fomented by the Colonial office agents. This I can vouch for from my own experience.

Patterson deplored "the inhumanity now being perpetrated by England against the unfortunate immigrants fleeing from worse than death to their homeland." He continued:

> I had the privilege of knowing the late F.D.R. and occasionally wrote him of the danger coming from Europe long before war broke out. I also knew the late Theodore Roosevelt, whose guest I have been, both at the White House and at Oyster Bay. If either of the two great men were in the White House today, I make bold to state that they would put their foot down on the inhumanity displayed by the English bureaucrats who now rule England. I would very humbly beg you, sir, to take this matter up boldly—the matter of justice, right and humanity—your stand would be upheld not

23. The Pattersons outside their last home in La Jolla, California, in the 1940s. Courtesy of Alan Patterson.

only by your people of America, but by the good people of England, also, who in their hearts hate the despicable position in which the bureaucrats have placed them.[13]

The *Exodus* incident aroused international opinion against the British, who never repeated this callous tactic of returning Jewish refugees to Germany. Although Truman did not reply to Patterson, his subsequent recognition of Israel as the Jewish homeland was the answer Patterson wanted.

Patterson was never to see the result of his efforts. When The Travis family planned a vacation in August 1947, Marion Travis wrote to Bryan's wife, Beatrice, asking her and her husband to come to California to take care of Patterson while they were away. But Bryan had a fixed agreement to go on an expedition during that time, and Beatrice had to care for their child.

The seventy-nine-year-old Patterson solved the problem by dying in his sleep on June 18, 1947. Six weeks later, his wife, Frances, died. They were both cremated. The *New York Times* reported Patterson's death in nine paragraphs, headlined

J. PATTERSON DIES

LED JEWISH LEGION

Commander in 1st World War

Was 80 [*sic*]—Big Game Hunter

Supporter of Zionism

Time gave a brief account of his life, and the American Zionist publication *New Palestine* published a tribute by Eliahu Ben-Horin, who described Patterson as "an unforgettable man, a great soldier, an outstanding champion of Zionism and a dearly beloved friend. He sacrificed a brilliant military career on the altar of Zionism without a word or a thought of complaint. The truth is that Patterson loved the Jew and thought more of the Jew than does many a Jew."[14] No British newspaper noted his death. But the chairman of the British New Zionists organized a memorial meeting at the Anglo-Palestine Club in London. He had invited the War Office to send a representative, but it declined.

Benjamin Netanyahu remembered his brother's godfather with affection in his book *A Place among the Nations: Israel and the World:*

> In addition to the hundreds of Jews who had served in the Allied armies [of World War I] the special Jewish Battalions formed by the Zionist leadership and led by Colonel John Henry Patterson, made a tangible contribution to the British campaigns against the Turks in Samaria, Galilee, and Transjordan.
>
> Patterson was a remarkable non-Jewish Zionist. A British officer, he commanded the first Jewish fighting unit in centuries—the Zion Mule Corps, founded by Joseph Trumpeldor—which participated in the Gallipoli campaign. . . . Patterson went on to command the Jewish Legion founded by Jabotinsky. Soldier and intellectual, he collaborated with my father in America at the outbreak of World War II, when my father came to the United States as a member of Jabotinsky's delegation, to campaign for the establishment of a Jewish state. Such was the friendship between them that my parents decided to call their first son Jonathan, the "Jon" in honor of Patterson and the "Nathan" in honor of my grandfather. Now and then, on special occasions, my family brings out a silver cup with the inscription "To my darling godson, Jonathan, from your godfather, John Henry Patterson."[15]

Nine months after Patterson's death, Eddie Jacobson visited his friend and former business partner Harry Truman in the White House, where he reminded him that the ailing Chaim Weizmann was anxious to see him. Despite the State Department's objections, Weizmann was secretly admitted through the east gate. He got a positive response: on May 14, 1948, David Ben-Gurion told some two hundred Palestinian Jews in Jerusalem's Municipal Museum that the State of Israel had come into being. Eleven minutes later the United States officially recognized the new state, as did most of the countries voting in the United Nations.

The Arabs did not recognize the new state. Five Arab armies, Egyptian, Syrian, Iraqi, Jordanian, and Lebanese, tried to destroy it. And its destruction seemed inevitable. In manpower, the two sides were almost equal: some thirty thousand Jews faced about twenty-six thousand Arabs. But the Jews were so outmatched by the attacking Arabs in armaments that British general Bernard Montgomery predicted the Jews would be defeated within two weeks.

The Jews had 1 tank, the Arabs 40; the Jews had 2 armored cars without cannon, the Arabs 200; the Jews had 120 armored cars with cannon, the Arabs 300; the Jews had 5 artillery pieces, the Arabs 140; the Jews had 24 AA guns, the Arabs 220; the Jews had no warplanes, the Arabs had 74; the Jews had 28 scout planes, the Arabs 57; the Jews had 3 armed ships, the Arabs had 12.[16]

Many British-trained Jewish Infantry Brigade veterans were among those who, against incredible odds, almost miraculously won the battle. Among them, thirty-five eventually became Israeli generals. Corporal Levi Shkolnik became, as Levi Eshkol, prime minister of Israel; Gershon Agronsky, as Agron, became Jerusalem's mayor. The Jewish Brigade's Sergeant Jacob Dostrowsky, under his Hebrew name, Yaakov Dori, was the Israeli Army's first chief of staff; Sergeant Bernard Joseph, as Dov Yosef, served as Jerusalem's military governor from 1948 to 1949.

Patterson's Legacy

Some sixty years after Patterson's death his parentage is still unknown; those in the know kept his secret. The seven lives he chose to live also helped him to remain something of a mystery to the public. Some who knew him as a big-game hunter had no idea that the same man was

leader of the Zion Mule Corps in Gallipoli, or of the Jewish Legion in Palestine. And many who knew him as a political advocate of Zionism had
no idea that the same man had built bridges, killed lions, and authored
best-selling books. Not to forget those individuals who knew Patterson
only as an inventor and entrepreneur. These differences might explain
why Lawrence of Arabia is universally known, whereas Patterson, whose
effect on the fate of the Jews is greater than Lawrence's on the fate of the
Arabs, is known only to a comparative handful. They might explain why
this book is the first full-scale biography of such a remarkable and influential man.

Although in his 1971 autobiography, *Israel: A Personal History*, David
Ben-Gurion did not mention Patterson or his Zion Mule Corps, he did
acknowledge that the Jewish Legion had helped to pave the way for an
independent country: "Without these soldiers and officers it is doubtful
we could have built the Israeli Defense Forces in such a short period and
such a stormy hour [to fight and win the 1948 war of independence]."[17]

Some Israelis have not forgotten what they owe to Patterson, and have
named a Jerusalem street after him and maintain two museums to keep
alive the details of some of his seven extraordinary lives. The largest is in
the Jabotinsky Institute and Museum in Tel Aviv, where there is a bust of
him, souvenirs from his hunting trips, a recording of a radio interview
he and Jabotinsky gave in New York, and a film of him laying the cor-
nerstone for the Jabotinsky House. The second, Beit Hagdudim (Jewish
Legion) Museum, is dedicated to Patterson's Zion Mule Corps and Jewish
Legion. His military uniform and skins of some of the animals he killed
are on display. A third museum, Chicago's Field Museum of Natural History, has a permanent exhibit of the infamous two man-eating lions that
he killed at Tsavo in British East Africa. He is also remembered at "Patterson's Safari Camp," in the Tsavo National Park.

As previously mentioned, while on a hunting trip in East Africa,
Ernest Hemingway was so intrigued by the gossip he heard about Pat-
terson's fatal safari that it inspired his "The Short Happy Life of Francis
Macomber." Filmed in 1947 as *The Macomber Affair*, it was directed by Zol-
tán Korda with Gregory Peck as Patterson, and with Joan Bennett and
Robert Preston.

The first movie based on Patterson's lion-hunting exploits at Tsavo was *Bwana Devil*, a 1952 United Artists production. The first color film made in 3-D, Arch Oboler wrote and directed it, with Robert Stack as Patterson, Barbara Britton, and Nigel Bruce.

In 1996 Jim Burroughs produced and directed a documentary, *Maneaters of Tsavo*, released by Winstar Home Entertainment. In it, the camera follows in the footsteps of Patterson as he built a bridge, extended the railroad, and fought the deadly marauding lions.

A year later Val Kilmer played Patterson in Paramount's *Ghost and the Darkness*, another simplified film version of *The Man-Eaters of Tsavo*, with Michael Douglas as the costar. William Goldman wrote the screenplay, and Stephen Hopkins directed the film, in which Douglas teams up with Kilmer because he knows how to lure the lions into a trap.

Eager to learn more about his grandfather, Alan Patterson, a Boston-based adviser on environmental affairs, visited the Jabotinsky Institute in Israel in 2002. There he searched the files and listened to Patterson's recorded voice, but found no clues to his mysterious childhood. He also discussed the Irish Zionist with Jabotinsky's grandson, Ze'ev; Peleg Tamir (whose grandmother was Jabotinsky's sister); Patterson and Jabotinsky's mutual Zionist friend, Professor Ben-Zion Netanyahu; and Jabotinsky's biographer and former secretary, Shmuel Katz.

It is possible, if not likely, that but for Patterson, Israel might never have survived. The success of his Zion Mule Corps led to the creation of the Jewish Legion in World War I and the Jewish Infantry Brigade in World War II. The latter's battle-trained soldiers formed the nucleus of a fighting force able to defend the embryonic State of Israel against five armies. And they, in turn, helped to create Israel's modern army and military tradition.

Who better than Shlomo Shamir to respond to the proposition that Colonel Patterson was the father of the Israeli Army, and that without the Jewish Legion, Israel itself might never have survived the attacks by Arab states? At twenty-eight, Shamir, a Russian-born former artist and electrician, had been a lieutenant in World War II's Jewish Infantry Brigade. What the British did not known was that he was also the leader of the Haganah members in his unit.

When the newly established Israel was under attack in 1948, Ben-Gurion appointed Shamir to command the Seventh Brigade, defending Jerusalem against the Arab Legion. Shamir recruited Chaim Hertzog, a former British army officer, as his chief of operations, and Chaim Laskov, a former teacher and captain in the Jewish Legion, to command Israel's first armored columns. (Later, Hertzog served twice as Israel's president, and Shamir became both commander of the Israeli Air Force and admiral of the Israeli Navy.)

The United Nations' recognition of Israel had not guaranteed its existence. With five Arab armies trying to obliterate the new nation, its survival depended on those individuals willing to fight for it. And where did they come from? Some were 450 young refugees who had just arrived from Europe or British detention camps in Cyprus. According to the authors of *O Jerusalem!* when told they were to defend Jerusalem, "The pale faces of the remnants of a condemned people suddenly came alive and from the mouths . . . rose a spontaneous, triumphant shout."[18] Despite their enthusiasm, most had probably never even handled a gun before, which was true of other recruits, including women. Fortunately, many of their leaders were veterans of the Jewish Legion and the Jewish Infantry Brigade. And they led their inexperienced but spirited troops to ultimate victory.

The successful record of Colonel Patterson's Zion Mule Corps and his Jewish Legion in World War I made the World War II brigade possible. And in Shlomo Shamir's opinion, without its experienced fighters, "Israel could have been only a Zionist dream."[19]

Afterword

ALAN PATTERSON

ON THE FIRST of the only two times I was in my grandfather's presence I was just a babe in arms. I should have been no match for an Anglo-Irishman with the traditional English stiff upper lip, a man who had finally tracked and killed man-eating lions, put down mutineers who were promising to kill him, and faced down a charging rhino. Nonetheless. I put him to rout. Being easily bored by the staid atmosphere of the dining room of the hotel he was staying in while passing through Chicago, I soon began to fuss and then to bawl. His first response was to advise my mother to shush the cranky infant. When that didn't work, out came the military order, "Bea, make that child be quiet." Neither I nor my mother gave much satisfaction, and soon he could take no more. The final order was given to decamp, and the two adults finished lunch in my grandfather's room, where I, presumably amused by all the furor and bustle I had inadvertently caused, promptly went to sleep.

Lt. Col. John Henry Patterson, DSO, the Colonel, as he was known in the family, Colonel Pat to some of his acquaintances, or simply JHP to save time and typing, has several public faces, most of them valiant, determined and military. One of the most satisfying aspects of Denis Brian's biography of JHP is the discovery and presentation of many of the less well-known aspects of the man of which there were many, even though JHP was in many ways a very public figure. He wrote four books, in all of which he was the central character. He has been portrayed three times in the movies, by Gregory Peck, Robert Stack, and Val Kilmer. Yet

223

with all that, remarkably little has been known about him, even within the family.

During the run up to *The Ghost and the Darkness*, the latest movie version about his experiences concerning *The Man-Eaters of Tsavo* (his first book), Joan Travis, daughter-in-law of JHP's California benefactor in the 1940s, contacted me to see if I could provide any additional information and photos for a short bio of the Colonel that would appear in the paperback version of *The Man-Eaters* to come out in conjunction with the movie. Aside from a few photos I could locate I was able to contribute little.

The effort did, however, rekindle my interest in my grandfather who had been a notable presence when I was very young. The man-eaters were on display at Chicago's Field Museum where my father had worked ever since first arriving in the States. I was regularly taken to the museum, with the two lions being one of the highlights of my visits. I was apparently so impressed that my first remembered dream is of a lion in our kitchen. The beast wandered around the table I was under but was careless enough to not look down, so I survived the episode with no harm or lingering fear. In fact, I was prone to babbling about JHP and the lions to perfect strangers, either in the museum or on the street. The Col.'s influence lasted a bit longer, as I recall having named in the eighth grade his friend Theodore Roosevelt as my most admired person.

In the past decade since the release of *The Ghost and the Darkness*, I, along with various others, have tried to determine who John Henry Patterson really was. I was initially skeptical that there was enough information to warrant a biography. Denis Brian (and before him, authors Patrick Streeter and Forbes Taylor—who provided the basic information for the short bio in the paperback version of *The Man-Eaters*) has uncovered a great deal of new information. As more and more people became interested in and started researching the Col., I wondered if any of us would be able to turn up the answers to three key questions that I have long wondered about: JHP's origins, how he managed to survive financially and to live well in Grove House in Iver (described by Taylor as the "stockbroker belt"), and finally how he came to be such a dedicated and ardent Zionist.

One of the maddening things about JHP is that he is so hard to pin down. Who or what was he? In the course of my efforts to learn more about him, I identified five possible roles—the bastard out of Ireland, Patterson of East Africa, the last Victorian gentleman, the Irish Zionist—and a last possible catchall category of undesirable characteristics: military martinet, bounder, murderer, perhaps even traitor.

Not that I personally thought that any or all of these were necessarily true. Most researchers subscribe to the idea that JHP was illegitimate. It's a valid hypothesis and may well be true. I consider it not proven and another hypothesis equally worthy of consideration: that he was in fact legitimate, from a family that was both militarily and religiously oriented, and that for some reason he severed relations before going off to join the army, underage in my opinion. I agree with everyone that his family connections were of use to him throughout his life, but whether he could have utilized them if he in fact was illegitimate is moot.

In terms of religion, he had a thorough Old Testament grounding, particularly in its military aspects. This would, of course, reflect a Protestant upbringing, probably within a strongly militarily oriented family environment, possibly either a religious military father, or a father who was either in the church or extremely religious, and who also had an army connection.

In my attempts at locating JHP's origins I decided to look mostly toward Northern Ireland, even though he gave his birthplace at time of enlistment in the army as a very small place in what is now the Republic of Ireland. I considered the information he gave on enlistment suspect for several reasons. First is the limited information about family, listing only an "aunt" who has never been traced. Second, for a lad of nineteen, the official enlistment age, he was quite slight, and not near his final growth, which by nineteen he should have been. Having tried on his dress uniform once, and finding it a near perfect for my 5'9½" frame, the 5'7" listed as his height made me doubt his stated age (and in fact has made me a bit skeptical of many of the "facts" about him).

In the Linen Hall Library in Belfast I discovered a self-printed family history of scientific and linen merchant Pattersons, some of the many of that name in the North. In addition to finding out that JHP's future father-in-law, as well as his future wife, then a young girl, attended from time to time that Patterson family home, I learned that a cousin of the family, Robert Stuart Patterson, also visited from time to time. I was most interested to note that RSP was in the Church of Ireland. Subsequent research on him showed that soon after taking his vows, he became a military chaplain who rose through the ranks, attaining the position of chief chaplain in Egypt in 1916 when JHP went out there to attempt to stir up a command position shortly before the Middle Eastern front opened up. Interestingly, RSP had over his lifetime some dozen children and three wives, two of whom died prematurely, with one being dramatically lost at sea. Within all the possibility of family change and turmoil, "evil" new stepmothers and the like, it could easily provide occasion for an adolescent boy to decide to leave home and join the army.

Such a relationship would nicely fit my assumptions about the Col.'s background, but unfortunately I have been able neither to prove nor to disprove this connection, or any other. RSP's will lists only two of his children as heirs. Although the man died in his nineties, still one would think that more than two of twelve would have survived him—unless he chose not to include them in his will. In any case, this hypothesis remains just that. And, of course, I am searching on the assumption that JHP was born a Patterson. Given the man's refusal to go into his origins, it would not surprise me at all if in fact he simply chose to be known as Patterson, for whatever reason. When pressed by my father to talk of his, JHP's, parents, he once allowed as how they came from the Curragh. My father could only surmise that since the Curragh was Ireland's premier horse-breeding area, his parents were perhaps horse thieves, hence the reticence. I rather doubt, however, that my father gave serious credence to the notion.

JHP is considered to be perhaps the first "great white hunter" by Kenneth Cameron, historian of the safari. Certainly, his exploits and trials in Kenya gave him a renown far beyond that of many others who worked at the trade for much longer than he. How did he arrive in Africa in the first place when he was no more than a sergeant after more than ten years in the Indian Army, for which there is no known record of exemplary service that might have led to his being hired as engineer for the proposed railway from Mombasa to Uganda? He may have sought the job. If he had railroad experience in India, it isn't shown on his service record, however. As it turned out, the section of the Mombasa-to-Uganda railway happened to encompass the territory of the man-eaters. As a result of his ultimately successful killing of two of them, his life changed abruptly and significantly.

Through the publicity (and undoubtedly some efforts at self-promotion) that resulted, he managed to obtain a position as adjutant with the tony Essex regiment with whom he then successfully served in the South African war, achieving battlefield promotions that led to his rising from lieutenant to lieutenant colonel in eight months. His decorations from service there, his connections with aristocratic members of the regiment, and natural leadership presumably led to his subsequent independent safaris and appointment as the first game warden for British East Africa. The death of a colleague from the regiment whom he had allowed to accompany him as he carried out a parks reconnaissance (the second son of a Lord Blyth) cut short his service as game warden, and illness and controversy in Kenya about Blyth's death led to his prompt return to England. Tales of those troubles continued to be told around safari campfires for years, with one retelling leading to a Hemingway short story. Almost fifty years later, another campfire tale, this time of the earlier Tsavo exploits, led screenwriter William Goldman to write a script on spec that ultimately resulted in *The Ghost and the Darkness*.

There is little connection between JHP's African and Zionist segments of his life and career except that his army experience in South Africa enabled him to obtain his World War I appointments with the Zion Mule Corps and the Jewish Legion. There is one amusing tale, however, that connects Tsavo with Zionist efforts. Long before the decision was made to concentrate efforts on what is now Israel, Zionists considered a number of alternative locations for establishing a Jewish homeland, one being East Africa. A small delegation came to Kenya to analyze its suitability and were in due course taken out into the countryside. Not surprisingly, lions were heard roaring at night. So around another campfire the tale of the Tsavo lions was again retold. It allegedly so unsettled the delegation members that they immediately crossed East Africa off their list and returned posthaste to Europe.

Had JHP been able to obtain a command position in the European front in World War I, the last third of his life would have been completely different, possibly even pedestrian. Denis Brian mentions JHP taking a trip to examine the front in Belgium. In the family, the story was a bit different. In our version—and who knows if it is correct—the Colonel, after lack of success in obtaining a commission in London, took off to the front in Belgium on his own to volunteer his services, significantly disconcerting the more conventional officers he encountered.

For whatever reason, and on whose advice we don't know, he subsequently went to Egypt to seek his luck there as the opening up of the Middle East front meant the likely need for additional officers. What was offered to him, the command of a mule corps that would serve in a nonfighting capacity was most certainly not what he had in mind. Considered reckless by some, he also had his rational side, and I am sure he realized that at near fifty, a somewhat "over the hill" cavalry officer, this was as good as he was likely to get. That the command would be of Jewish soldiers was probably a nonconsideration in his decision to accept the commission. As far as he knew, he had never met any Jews before, although he was thoroughly conversant with Old Testament tales.

Command of the Zion Mule Corps led to command of the Jewish Legion, three regiments planned as an actual fighting force. The Mule Corps was an ironic start to what turned out to be the raison d'être for the remainder of his professional and civic life. He related his World War I experiences in his last two books. I believe it was his admiration for his troops that he related in the books, and their transformation from fairly meek, mostly ghetto dwellers into hardened serious soldiers, together with his work with the remarkable Zionist Ze'ev (Vladimir) Jabotinsky (who provided the political and organizational skill and effort necessary to establish the legion and who served in the legion with JHP as a sort of aide-de-camp) that led him to his lifelong dedication to Zionism, filling some unknown void in his life.

People have often wondered about the relationship between my father and JHP. In his army career, at Tsavo, and as a Zionist, JHP was a man of action. It was perhaps galling to him that my father didn't appear to be cut from the same cloth, and was much more interested in anything and everything having to do with nature. In this he was undoubtedly encouraged and abetted by his mother, Frances Helena (Gray), the first of whose three university degrees was in biology. (She was the first woman in the United Kingdom to receive a master's of law degree, although she was not allowed to practice. Instead, she became a teacher and then head mistress of several schools.) JHP was often to lament to my father that he would never be anything but a "hewer of wood and a carrier of water." He perhaps tried to inculcate some military values into my father, without pushing it too far, and may have been willing to be tolerant of a young boy. It was my father's occasional duty to polish boots, and he wasn't always up to doing an adequate job. My father once countered the complaint that the heels were totally bereft of polish with the dubious justification, "But sir, a good soldier never looks behind him," and got away with it. (On the other hand, when if fell to me to do my father's shoes, heels were the first to be checked.)

My father was homeschooled by his mother until he was about twelve and then sent off to Malvern, for three years at Malvern Preparatory and another three years at the college. Whether continuing to despair of reasonable life prospects for my father, simply not being willing to sink any more money into education that appeared unlikely to lead to productive employment, or, more likely, both reasons, perhaps coupled with one of his periodical financial reverses, the Col. decided to pull his son from school at age seventeen and send him off to the United States to seek his future.

In my early imaginings about my father's coming to the States, I concocted the notion that the two of them went off to the docks at Southampton, and JHP saw to my father's being ensconced in steerage class, advising him to avoid the fleshpots of New York and go directly to Chicago where possibly there might be a museum job for him. Reality was less romantic or uncertain. As I did my research, I learned that the Col. accompanied his boy to Chicago—and surely not in steerage—sat him down with the director of the Field Museum, and reminded the director of his promise of several years back that they could always find a place for a keen young man of broad interest but a lot of attention to detail. Among the staff who were queried as to who could best employ the lad, the curator of fossil mammals made the best presentation, which was how my father became a paleontologist and not a herpetologist or fungus expert. Satisfied that his son would have a job of sorts and a small income, JHP proceeded to ensure that his living arrangements would be healthy and moral. Through unknown connections, he arranged for my father to room with some of the curates at Chicago's Episcopal Cathedral (where I in time was duly christened).

The Col. probably felt that he had done all he needed to or could do for his son and it was up to him to sink or swim. The two maintained some contact (probably random), but the Col. was able in the late 1930s to give him some vital advice. My father had the notion that he should enlist in the International Brigade and go to Spain. The Col.'s response on learning of this was immediate and negative, something along the lines of "Don't be a bloody fool, my boy." My father accepted this sound advice, and given the mortality among the *brigadistas,* perhaps it is what made possible my birth five years thereafter. The Col., but not Francie, would have undoubtedly been amazed when a few years after their death, their son was appointed to a chair at Harvard.

Their relationship was probably as good and as close as one could find, given the time and country and English middle class that they represented, particularly since the Col. was often away—and almost continuously so from 1914 to 1920, my father's years from age five through eleven—and my father was away at school for almost all the time thereafter. Still, my father had developed a great respect for his father. He wisely listened to him about Spain and was enraged in the 1980s when a mostly fictional book (offered as reality) about the building of the Mombasa-Uganda Railway portrayed JHP as an unmitigatedly cold martinet, almost a slave driver. He spent quite a bit of effort and money through private investigation in Nairobi in an attempt to locate the persons and sources cited in *The Iron Snake* that were the basis for this mischaracterization of the Col. No proof that they existed could be found. A lawyer friend advised that action for defamation of character would be futile and costly, so my father had to content himself with the partial satisfaction of knowing that the author had misrepresented JHP simply because he felt he needed a villain to enliven his book.

The relationship is perhaps represented by stamps. From early on my father collected stamps, many of which must have been sent by the Col. from his wide travels. Some remain attached to postcards from such places as Victoria Falls and the ruins of Zimbabwe. Certainly, the Col. saw this as one way of keeping contact, or even telling a story about his dealings. When my father was well into his thirties (and JHP in his late sixties) he received a series of a dozen postcards from the area of Mexico where the Col. and his associates were attempting to mine gold. The cards, additional snapshots, and brief messages on the back told a bit about the dig, and one referenced my father's tree-climbing exploits as a child. But none told of any significant amount of gold found. All were stored away, as were all the foreign stamps that my father received over the years through professional communication.

JHP had, and still has with some, a reputation, if not as a lady's man, certainly a man with an eye for the ladies. In some fashion this has led to his turning up in a contemporary novel, *The Hanging Tree,* about a young female South African paleontologist in Kenya, who as dubious preparation for her trip there is reading the Col.'s second Kenya book, about his experiences as game warden and leader of the ill-fated safari during which the second son of Lord Blyth is found dead in his tent. JHP in the novel is a ghost, but not a pale and bloodless one, but rather a startlingly (and I must admit a somewhat disconcertingly) sexy one. Perhaps JHP was the personification of the old song lyrics, that if "he's not near to the girl he loves, he loves the girl he's near." At the very least, he most definitely enjoyed female company.

One rumor going around Kenya after the safari returned to Nairobi was that JHP had killed the man in order to have an affair with the wife. I simply cannot believe that of JHP. That he may have had an affair with her is less easy to discount. Or even that Effie (Ethel) Blyth, the widow, may be my biological grandmother. And if so, what? I have been advised that with either Francie or Effie I have an excellent forebear, and I would agree. Whichever of them actually gave birth to my father is almost immaterial. I feel a very strong link to Francie, more so actually than with JHP. I feel that from her, through my father, I inherited my love of nature and my resulting career as an environmental planner and analyst. As regards

Effie, should she prove to be the biological grandmother, all it does is give me a very weak link to a lordship, essentially nonexistent since inheritance through the maternal line is no longer considered valid. In centuries past it might have been worth fighting for, but these days it's just a curious conversation piece.

Many people have expressed surprise that JHP never showed any particular interest in the Irish cause. He was not anti-Irish and during difficult times at Tsavo longed to be back in Ireland (as well as with Francie). But I suspect that his presumably Protestant and Northern Irish orientation, together with his probably awkward childhood, blocked any real possibilities for Irish sensibilities or identification. Nonetheless, he was not unaware or outwardly unsympathetic to the Irish. He undoubtedly served with many in India. Before appointment to lead the Jewish Legion, he had a basically administrative command outside Dublin. There he told his troops that "in the barracks you can sing of the 'wearin' o' the green' to your heart's content, but on parade it's spit and polish and up the King." I believe that this at least partial identification with the Irish was honestly felt. In general he was able to forge good relations with many different people, Boers in South Africa and both Indians and Africans in Kenya, even if his command of Hindi and Swahili, like Hebrew later on, was tenuous at best. My sense of JHP is of an Englishman. He served in the king's army, lived in England, served the empire, and had British citizenship. Strangely, it was with the English that he seemed to encounter the greatest difficulties.

If JHP's identification with things Irish was weak, his somewhat contradictory personality traits are quite suggestive. He could be both modest and arrogant. His temper could be volatile and his actions on occasion reckless, yet in times of crisis or frustration he could be calm and even optimistic, proposing his habitual toast, "Here's to trouble." He was steadfastly loyal to the Zionism that so often appeared to be a lost cause, and even within that movement he was loyal to his friends and colleagues within the underdog Revisionist Zionists, the followers of Jabotinsky.

His attitude toward authority was at times cavalier (at best) or outrageous, and was undoubtedly the reason for never advancing beyond lieutenant colonel, in spite of experience and command responsibility. On the spur of the moment, he could order his troops to surround with lowered

bayonets the visiting general who had unjustly insulted one of his Jewish soldiers and demand (and receive) an instant apology. Or tiring of his
father-in-law's overlong description of a recent tricolite (a fossil of an extinct
marine arthropod) find, he could just as easily grab one of the scones at the
tea table and, in hopes of at least slowing the torrent of words, thrust it at
his esteemed relative and suggest, "'Ere, trile a bite o' this."

In defense of Zionist goals he publicly excoriated Churchill, a man
he genuinely admired. Zionist fund-raising in the 1920s for general and
humanitarian goals continued and shifted, so that by the late '30s he was
part of the Irgun efforts that led to the first ships to take "illegal" Jewish
immigrants to Palestine and helped in arming groups that in the future
would be shooting in earnest at British troops there.

Despite his refined English accent, its orientation toward the Ulster
provinces of the North of Ireland, JHP nonetheless represented any number of the traits and qualities so often associated with the Irish. It's not
surprising that many in England thought of him as "Irish." Contrariwise,
others thought of him as a strong Ulsterman. However others, or he,
thought of him, I've often felt that one of his qualities was affection for
and support of the underdog. If he hadn't become so deeply involved in
Zionism, I strongly suspect that he would have become strongly associated with some other cause or peoples.

I will probably never know what exactly motivated my grandfather
to become such a dedicated and determined Zionist. I have my idea, his
connection with his troops and some need for a cause. Then again, it may
also be that it gave him an opportunity to be involved, be part of some
action again, perhaps even to still be able to enjoy the limelight from time
to time. When I began my research on JHP, I wondered if he was anything more than just a footnote to history, albeit a rather interesting one,
and always good for a tale around the campfire. Denis Brian's biography
clearly shows that he was more than just a footnote.

And in the family, he was always good for the occasional unexpected
encounter outside of the literary realm. When I was ten, the family spent
a year in Argentina while my father was studying Argentine fossils. I and
other members of my Boy Scout–like organization went to a downtown
athletic and social club for swimming lessons. Arriving early one day I

was idly flipping through the guest register and was startled and rather excited to come across the Col.'s signature. A few years later at a conference in Alexandria, my father was one day approached by the government's official minder. "Ah, yes, Professor Patterson, we knew your father very well." Shaking a finger he continued, "We have a very thick dossier on him." Ah, to be able to read Arabic and to have access to the archives of the Ministry of the Interior!

The first movie about the man-eaters, *Bwana Devil*, was not a good movie, but did offer the novelty of being the first commercial 3-D movie. From time to time I still encounter posters of the *Life* magazine cover showing the audience at one of the early screenings, all decked out in paper-and-plastic two-color glasses that enabled everyone to see the third dimension. And just as I was writing this afterword, an item appeared on the Internet announcing that JHP had four much older brothers. Rather than provide the answer to JHP's parentage, the claim turned out to be based on a misunderstood e-mail from Ireland to Israel talking about Patrick Streeter's hypothesis on JHP's birth and illegitimacy.

The final chapter of JHP's life was more tranquil than the earlier ones, although not without interest. Jabotinsky and the Revisionist Zionists, in their quest to create a new Jewish Legion for World War II, decided that they were more likely to have success in the United States than in England. The Revisionists established themselves in New York. In a sense, JHP went along. Francie's health was deteriorating, not helped by the English climate, and she and the Col. ended up in a small bungalow by the seaside in La Jolla, California. If the bungalow had been in Brighton or Hove, it would have been a fairly typical British military retirement setting. Or if it had been on Long Island, New York, it would have been much more convenient, as JHP needed to travel fairly often across the country to attend and sometimes headline various Zionist meetings and rallies. But no matter where the bungalow, it was a far cry from Grove House. Still, there were enough memorabilia to remind them both of what had gone before. Interestingly, little of it related to either Ireland or Israel. From the former there was an ornate Victorian fruit compote, complete with cherubs and musical instruments (a long-ago gift to Francie's father from the Belfast Amateur Naturalist's Club) and Francie's three diplomas. From Israel there were only two illuminated scrolls presented to JHP in

Jerusalem in 1920. From the army, he had kept his medals, dress uniform, swords, and field tea kettle. From Africa he had Masai spears and shields, smaller spears from the Wanderobo tribe, a lion and zebra skin apiece, and an unpublished (and not very good) novel set in South Africa. Many more animal trophies remained behind in England that he never succeeded in transporting to America. Unfortunately, none of his pre-California correspondence made the journey to the United States. Aside from the occasional letters to and from the Revisionist Zionist headquarters in New York, his correspondence reflected a typical expatriate's or exile's communication with far-flung friend from Alexandria to Argentina, as well as neighbors in Iver, chatting about health, family, and life in general. No letters from Ireland were found.

Unfortunately, while in the States he was not able to receive his pension. The army bureaucracy claimed that because of the war it was not possible to send it, although the occasional meager royalty from *The Man-Eaters* managed to dribble in. It may well be that the army simply couldn't be bothered to make the effort, or was so bothered by his occasional broadsides against British policy that they consciously chose not to make the effort. In any case, he and Francie were seriously strapped for cash. He was forced to borrow over time some five to six thousand dollars from his fellow Zionist and supporter Marion Travis, money that he would never be able to repay. Knowing this, he left all the rights to his books to Travis, which provided no return until the making of *The Ghost and the Darkness*. He was effectively a pauper. Francie's health deteriorated, and she had to enter a nursing home. JHP then moved up the coast and in with the Travis family, where he died a few months later, broke but living in a mansion in Bel Air. Francie died in another six weeks, and their ashes were placed in a Jewish cemetery in Los Angeles.

The three major questions that I posed to myself when I set out on my research have not yet been answered in any definitive way. His origins are still unproven, and I suspect that they always will be. Either there was never any documentary trace to be found, or else he covered his tracks so skillfully that it could never be uncovered.

Concerning his finances and how he managed to live so well, I doubt much more will be learned, although it's possible that Francie may have been able to contribute in this regard, perhaps through the sale of one or more of the buildings in which she operated her schools. Royalties from the "Patterson Equipment," a widely adopted device he invented allowing a cavalryman to dismount with his rifle still attached, undoubtedly helped, at least as long as there still existed cavalries. That and initial payment for *The Man-Eaters* presumably provided funds that allowed for obtaining Grove House around 1908. Otherwise, it was through his book royalties, magazine articles, speaking tours, and modest pension that he managed to keep house and home together, if just barely. None of his major overseas efforts to make money panned out, whether oil in the Middle East, hydropower in West Africa, or gold in the Yukon and Mexico.

As to his dedicated Zionism, I have my theories and feel that they must be right, at least in part. Solving the question of his origins would certainly help to understand or intuit some of his emotional makeup and thus to clarify his Zionism. I have a few leads yet to track down, although I have low expectations. There are still extensive records of the Church of Ireland to plow through, and I have a lead on several military Pattersons with a connection to Ireland. And possibly I can find something out about the schools where Francie was headmistress, whether she owned the buildings, and whether their sale could have helped obtain and keep Grove House.

Two additional tasks remain for me. There lives in England a possible Cousin Maude, the grandniece of Effie, widow of the son of Lord Blythe. If I can manage to track down and extricate from a distant laboratory storage a biopsy taken of my father, it would provide a better DNA comparison with Maude's than would mine (which is from a generation further removed from the maternal line to be examined). The last is to organize removal of JHP's and Francie's remains and relocate them suitably in Israel. One of his last wishes was to be buried with his troops. Near the Beit Hagdudim Museum, dedicated to the Jewish Legion, there is a cemetery where many of the legionnaires are buried, and this presumably would be the most appropriate place, provided that Francie could be interred there as well. This will, I fear, entail significant dealings with bureaucrats. The Col. was used to bulldozing through, skirting or, when essential, ignoring bureaucracy and its requirements, skills that could prove very useful to me now.

Appendixes

Notes

Bibliography

Index

American and Canadian Members
of the Jewish Legion

IN FEBRUARY 1918, after Supreme Court Justice Brandeis obtained permission, Britain opened a military recruiting headquarters at 280 Broadway. New York City, and two other recruiting offices for the newly approved 39th Battalion. It was to be composed of Jews aged 18 1/2 to 45, residing in the U.S. who were not American citizens, or could not be drafted into the American Army. By mid-February over one hundred had signed up, including Kelly, an Irish American from Baltimore, who was over 45 and a former captain in the U.S. Army. He would become a sergeant in the Jewish Legion. Another volunteer was an Anglo-African, Lo Bagola, who claimed to be a Black Jew.

On February 28 the first contingent of 150 men marched down Fifth Avenue, took the Sixth Avenue L to Cortland Street, and sailed for Canada with a stop at Boston, where 168 more recruits joined them. Hadassah women distributed sandwiches, coffee and chocolates. The men then boarded their ship singing "Hatikvah," and "Ahm Yisrael Chai," and sailed to Windsor, Canada, where they disembarked in a drizzle for two months training with Canadian recruits.

In March 1918 Batya Albert from Brownsville volunteered, but was rejected—as was Golda Meir, in Milwaukee—because there was no women's Battalion. Batya then asked to serve as a nurse with the 39th Battalion, but refused to wear the emblem of the Red Cross since she was Orthodox. She proposed, instead, the formation of a Jewish counterpart to be called the Red Mogen David with a red

From Dr. Oscar Kraines, "Jabotinsky: Hero or Villain?" *Beth* Sholom Bulletin 42, no. 9 (January 1–15, 1987): 8–12.

star of David. Rae Raskin, wife of an artist, Saul Raskin, then organized the first branch of the Red Mogen David with headquarters on East Broadway.

Ben-Gurion signed up with the 39th on April 26 and on May 29 the second contingent of 300 men, including Ben-Gurion and Ben-Zvi, marched down Fifth Avenue with bands playing as they left for Canada. After their training, the 39th left for England, arriving at Plymouth on July 23, 1918, and shortly after sailed for Egypt where Lt. Colonel Margolin of the Australian Army assumed command.

Oscar Kraines' 1940 Interview with Vladimir Jabotinsky

JABOTINSKY WAS 59 years old and I was 26. He was of medium height and erect and wore glasses. He introduced his wife, Jyanna, who said that their only child, a son, Eri, was then in a British prison in Palestine for smuggling in Jewish refugees. Speaking softly but intensely, walking restlessly around the desk and my chair, and clenching his right fist for emphasis, he described briefly what life was like for Jews in Czarist Russia and said he understood why so many became socialists. He himself had been a socialist, secularist and proletarian novelist when Maxim Gorky befriended him and urged him to concentrate in writing in Russian. However, the pogroms of 1902–1905 changed him, and he realized that the Jews must have their own land, that it had to be the Biblical homeland, and now being a Zionist he could never live permanently in Russia.

K. Is it likely that we will see the Jewish state in our lifetime?

J. Britain is not doing well in this war and may come out of it weak and have to give up many of its colonies, including the Mandate for Palestine. We must prepare for such an event, not only politically but also militarily and have armed, trained forces to fight the Arabs of both Palestine and the surrounding countries. I haven't the slightest doubt that the Arabs will not accept the Jewish state and will try to destroy it. . . . It will be very important for Jews to settle in the Jewish state because there is great danger that the Arabs will outnumber the Jewish population.

Material from this interview was incorporated into a talk by Dr. Oscar Kraines, published as "Jabotinsky: Hero or Villain?" *Beth Sholom Bulletin* 42, no. 9 (January 1–15, 1987): 8–12.

I am not that naïve to think that Britain will eagerly create the promised homeland and help us defend ourselves against the Arabs. I have argued before British commissions that Britain should create the Jewish state with the same attitude and smoothness as its other colonization efforts, and that it should allow the Jews to arm themselves openly against Arab attacks. Just as the white European settlers in Kenya were allowed to arm themselves against the blacks. . . .

But now our most important job is rescuing European Jews and smuggling them into Palestine; and this requires armed, trained rescuers and ships. Do you think Britain and France are committed to rescuing Jews, or will risk antagonizing the Arabs, especially when the Germans may be marching against Egypt and the entire Near East? Wars arouse nationalism; and just as Ukraine nationalism was inflamed by the World War and Russian revolutions, so may Arab nationalism long dormant, be aroused by the present war and by the creation of the Jewish state. We must be prepared for this.

K. Why do you believe socialism is no good for Zionism?

J. I want the Jewish state to be a modern, westernized land, not a Near Eastern nation of shepherds and farmers only. I want skyscrapers and airplanes, not mud huts and camels. This will require incentives for large investments of capital to import resources and to develop and industrialize Palestine. Socialism's anticapitalist doctrines will discourage such investments, and will produce a nation of labor organizations and bureaucrats and splintered socialist factions each with its own Karl Marx.

Besides, the international socialist and communist movements are anti-Zionist. Even the socialist Jewish Bundists are anti-Zionist. When the Arabs murdered Jewish settlers in 1936, 1938 and 1939. socialist Zionists were shocked that gentile socialists and communists, including Jewish communists, described these massacres as nationalist uprisings against imperialism. Also, socialist Zionists are too pacifistic.

The world has yet to accept Jews as fighters, trained and disciplined soldiers who know how to use weapons.

K. Is unity among Zionists possible despite differences in ideology and strategy? Why battle *now* over whether the *future* state should include all Biblical boundaries and whether strikes should be banned? Was Stalin right when he said the Jewish obsession with endless argumentation would eventually cause any Jewish state, Birobidzhan or Palestine, to fail?

J. We Zionists are entitled to disagree among ourselves because the type of state we will build someday will depend on which group of Zionists governs.

But one thing I am sure of—we won't have purges, terror and imprisonment for disagreeing as under Stalin. What Stalin describes as endless argumentation we consider freedom of thought and speech. We Jews have a Talmudic tradition of analyzing everything and giving our own commentary. Is there unity among communists, among socialists? Is the Nazi-Soviet pact an example of Stalin's concept of unity? I'm sure that in the case of grave danger we Zionists will unite for survival.

Remember that our arguments are within the Zionist family. It is when the non-Zionist Jews. especially the leftists, attack us that I am disturbed.

What kind of advice is it to tell Jews who are being slaughtered by gentiles to stay put and build a classless society together with non-Jews? Whose culture do you think will disappear?

I believe we Jews are a superior race with a great national culture, and what we now need is a territorial nation in Palestine. So this is the nationalism that frightens so many of you!

I am frightened by assimilation, especially among the socialist and communist Jews who believe in a class unity, not national unity. What do you think is happening to our national culture in Russia? This is why I long ago praised the Ukranian nationalists who opposed Russification and fought for independence from the Soviets, I was not blind to their anti-Semitism and pogroms under Petlura. But they fought to preserve their national culture. I don't see the Jewish communists acting to preserve Jewish culture.

I think that someday the "great" October revolution of 1917 will be seen as the downfall of Russian Jewry.

Notes

Preface

    1. *Spectator,* March 3, 1900.

    2. General Sir Ian Hamilton, *Gallipoli Diary,* 84.

1. The Man-Eaters of Tsavo, 1896–1901

    1. James Morris, "Long Live Imperialism," *Saturday Evening Post,* 10.

    2. Charles Miller, *The Lunatic Express: An Entertainment in Imperialism,* 286.

    3. Theodore Roosevelt, *African Game Trails: An Account of the African Wanderings of an American Hunter-Naturalist,* 12, 2.

    4. Ibid., 519, 527.

    5. C. Miller, *Lunatic Express,* 286.

    6. Ibid., 318.

    7. Patrick Streeter, *Mad for Zion: A Biography of Colonel J. H. Patterson,* 1, 2, 3.

    8. C. Miller, *Lunatic Express,* 192, 193.

    9. John Henry Patterson, *The Man-Eaters of Tsavo and Other East African Adventures,* 20, 21.

    10. Ibid., 21, 22.

    11. Ibid., 22, 23, 24.

    12. Ibid., 29.

    13. Ibid., 34, 35.

    14. Ibid., 35, 36.

    15. Ibid., 38, 29, 40.

    16. Ibid., 40.

    17. Patterson's diary, April 23, 1898.

    18. C. Miller, *Lunatic Express,* 331.

    19. Patterson, *Man-Eaters of Tsavo,* 55–59.

    20. Ibid., 59.

    21. Ibid., 67, 68.

22. Ibid., 78, 79, 80.

23. Ibid., 82.

24. Ibid., 90–91.

25. Ibid., 99, 100.

26. Streeter, *Mad for Zion*, 28.

27. C. Miller, *Lunatic Express*, 343.

28. Streeter, *Mad for Zion*, 27.

29. C. Miller, *Lunatic Express*, 345.

30. Patterson, *Man-Eaters of Tsavo*, 212, 213.

31. Ibid., 117, 126.

32. C. Miller, *Lunatic Express*, 368.

33. Patterson, *Man-Eaters of Tsavo*, 294, 295.

34. C. Miller, *Lunatic Express*, 390, 391.

2. Boer War Bravado, 1900–1907

1. J. H. Patterson, *In the Grip of the Nyika*, preface.

2. This letter and all others from Mrs. Patterson to her parents are from the author's collection.

3. J. H. Patterson, *Man-Eaters of Tsavo*, 327.

4. Peter Capsick, ed., *Tsavo*, 306.

3. Theodore Roosevelt's Friendship, 1907

1. J. H. Patterson, *Grip of the Nyika*, 295.

2. Randolph S. Churchill, *Winston S. Churchill*, 231.

4. Fatal Safari Leader, 1908

1. J. H. Patterson, *Grip of the Nyika*, 295.

2. Ibid., 296.

3. Ibid., 301.

4. Ibid., 302.

5. Ibid., 306.

6. Ibid., 308.

7. Ibid., 321.

8. Ibid., 319.

9. Ibid., 379.

10. Ibid., 380.

5. Rumors of a "Sinister Character," 1908–1909

1. British Public Record Office, Co 533/45/6791; and British Public Record Office, Reference Co 533/57 8348.

2. John Henry Patterson, *With the Zionists in Gallipoli*, preface.

3. William Crozier to John Henry Patterson, December 31, 1908, author's collection.

4. Testimony of Saiewa Masai, author's collection.

5. Streeter, *Mad for Zion,* 67–68.

6. Ibid.

7. Alan Patterson, telephone interview by author, June 6, 2005.

8. Streeter, *Mad for Zion,* 76–77.

9. Ibid., 74, 75.

10. *Times* (London), April 2, 1909.

11. *Spectrum Guide to Kenya,* 291.

12. Patrick Hemingway, telephone interview by author, May 9, 2005.

13. Beatrice Patterson, telephone interview by author, November 15, 1987.

14. F. E. Smith letter to Churchill, December 26, 1907, CHAR 2/29/122-123; Churchill Archives; See also Streeter, *Mad for Zion,* 71, 72.

6. Adventures in Africa and among the High and Mighty, 1909–1914

1. Roosevelt, *African Game Trails,* 12.

2. Ibid., 120–21.

3. Streeter, *Mad for Zion,* 83.

4. J. H. Patterson, *With the Zionists,* 25.

7. World War I, Patterson Leads the Zion Mule Corps, 1914–1916

1. Vladimir Jabotinsky, *The Story of the Jewish Legion,* 41–42.

2. J. H. Patterson, *With the Zionists,* 46, 47.

3. Elias Gilner, *War and Hope: The History of the Jewish Legion,* 403, 33. See also Martin Sugarman, "The Zion Muleteers of Gallipoli, March 1915–May 1916," 299.

4. Gilner, *War and Hope,* 37.

5. J. H. Patterson, *With the Zionists,* 53, 54.

6. Ibid., 54.

7. Quoted in Benis M. Frank, chief historian of the U.S. Marine Corps, "The Jewish Company of the Shanghai Volunteer Corps Compared with Other Jewish Diaspora Fighting Units," n.p.

8. J. H. Patterson, *With the Zionists,* 131, 132.

9. Ibid., 135, 205.

10. Ibid., 204, 208.

11. Ibid., 202.

12. Ibid., 201.

13. Arthur Behrend, *Make Me a Soldier: A Platoon Commander in Gallipoli.*

14. Gilner, *War and Hope,* 73–75.

15. Alan Moorehead, *Gallipoli,* 234.

16. *Encyclopedia Judaica,* s.v. "Jewish Legion."

17. J. H. Patterson, *With the Zionists,* 208–9.

18. Letter to author from Charles S. Schwartz, September 1, 1987. Schwartz interviewed the deserter in Los Angeles.

19. Gilner, *War and Hope*, 61, 66.

20. J. H. Patterson, *With the Zionists*, 241.

21. *Jewish Chronicle*, September 10, 1915.

22. J. H. Patterson, *With the Zionists*, 250.

23. Ibid., 253.

24. Ibid., 281.

25. Ibid., 137.

26. "Fifty Thousand Miles on a Hospital Ship, by 'The Padre,' 1917–1918," 188.

27. J. H. Patterson, *With the Zionists*, 294.

28. Shmuel Katz, *Lone Wolf: A Biography of Vladimir (Ze'ev) Jabotinsky*, 224.

29. Ibid., 201, 202.

8. Patterson's Fight to Create a Jewish Legion, 1916–1918

1. Jabotinsky, *Story of the Jewish Legion*, 69–70.

2. Ibid., 78.

3. Ibid.

4. Ibid., 88–89.

5. Ibid., 20.

6. Katz, *Lone Wolf*, 292.

7. Ibid.

8. Streeter, *Mad for Zion*, 103.

9. Katz, *Lone Wolf*, 294–95.

10. Ibid., 298.

11. Ibid., 298–29.

12. Ibid., 301.

13. Ibid., 309.

14. Meyer W. Weisgal and Joel Carmichael, eds., *Chaim Weizmann: A Biography by Several Hands*, 164.

15. Katz, *Lone Wolf*, 323.

16. Abba Eban, *An Autobiography*, 6–7.

17. Martin Watts, *The Jewish Legion and the First World War*, 6–7.

18. Patterson, *With the Judeans in the Palestine Campaign*, 34.

19. Terence Prittie, *Eshkol: The Man and the Nation*, 32.

20. Katz, *Lone Wolf*, 338.

21. Ibid., 338–39.

9. Patterson's Jewish Legion Fights for Palestine, 1918–1919

1. Katz, *Lone Wolf*, 340–41.

2. Ibid., 341, 342.

3. Ibid., 346.

4. J. H. Patterson, *With the Judeans*, 64–65.

5. Colonel Richard Meinertzhagen, *Middle East Diary*, 128.

6. J. H. Patterson, *With the Judeans*, 318, 219, 220, 221.

7. Ibid., ix.

8. Ibid., 75–76.

9. Ibid., 79.

10. Ibid., 95.

11. Ibid., 98.

12. Ibid., 98, 99.

13. Ibid., 99.

14. Ibid., 101.

15. Ibid., 103–4.

16. Ibid., 111.

17. Ibid., 115.

18. Ibid., 125–26.

19. Katz, *Lone Wolf*, 382.

20. Lowell Thomas, *With Lawrence in Arabia*, 254, 256, 259, 260.

21. Jabotinsky, *Story of the Jewish Legion*, 139–40.

22. Ibid., 139.

23. Ibid., 140, 141.

24. J. H. Patterson, *With the Judeans*, 129, 131.

25. Ibid., 148.

26. Ibid., 160.

27. Ibid., 162.

28. Ibid., 183.

29. William B. Ziff, *The Rape of Palestine*, 202, 203; Ronald Storrs, *The Memoirs of Sir Ronald Storrs*.

10. Patterson's Command of the Sinai, 1919–1920

1. From a 1939 Patterson speech (author's collection) and Yitshaq Ben-Ami, *Years of Wrath*, 543, 544.

2. Benjamin Netanyahu, *A Place among the Nations: Israel and the World*, 54.

3. Ibid.

4. Schechtman, *The Jabotinsky Story: Fighter and Prophet, the Last Years*, 280.

5. J. H. Patterson, *With the Judeans*, 243–44.

6. Ibid., 186–87.

7. Ibid., 187–88.

8. Ibid., 191.

9. Ibid., 103.

10. Katz, *Lone Wolf,* 506–7.

11. Ibid., 507.

12. J. H. Patterson, *With the Judeans,* 231.

11. Defending the Jewish Homeland, 1919–1930

1. Howard M. Sachar, *A History of Israel from the Rise of Zionism to Our Time,* 122.

2. Netanyahu, *Place among the Nations,* 543.

3. Sachar, *History of Israel,* 122.

4. Schechtman, *Jabotinsky Story,* 324, 325.

5. Meinertzhagen, *Middle East Diary,* 81–82.

6. Ben-Ami, *Years of Wrath,* 547, 548.

7. Katz, *Lone Wolf,* 620.

8. Norman Rose, *Weizmann,* 203.

9. Streeter, *Mad for Zion,* 132.

10. Katz, *Lone Wolf,* 626.

11. Streeter, *Mad for Zion,* 135.

12. Ibid., 136.

13. Ibid.

14. Ibid., 137.

15. Ibid.

16. Ben-Ami, *Years of Wrath,* 546.

17. Katz, *Lone Wolf,* 836–37.

18. Ben-Ami, *Years of Wrath,* 38.

19. Dr. Oscar Kraines, "Soldiers of Zion: The Jewish Legion, 1915–1921," 17.

20. Streeter, *Mad for Zion,* 140.

21. Ibid.

22. Ibid., 138.

23. Patterson to Barnard Stone, January 10, 1922, Chaim Weizmann Archives.

24. Ibid., February 2, 1922.

25. Patterson to Weizmann, May 30, 1922, ibid.

26. Denis Brian, *Einstein: A Life,* 124–25.

27. Martin Gilbert, *Winston S. Churchill: The Stricken World, 1916–1922,* 649, 650.

28. Meinertzhagen, *Middle East Diary.*

29. Gilbert, *Winston S. Churchill,* 660–62.

30. Streeter, *Mad for Zion,* 141.

31. Ibid. See also British Public Record Office, PRO.CO/733/3/411.

12. Murder on a Tel Aviv Beach and the Start of World War II, 1931–1939

1. Rose, *Weizmann,* 290.

2. Prittie, *Eshkol,* 88.

3. Streeter, *Mad for Zion,* 147.

4. Golda Meir, *My Life,* 115–16.

5. Streeter, *Mad for Zion,* 150. See also Jabotinsky Institute archives.

6. Ben-Ami, *Years of Wrath,* 314.

7. Letter from Harriet Schlosberg's daughter, Janet Hillman, to the author, August 11, 2003.

8. Streeter, *Mad for Zion,* 151.

9. Ibid., 153.

10. Prittie, *Eshkol,* 108–9.

11. Streeter, *Mad for Zion,* 154.

12. The Peel Commission Report, Jewish Virtual Library, 10; David Ben-Gurion, *Israel: A Personal History,* 49.

13. Letters from Irene White (Ilse Michelsohn's Anglicized married name) to the author, September 7, November 20, 1987.

14. http://www.ou.org/chagim/yomhaatzmauth/jabo.htm.

15. Ben-Ami, *Years of Wrath,* 193.

16. Ibid., 215–16.

17. Publication of the American Friends for a Jewish Palestine, *Appeal to American Jewry,* 544, 545 (author's collection).

18. Ibid.

19. Ben-Ami, *Years of Wrath,* 544–45.

20. Ibid., 211.

13. World War II and a Recruiting Drive for a Jewish Army, 1939–1944

1. Meinertzhagen, *Middle East Diary,* 179.

2. Vladimir Jabotinsky, *The Jewish War Front,* introduction (n.p.).

3. E-mail on September 8, 2005, from Sir Martin Gilbert to author, confirming this material is to be found in his *Churchill War Papers: Never Surrender,* volume for May to December 1940.

4. Patterson to Dr. Jose Mirelman, Buenos Aires, June 8, 1940, author's collection. Mirelman was president of the Argentine New Zionist Organization (Katz, *Lone Wolf,* 1760).

5. Patterson to Ilse Michelsohn, June 8, 1840, author's collection.

6. Patterson to Lothian, June 18, 1940, Patterson Papers, Jabotinsky Institute.

7. *New York Times,* June 20, 1940, 12.

8. Letter from Jose Mirelman to author, October 5, 1997.

9. Patterson Papers, Jabotinsky Institute.

10. Jabotinsky, *Story of the Jewish Legion,* 152.

11. Frances Patterson to Ilse Michelsohn, November 13, 1941, author's collection.

12. Streeter, *Mad for Zion,* 167.

13. Ben-Ami, *Years of Wrath,* 250–51.

14. FBI report March 6, 1942, 100-91095-1X.

15. Ibid.

16. Ibid.

17. Streeter, *Mad for Zion,* 162–63.

18. Ben Hecht, *A Child of the Century,* 509, 510.

19. Michael Ignatieff, *A Life of Isaiah Berlin,* 114, 117.

20. Streeter, *Mad for Zion,* 164.

21. Wise, *The Personal Letters of Stephen Wise,* 260.

22. "Proclamation of the Moral Rights of Stateless and Palestine Jews," *New York Times,* November 17, 1942, 15.

23. Author's collection.

24. Philip K. Hitti, "Bridge Between Two Worlds," 15; Hitti, letter to the editor, October 31, 1943, 38.

25. Streeter, *Mad for Zion,* 167.

14. Victory, 1944–1948

1. Mitchell Bard, *The Complete Idiot's Guide to Middle East Conflict,* 199, 130.

2. Streeter, *Mad for Zion,* 167.

3. Ibid., 167, 168.

4. Ibid., 168.

5. Ibid., 170.

6. http://www.olinfilms.com, 2, 3.

7. Martin Gilbert, *Exile and Return: The Struggle for a Jewish Homeland.*

8. Morris Beckman, *The Jewish Brigade: An Army with Two Masters, 1944–1945,* 171.

9. Beatrice Patterson, telephone interview by author, October 22, 1987.

10. Ben-Ami, *Years of Wrath,* 542.

11. Elaine Bloomberg, telephone interview by author, May 21, 1988; Ava Zimmerman, telephone interview by author, May 21, 1988; Roy Travis, telephone interview by author, December 5, 1987; Joan Travis, telephone interview by author, January 6, 1988.

12. Dan Kurzman, *Ben-Gurion, Prophet of Fire,* 265.

13. Author's collection, from Joan Travis.

14. Streeter, *Mad for Zion,* 174.

15. Benjamin Netanyahu, *A Place among the Nations: Israel and the World,* 47.

16. Jehuda Wallach, ed., "Not on a Silver Platter: History of Israel, 1900–2000," n.p. Wallach is president of the Israeli Society for Military History.

17. http://www.olinfilms.com, 4.

18. Larry Collins and Dominique Lapierre, *O Jerusalem!* 491.

19. Gad Nahshon, "The Jewish Brigade: The Mother of the State of Israel," *Jewish Post of New York,* http://www.jewishpost.com/archives/news/thejewishbrigade.html.

Bibliography

Manuscript Collections

British Public Record Office. Kew, London.

Central Zionist Archives. Jerusalem, Israel.

Churchill, Winston. Archives. Cambridge, England.

Essex Regiment Museum. Chelmsford, Essex.

India Office Library. British Library, London.

Jewish Legion Museum. Avihayil, Israel.

Patterson, John Henry. Diary. Author's collection.

————. File. Jabotinsky Institute. Tel Aviv, Israel.

Roosevelt, Theodore. Collection. Houghton Library, Harvard University, Cambridge.

Weizmann Institute. Archives. Rehovot, Israel.

Other Sources

Alion, Yigel. *Shield of David: The Story of Israel's Armed Forces.* New York: Random House, 1970.

Bard, Mitchell. *The Complete Idiot's Guide to Middle East Conflict.* New York: Alpha Books, 1999.

Bauer, Yehuda. *Jews for Sale? Nazi-Jewish Negotiations, 1933–1945.* New Haven: Yale University Press, 1994.

Beckman, Morris. *The Jewish Brigade: An Army with Two Masters, 1944–1945.* Rockville Centre, N.Y.: Sarpedon, 1999.

Begin, Menachem. *The Revolt.* New York: Nash, 1977.

Behrend, Arthur. *Make Me a Soldier: A Platoon Commander in Gallipoli.* London: Eyre and Spottiswoode, 1961.

Bein, Alex. *Theodore Herzl: A Biography.* Translated by Maurice Samuel. New York: World Publishing and the Jewish Publication Society of America, 1962.

Ben-Ami, Yitshaq. *Years of Wrath, Days of Glory: Memoirs of the Irgun.* New York: Robert Speller, 1982.

Ben-Gurion, David. *Israel: A Personal Story.* Translated by Nechemia Meyers and Uzy Nysta. New York: Funk and Wagnalls, 1971.

Ben-Horin, Eliahu. *The Middle East Crossroads of History.* New York: W. W. Norton, 1943.

Blomberg, Stanley A., and Gwian Owens. *The Survival Factor: Israeli Intelligence from World War I to the Present.* New York: Putnams, 1981.

Boyles, Denis. *Man Eaters Motel.* New York: Tickner and Fields, 1991.

Brian, Denis. *Einstein: A Life.* New York: John Wiley, 1996.

Briscoe, Robert. *For the Life of Me.* London: Longmans, 1959.

Bush, Eric Wheler. *Gallipoli.* London: Allen and Unwin, 1975.

Capsick, Peter, ed. *Tsavo.* New York: St. Martin's Press, 1986.

Carter, Jimmy. *The Blood of Abraham: Insights into the Middle East.* Boston: Houghton Mifflin, 1988.

Casada, Jim. "Great Hunters in History: John Henry Patterson (1867?–1947)." *Sports Afield,* November 1, 2004.

Churchill, Randolph S. *Winston S. Churchill.* Vol. 2, *Young Statesman, 1901–1914.* London: Heinemann, 1967.

Churchill, Winston S. *Their Finest Hour: The Second World War.* Boston: Houghton Mifflin, 1981.

———. *Triumph and Tragedy.* Boston: Houghton Mifflin, 1953.

Collins, Larry, and Dominique Lapierre. *O Jerusalem!* New York: Simon and Schuster, 1972.

Congressional Record. "Salute to the Veterans of the Judean Battalion," by Senator Cranston, June 3, 1966.

Eban, Abba. *An Autobiography.* New York: Random House, 1997.

———. *Personal Witness: Israel Through My Eyes.* New York: Putnam's, 1992.

Edgerton, Robert R. *Nau Mau: An African Crucible.* New York: Free Press, 1989.

Eskenazi, Joe. "Jews in Ireland." *Jewish Bulletin* (northern California) (2003).

"Fifty Thousand Miles on a Hospital Ship, by 'The Padre,' 1917–1918." *Religious Tract Society* (St. Paul's Churchyard, London) (1918).

Frank, Benis M. "The Jewish Company of the Shanghai Volunteer Corps Compared with Other Jewish Diaspora Fighting Units." http://net.hb.byu.edu/ww/comment/svc.htm, 1992.

Friedman, Isaiah. *The Question of Palestine, 1914–1918: British-Jewish-Arab Relations.* New York: Schocken, 1973.

Gilbert, Martin. *Churchill War Diaries: Never Surrender, May 1940–December 1940.* New York: W. W. Norton, 1995.

———. *Exile and Return: The Struggle for a Jewish Homeland.* New York: Lippincott, 1978.

———. *Winston S. Churchill: The Stricken World, 1916–1922.* Boston: Houghton Mifflin, 1975.

Gilner, Elias. *War and Hope: The History of the Jewish Legion.* New York: Herzl Press, 1969.

Hamilton, Sir Ian. *Gallipoli Diary.* New York: George H. Doran, 1920.

Hecht, Ben. *A Child of the Century.* New York: Simon and Schuster, 1954.

Hemingway, Ernest. *The Short Happy Life of Francis Macomber: The First Forty-nine Stories.* London: Arrow Books, 1993.

Hentoff, Nat. "Fierce Israeli Dove Hunts for American Allies." *Village Voice,* October 25, 1976, 39–42.

Hirschler, Gertrude, and Lester S. Eckman. *Menachem Begin.* New York: Shengold, 1979.

Hitti, Philip K. "Bridge Between Two Worlds." *New York Times Book Review,* September 12, 1943, 15.

———. *History of the Arabs: From the Earliest Times to the Present.* New York: Palgrave Macmillan, 1937.

Hurwitz, David Lyon. "Churchill and Palestine." *Judaism* (Winter 1995).

Ignatieff, Michael. *A Life of Isaiah Berlin.* New York: Henry Holt, 1998.

Jabotinsky, Vladimir. *The Jewish War Front.* London: George Allen and Unwin, 1940.

———. *The Story of the Jewish Legion.* Translated by Samuel Katz. New York: Bernard Ackerman, 1945.

———. "The Threatened Partition of Palestine." Address to members of the British Parliament, July 13, 1937.

———. *The War and the Jew.* With a foreword by Pierre van Passen and a conclusion by Colonel John Henry Patterson, DSO. New York: Dial Press, 1942.

Jerusalem Report Staff. *Shalom Friend: The Life and Legacy of Yitzhak Rabin.* Edited by David Horovitz. New York: Newmarket Press, 1996.

Katz, Shmuel. *Lone Wolf: A Biography of Vladimir (Ze'ev) Jabotinsky.* Vol. 1. New York: Barricade Books, 1996.

Klabunde, Anja. *Magda Goebbels.* New York: Time Warner, 2004.

Kraines, Dr. Oscar. "Soldiers of Zion: The Jewish Legion, 1915–1921." *Beth Sholom Bulletin* 41, no. 6 (December 1–15, 1985): 17.

———. "A Talk at Temple Beth Sholom, Miami Beach." *Beth Sholom Bulletin,* December 8, 1985.

Kurzman, Dan. *Ben-Gurion, Prophet of Fire.* New York: Simon and Schuster, 1983.

Lewis, David Levering. *The Race to Fashoda: European Colonialism and African Resistance to the Scramble for Africa.* New York: Weidenfeld and Nicolson, 1988.

Meinertzhagen, Colonel Richard. *Middle East Diary.* London: Cresset Press, 1959.

Meir, Golda. *My Life.* New York: Futura, 1977.

Meyers, Jeffrey. *Hemingway.* New York: Harper and Row, 1985.

Miller, Charles. *The Lunatic Express: An Entertainment in Imperialism.* New York: Macmillan, 1971.

Miller, Merle. *Plain Speaking: An Oral Biography of Harry S. Truman.* New York: Berkeley, 1977.

Montgomery, Bernard. *The Memoirs of Field Marshal Montgomery.* New York: Fontana Monarchs, 1960.

Moorehead, Alan. *Gallipoli.* New York: Harper and Row, 1956.

Morgenthau, Henry, III. *Mostly Morgenthaus: A Family History.* New York: Tickner and Fields, 1991.

Morris, James. "Long Live Imperialism." *Saturday Evening Post,* 10.

Nahshon, Gad. "The Jewish Brigade: The Mother of the State of Israel." *Jewish Post,* September 2, 2003.

Netanyahu, Benjamin. *A Place among the Nations: Israel and the World.* New York: Bantam Books, 1993.

Patterson, Bruce. *The Lions of Tsavo: Exploring the Legacy of Africa's Notorious Man-Eaters.* New York: McGraw-Hill, 2004.

Patterson, John Henry. *In the Grip of the Nyika.* London: Macmillan, 1909.

———. *The Man-Eaters of Tsavo and Other East African Adventures.* London: Macmillan, 1907.

———. *With the Judeans in the Palestine Campaign.* London: Hutchinson, 1922.

———. *With the Zionists in Gallipoli.* London: Hutchinson, 1916.

Perlmutter, Amos. *The Life and Times of Menachem Begin.* Garden City, N.Y.: Doubleday, 1987.

Prittie, Terence. *Eshkol: The Man and the Nation.* New York: Pittman, 1969.

Rapaport, Louis. *Shake Heaven and Earth: Peter Bergson and the Struggle to Rescue the Jews of Europe.* Jerusalem: Gefen Publishing House, 1999.

Roosevelt, Theodore. *African Game Trails: An Account of the African Wanderings of an American Hunter-Naturalist.* New York: Scribner's, 1910.

Rose, Norman. *Weizmann.* London: Weidenfeld and Nicolson, 1987.

Roth, Cecil. "Fifty Years of Jewry, 1918–1968." *Jewish Chronicle* (November 22, 1968).

Rubinstein, William D. "The Secret of Leopold Amery." *History Today* (February 1999).

Sacher, Howard M. *The Course of Modern Jewish History*. New York: Delta, 1957.

———. *A History of Israel from the Rise of Zionism to Our Time*, New York: Alfred A. Knopf, 1996.

Said, Edward W. *The Case for Palestine*. New York: Times Books, 1980.

St. John, Robert. *Ben-Gurion: The Biography of an Extraordinary Man*. Garden City, N.Y.: Doubleday, 1959.

———. *They Came from Everywhere*. New York: Coward McCann, 1962.

Sarner, Harvey. *The Jews of Gallipoli*. Cathedral City, Calif.: Brunswick Press, 2000.

Schechtman, Joseph B. *The Jabotinsky Story: Fighter and Prophet, the Last Years*. New York: Thomas Yoseloff, 1961.

Silvertown, Cyril. "The 'Righteous' Colonel and the Jewish Legion." *Jewish Quarterly* 32, no. 2 (1985).

Spectrum Guide to Kenya. Nairobi: Hunter Publishing, 1993.

Storrs, Ronald. *The Memoirs of Sir Ronald Storrs*. North Stratford, N.H.: Ayer, 1972.

Streeter, Patrick. *Mad for Zion: A Biography of Colonel J. H. Patterson*. Harlow: Matching Press, 2004.

Sugarman, Martin. "The Zion Muleteers of Gallipoli, March 1915–May 1916." *Jewish Historical Society of England* 36 (1999–2000).

Taylor, A. J. P. *Beaverbrook: A Biography*. New York: Simon and Schuster, 1972.

Thomas, Lowell. *With Lawrence in Arabia*. New York: Collier, 1924.

Wallach, Jehuda, ed. "Not on a Silver Platter: History of Israel, 1900–2000." Jerusalem: Carta, 2000.

Watts, Martin. *The Jewish Legion in the First World War*. New York: Palgrave Macmillan, 2005.

Weisgal, Meyer W., ed. *Chaim Weizmann: Statesman, Scientist, Builder of the Jewish Commonwealth*. New York: Dial Press, 1944.

Weisgal, Meyer W., and Joel Carmichael, eds. *Chaim Weizmann: A Biography by Several Hands*. New York: Atheneum, 1963.

Weizmann, Chaim. *Trial and Error*. Philadelphia: Jewish Publication Society of America, 1949.

Wise, Stephen. *The Personal Letters of Stephen Wise*. Edited by Justine Wise Polier and James Waterman Wise. Boston: Beacon Press, 1956.

Wyman, David S., and Rafael Medoff. *A Race Against Death: Peter Bergson, America, and the Holocaust.* New York: New Press, 2002.

Yahil, Leni. *The Fate of European Jewry, 1932–1945.* Translated by Ina Friedman and Haya Galai. New York: Oxford University Press, 1990.

Ziff, William B. *The Rape of Palestine.* New York: Longmans, Green, 1938.

Index

Italic page number denotes illustration.